The authors

Alison Gillies is a welfare rights worker at CPAG Scotland.

Alan Murdie LL.B(Hons), Barrister is director of McKenzie Friends with the Zacchaeus 2000 Trust. He writes and lectures extensively on debt and finance issues and is involved with many test cases relating to poverty issues.

Cecilia Torsney has specialised in debt advice since 1997, working in a variety of supervisory and management roles. Cecilia curently works for the Mary Ward Legal Centre in London.

Energy Action Scotland is the national charity working for an end to fuel poverty and to promote warm, dry homes for all in Scotland.

Acknowledgements

The authors would like to thank everyone who has contributed to this book. In particular, thanks are due to Consumer Focus, Elizabeth Gore and Edward Graham for their invaluable comments and assistance. Thanks also to the previous authors for their contribution to the book.

We would also like to thank Nicola Johnston for editing and managing the production of the book and Clare Gardner for the index and proofreading the text.

The law covered in this book was correct on 1 November 2012 and includes regulations laid up to this date.

Fuel Rights Handbook

16th edition

**Alan Murdie, Cecilia Torsney, Alison Gillies and
Energy Action Scotland**

CPAG promotes action for the prevention and relief of poverty among children and families with children. To achieve this, CPAG aims to raise awareness of the causes, extent, nature and impact of poverty, and strategies for its eradication and prevention; bring about positive policy changes for families with children in poverty; and enable those eligible for income maintenance to have access to their full entitlement. If you are not already supporting us, please consider making a donation, or ask for details of our membership schemes, training courses and publications.

Published by Child Poverty Action Group
94 White Lion Street
London N1 9PF
Tel: 020 7837 7979
staff@cpag.org.uk
www.cpag.org.uk

A CIP record for this book is available from the British Library

ISBN: 978 1 906076 68 9

Child Poverty Action Group is a charity registered in England and Wales (registration number 294841) and in Scotland (registration number SC039339), and is a company limited by guarantee, registered in England (registration number 1993854). VAT number: 690 808117

Cover design by Devious Designs
Cover photo by Duncan Phillips www.reportgital.co.uk
Typeset by David Lewis XML Associates Ltd
Printed in the UK by CPI William Clowes

Contents

Contents

Abbreviations

AA	attendance allowance
CA	carer's allowance
CERT	Carbon Emissions Reduction Target
CTC	child tax credit
CTB	council tax benefit
DECC	Department of Energy and Climate Change
DEO	debt relief order
DLA	disability living allowance
DNO	distribution network operator
DWP	Department for Work and Pensions
ECO	Energy Company Obligation
EPC	energy performance certificate
ESA	employment and support allowance
EHU	extra help unit
EST	Energy Saving Trust
FITs	feed-in tariffs
HB	housing benefit
IB	incapacity benefit
IS	income support
JSA	jobseeker's allowance
kWh	kilowatt hour
LESA	landlord's energy saving allowance
LVT	leasehold valuation tribunal
OFT	Office of Fair Trading
PC	pension credit
PRHP	Private Rented Housing Panel
SLC	standard licence conditions
WHD	Warm Home Discount
WTC	working tax credit

Foreword

This is the 16th edition of CPAG's *Fuel Rights Handbook* and details a number of significant changes in law and practice since the last edition in 2011.

This edition book follows the pattern of previous editions of the handbook since the year 2000, incorporating changes in energy regulation and the protection mechanisms for consumers who have their energy supplied under contracts. The handbook is compiled with particular emphasis upon the position of consumers in fuel poverty, appearing in the context of rising fuel prices, with the largest suppliers increasing fuel prices in the autumn of 2012, ahead of significant planned cuts to welfare benefits expected in 2013.

Well-publicised price increases by energy suppliers prompted Prime Minister David Cameron to announce on 17 October 2012 that the complicated system of differing tariffs which has created a bewildering range of prices and schemes for consumers is to be drastically reformed, with the options on tariffs to be reduced to four. Reform of the system is ultimately unlikely to be as dramatic but it appears that a British government is at last considering intervening in the area of consumer pricing and contracts, market forces having failed to deliver the lower prices that were once promised. What is clear is that the strategy pursued by successive governments over the last decade, based upon the notion that a permitting a free market in energy supply would reduce fuel poverty by providing consumer choice, is not only flawed but has failed completely.

In the meantime, millions of consumers remain tied to existing contracts, with increasing poverty across the UK arising from unemployment and changes in welfare provision which mean that increasing numbers of poor consumers are being forced into greater debt and poverty. Fuel poverty has more than quadrupled since the year 2000 and successive investigations by Ofgem to examine the causes of fuel poverty have failed to face the fact that energy policy cannot be separated from the question of inadequate incomes and wholly unforeseen effects of the privatisations state energy suppliers during the 1980s and 1990s. After initial waves of enthusiasm by small investors in buying shares in British Gas and state-owned electricity companies in the 1980s, ownership has moved from individual shareholders to financial institutions and then to foreign energy companies. Five of the 'Big Six' energy companies which supply 99 per cent of UK households are now owned by companies based outside the UK. For instance, Eon is based in Germany and British Gas is owned by a Spanish company. It would be optimistic to imagine that social policy in Britain is near the top of any list of concerns regarding their pricing strategies. Indeed, the rise in prices may well be seen as a deliberate strategy to mitigate the effects on the squeeze on incomes which will occur in 2013 with the overall benefit cap, the abolition of council tax benefit and caps on housing benefit. Energy companies have acted to maximise profits by seeking to raise prices before welfare cuts bite.

Welcome as signs are that the light approach to regulatory intervention practised by successive governments is now on the wane, there still remains an on-going reluctance to face up to other reasons as to why an increasing numbers of households are in fuel poverty. A belated recognition of the failure of the fuel poverty strategy was made by David Kidney, the Secretary of State for Energy, under last Labour government with an admission that various strategies adopted by the government had not succeeded and that an increase in fuel poverty was occurring. His 2009 report highlighted that low incomes played a significant part, but these realisation did not translate into any awareness that welfare cutbacks and restrictions – many supported by both sides of the House of Commons under a guise of 'reform' – may have been a significant factor in contributing to fuel poverty.

Although some parts of the welfare system, such as winter fuel payments, operate efficiently and assist pensioners with few noticeable problems, many others on means-tested benefits find their situation exacerbated by changes in other parts of the benefit system, which have impact upon their ability to deal with energy bills without going into debt. This has yet to be realised by the Coalition government which has made various announcements since its establishment following the General Election in April 2010. Soon after the Coalition took power, Energy Secretary Chris Huhne announced the first ever Annual Energy Statement to Parliament setting out 32 actions 'taken to accelerate the transformation of the energy system and wider economy' and the following year enacted the Energy Act 2011. However, these strategic steps have had little demonstrable impact as yet on fuel poverty, being primarily concerned with cutting of carbon emissions and move towards a low carbon energy system and wider economy. Similarly, the Energy Act 2011 contains extensive regulation making powers in respect of domestic energy efficiency in England and Wales, with corresponding powers for Scottish Ministers but these do not address the core problem of the costs of fuel and the inadequacy of incomes to pay for it.

Only in September 2012, the Energy and Climate Change Secretary, Edward Davey, set out measures to help ensure that energy consumers are treated fairly and make it easier for households get a better energy deal. In the long-term proposed measures include a power for Ofgem to order compensation directly to customers who have suffered loss as a result of a supplier's breach of a licence condition, rather than fines being paid direct to the Treasury.

From 1 November 2012, the switching threshold for customers with prepayment meters with debts has been raised from £200 to £500. However, this remains a voluntary arrangement with suppliers and may be more difficult to obtain in practice for customers in debt; it will also depend upon the willingness of suppliers to accept customers with existing debt levels and if they find a cheaper deal. Proposals to establish schemes for 'collective switching' involving groups of consumers are also being contemplated but details as yet are sketchy. Unfortunately, any improvements may well be undermined by wider changes in the welfare system expected in 2013 and which are detailed in other CPAG publications and guides. The reduction in benefits in real terms for many on benefits may well extinguish progress made in other areas to reduce fuel costs and bills.

However, away from the role of government, it is important to note that there have been some improvements in the way energy companies handle customers in fuel poverty, allowing a greater flexibility with many debt situations and the use of discretion. The Energy Ombudsman Service has also provided an important source of help in resolving a wide range of complaints, the role of the Ombudsman being enhanced by the scope and effect of the Gas and Electricity (Consumer Complaints Handling Standards) Regulations 2008 which have become more widely known and impose consistent standards across the industry.

Page 9 of the National Standards for Enforcement Agents remains important as guidance with respect to the pursuit of debts and referral back to suppliers when vulnerable situations are encountered. Third party deductions using the Fuel Direct scheme continues to be used as a last resort by suppliers in recovering fuel debts – though its efficacy as a measure has been seriously undermined by the practice of sanctioning qualifying benefits under the Welfare Reform Acts 2009 and 2012.

While the system for applying for warrants for disconnection remains antiquated, the number of disconnections undertaken by certain suppliers has shown a general trend downwards, though Ofgem has expressed concern about certain patterns and practices in the records of individual suppliers in certain areas. However, a person who faces arrears enforcement before the magistrates' court in England and Wales is now more likely to face the installation of a pre-payment meter, rather than an out-right cut off of fuel supply as occurred in the past or threatening and wholly misleading correspondence implying that the police might be in attendance.

The case of *Ferguson v British Gas* [2009], in which the Court of Appeal ruled that British Gas could be subject to both civil and criminal proceedings for harassment of a consumer, remains as a milestone in the law with respect to the position of the customer against heavy-handed enforcement. Ultimately, if problems and complaints cannot be resolved by negotiation, the courts remain the remedy of last resort and experience suggests that despite their size and wealth energy companies are often ill equipped to deal with claims in the courts.

With respect to consumer protection, the Citizens Advice is coming to play an ever more significant role, with the advice line and website of the former Consumer Direct service transferred under its umbrella in April 2012. In 2013

Consumer Focus (the successor to the previous statutory consumer champion Energywatch) will be re-organised as the Regulated Industries Unit with responsibility for energy and postal services in England, Scotland and Wales, for post in Northern Ireland and also for water in Scotland. It is envisaged that in turn this may also become part of Citizens Advice in 2014.

It remains to be seen how Citizens Advice will operate with these added responsibilities; but there will be at least be an awareness of the impact of welfare cuts on the fuel poor among many advisers. Such awareness will undoubtedly inform and assist the increasingly robust advocacy which is going to become necessary in the interests of the fuel poor in the years ahead.

Alan Murdie

Chapter 1

Introduction

This chapter covers:
1. Sources for your rights (below)
2. The structure of the industry (p2)
3. How to use this book (p5)

1. Sources for your rights

The sources to refer to for your rights, in respect of the supply of gas and electricity, are:

- primary legislation – principally Acts of Parliament, the Gas Acts 1986 and 1995, the Electricity Act 1989, the Competition and Services (Utilities) Act 1992, the Utilities Act 2000, the Energy Act 2010, the Energy Act 2011 and the Energy Bill published in 2012 which will become the Energy Act 2013; the legislation particular to Wales is also passed by the Welsh government and in Scotland by the Scottish government;
- statutory instruments – regulations made under legislation – eg, the Electricity (Standards of Performance) Regulations 2010 SI No.698;
- law reports/court decisions;
- licences – the Utilities Act 2000 amended both the Gas Act 1986 and the Electricity Act 1989, changing the licensing regimes for both the gas and electricity industries;
- your contract with your supplier – if you get your electricity from one of the licensed gas or electricity suppliers (eg, British Gas, E.ON, etc) the rules governing your relationship with that supplier are in the legislation, in statutory instruments or arise from the contract. Gas and electricity customers have a contract with the supplier. The standard terms and conditions for that contract must be freely available from the relevant supplier;
- codes of practice – each supplier publishes its own code of practice or statement of policy for various processes, such as complaint handling, marketing or billing. The codes are not legally binding by themselves, but they do indicate how a supplier should and usually will behave in certain situations. You may be able to get a remedy against a supplier's practice or particular action simply

because it breaches one of the relevant codes of practice. Copies of the complaint handling code of practice should be made available to any person that requests it and should also be published on the supplier's website. Regular advisers in this field should have the relevant codes for the main suppliers in their locality;

- the gas and electricity minimum standards of performance regulations. Regulations passed by Parliament lay down minimum standards for the performance of gas and electricity supply companies and distributors for various situations (see Appendix 2);
- decisions of the Energy Ombudsman – although not binding these give an indication of the standards expected and can help assess the adequacy of responses to complaints.

2. **The structure of the industry**

Since 1999, all gas and electricity customers in Great Britain have been able to choose the company from which they buy their fuel supplies. The largest energy companies are multinational businesses based outside the UK with subsidiary companies operating within the UK.

Gas

The gas industry is split into three parts – shippers, transporters and suppliers – with a requirement on those operating in each part to be licensed. Shippers buy gas and put it into the pipes, transporters convey it to your meter and suppliers actually sell the gas to you (shipping and supplying is normally done by different parts of the same company).

The main effect for you is that the supplier who sends the gas bill does not actually handle the gas itself – that is the role of the transporter. If there is a gas leak, for example, you should contact the transporter, not the supplier. The main gas transportation network is split up into four companies:

- National Grid (formerly Transco), now transports gas in four areas of England: north west England, London, eastern England and the West Midlands covering approximately 11 million users;
- Northern Gas Networks cover 2.6 million users in the north of England;
- Scotia Gas Networks cover 5.8 million users in Scotland and southern England;
- Wales and West Utilities are available throughout Wales and the west of England.

In addition, there are also a number of independent gas transporters that have various smaller networks throughout Britain. All emergencies, including gas leaks, emissions of carbon monoxide and fires and explosions, throughout Britain are reported directly to the National Grid Gas Emergency Line on 0800 111 999, no matter who the gas transportation company is.

Electricity

The companies involved in the generation, transmission, distribution and supply of electricity are required to be licensed. There are no longer regional monopolies. Although local distribution is still done by one of the 14 former public electricity companies, the supply of electricity is entirely commercial, and therefore (in theory) competitive and you are able to select the supplier from whom you buy your electricity and transfer from one to another. In the majority of cases this may be reduced to a right to choose between one of six major suppliers, unless you are able to access a smaller supply or establish some degree of independent generation of energy.

Contracts

Your gas and electricity is supplied under a contract or deemed contract from the supplier/s of your choice. 'Dual fuel' contract suppliers can supply both gas and electricity under contract.

In theory, contracts are reached by negotiation and agreement. In practice, most terms and conditions are presented to consumers on a 'take it or leave it' basis. The use of contracts means that finding out about your rights is now far more complicated than it used to be prior to privatisation of the energy industry. Terms of energy supply for individual consumers are set down in contracts which have to be within the framework of general licensing conditions imposed upon supply companies. You need to look particularly at the contract given to you by your supplier. There will be important differences in the terms of the contract when compared with those of other suppliers.

Ofgem – the industry regulator

Ofgem was set up in March 2000 to replace the separate regulatory bodies for the gas and electricity industries. The main functions of Ofgem are promoting competition in all parts of the gas and electricity industries and regulating them.

Ofgem's regulatory functions include granting licences in both industries, monitoring performance, regulating the areas where competition is not so effective (such as the monopoly on 'pipes and wires') and determining the strategy for the fuel industry.

Ofgem currently has the power to fine energy companies up to 10 per cent of their annual turnover for regulatory breaches. Those requirements are principally set out in the Electricity Act 1989, Gas Act 1986 and regulated company licenses, and include rules on sales practices and complaint handling.

Ofgem is to be given powers to seek consumer redress in 2013 which will allow it to give direct compensation to consumers who have been adversely affected by breaches of licence conditions by suppliers (see p46).

Consumer protection

Consumer Focus (formerly Energywatch and the National Consumer Council) is being abolished and replaced by a service provided by Citizens Advice. In April 2012 it was announced that Citizens Advice and Citizens Advice Scotland will take on responsibilities and resources from the Office for Fair Trading (OFT) and Consumer Focus. The process has already started, and a new advice line succeeding Consumer Direct, the Citizens Advice consumer service, was launched on 2 April 2012.

Citizens Advice will also take on responsibility from Consumer Focus for representing consumers' interests in unregulated sectors. From April 2013 this will leave a new, technical Regulated Industries Unit working with the energy and postal services sectors and their regulators, replacing Consumer Focus. The Regulated Industries Unit will also transfer to Citizens Advice in April 2014.

The timing of these changes in Scotland will depend on the outcome of the Scottish government's request for the UK government to consider devolving responsibility for consumer issues to them. The government has said that there will be no reduction in consumer representation in Wales and Scotland as a result of the changes which apply from April 2013.

Companies can voluntarily choose to compensate consumers who lose out as a result of their wrongdoing. The Energy Ombudsman can also force the firms to pay consumers up to £5,000 if it deems complaints about 'energy bills, sales activities, problems arising from switching supplier or with the supply of gas and electricity' to be legitimate. You may also seek redress for some aspects of wrongdoing, such as breach of contract, through the courts.

Minimum standards of performance

Minimum standards of performance for energy suppliers and distributors are set out in regulations. The Electricity (Standards of Performance) Regulations 2010, the Electricity (Connection Standards of Performance) Regulations 2010 and the Gas (Standards of Performance) Regulations 2005 set out minimum standards of service for consumers. If a supplier or distributor fails to meet these standards of performance, compensation is payable to the consumer as set down in the regulations. Section 14 of the Supply of Goods and Services Act 1982 provides that a term requiring that a service to a consumer is undertaken with reasonable competence and skill must be included in every consumer contract.

Energy efficiency and renewable energy

Over the last decade the government has placed greater emphasis on the role of energy efficiency in achieving a number of strategic aims, including the establishment of a sustainable energy policy for the UK, with policy goals being pursued to 2030 and in some cases to 2050.

The Department of Energy and Climate Change has a commitment to renewable energy and low-carbon industrial strategy to move the country towards a low-carbon economy, with a target of reducing carbon emissions by 34 per cent compared to 1990 levels by 2020. Plans included new loan schemes to encourage households to invest in energy efficient, low-carbon improvements, which would be paid back through energy bill savings. The Department publishes an Annual Energy Statement setting out policies and goals and progress made.

The Energy Act 2011 created a new financing framework for the provision of fixed improvements to the energy efficiency of homes, funded by a charge on energy bills that avoids the need for consumers to pay upfront costs (see p175).

In the 2012 Annual Energy Statement, the government set out its goals to create a competitive, low carbon economy and to cut greenhouse gas emissions by at least 80 per cent by 2050, and to source 15 per cent of UK energy from renewable sources by 2020. The government stated that its objective is to 'ensure that the costs and benefits of our policies are distributed fairly, so that we protect the most vulnerable and fuel poor households'.[1]

3. **How to use this book**

Unless specified, everything in this book applies to both gas and electricity. The main legislation applies to Great Britain (England, Wales and Scotland) only. Northern Ireland is, therefore, not covered. Where the law in Scotland differs, this is noted.

Use this book principally for help in tackling fuel poverty – ie, the inability to afford adequate warmth in the home. That has always been this *Handbook's* main purpose. It does not aim to cover policy issues or examine background information in detail, but to act as a guide to the rights of consumers. Other publications and organisations which may be able to help are listed in Appendix 1. This *Handbook* consists of two parts:

- chapters dealing with various topics. Look at the contents at the beginning of each chapter and consult the index to find the topic you are seeking. References at the end of each chapter give the sources of information so that you can use them as an authority for actions;
- appendices, which contain supplementary material and information.

There are references in the text to other CPAG handbooks which provide more detail on specific topics, such as benefits and dealing with debt. Where detailed information is required, such as eligibility criteria for benefits, consult the specialist handbook.

Abbreviations are used in the text to save space. The abbreviated term is explained in full the first time it is used in a section, and on pviii there is a list of all the abbreviations used.

The references in the text and notes to Standard Licence Conditions refer to the version which was published on 31 October 2012 and subject to amendment on 28 January 2013. Generally, the numbering for gas and electricity is the same, but where it differs, both numbers are shown.

Notes

1 Annual Energy Statement 2012,
   Department of Energy and Climate
   Change, 29 November 2012

Chapter 2

Choosing a supplier

This chapter covers:
1. Suppliers (below)
2. Marketing and sales (p11)
3. Contracts (p14)

1. Suppliers

Since 1999, consumers have been able to choose their supplier for gas and electricity and over the past decade over 50 per cent of consumers have changed their energy supplier at least once. Some customers now choose to take both gas and electricity from the same company – this is known as 'dual-fuel supply' (see p17). In 2002, there were 14 privatised electricity suppliers for electricity but the industry has since been consolidated into six major suppliers (British Gas/Scottish Gas, Npower, ScottishPower, SSE/Scottish and Southern Energy, EDF and E.ON), who provide approximately 99 per cent of consumer supply. The remaining 1 per cent consists of several smaller suppliers, such as Good Energy and the Utility Warehouse. Scotland has had a single wholesale market for electricity since April 2005.

Switching suppliers

In theory, switching supplier is fairly simple, although the process usually takes four to six weeks to complete. Suppliers are responsible for managing the switch and all have signed up to a switching supplier peace of mind guarantee.[1]

The process

Step 1

Gather information about your current tariff, payment method and usage over the last year – you can find this on your fuel bill or on your annual statement from your supplier. Use this information to compare suppliers (see p8).

Step 2

When you have found the best deal for you, agree a contract with a new supplier. The new supplier will write to you within seven working days to confirm the details. The new supplier will contact your current supplier for you.

Step 3

The new supplier will request a meter reading from you so that your old supplier can issue your final bill and your new supplier has the correct figure for your new bill. The new supplier will inform you of the date when your supply will be switched.

Step 4

Check your final bill from your old supplier.

On your gas or electricity bill, there is a gas meter point reference number (known as an 'M number') or an electricity supply number which is unique to your address. Once you have signed a contract which bears this number with the new supplier, the switch can take place – this should be sorted out between the new and old suppliers, although you can normally help by providing the M number or the supply number. Your present supplier may object to the transfer if you are in debt but you are still entitled to switch where the debt is below £500 and you have a prepayment meter (see p78). Above a £100 debt, a company has discretion whether to take you as a customer, and may do so if you have previously been a customer with a good credit history. The supplier may object where any debt is older than 28 days. In such cases, it may be difficult to switch, although the supplier should at least allow you to move on to the most favourable tariff available for the area in which you live.

It is also possible to stay with your current supplier and switch to a tariff which is better for you.

The following sections look at what to consider when deciding whether or not to switch and which supplier to choose.

Price

To most people, the price of their supply of gas and electricity is the most important factor in deciding which supplier to use.

See Chapter 4 for the types of meters and payment methods available. Suppliers must offer a full range of options, including prepayment meters and various payment methods, even if they do not publicise them all.[2] Consumer Focus publishes regional breakdowns of supplier prices so you can compare prices depending on how you pay, your type of meter and your average usage.[3]

When considering what the various suppliers are offering, look at:

- **standing charges** – some suppliers offer deals with no standing charges at all. However, the lower the standing charge, the higher the unit price is likely to be. If you are a particularly low user of gas or electricity, then a low or no standing charge with a high unit price might be suitable for you;

- **unit charges** – the price for each unit of fuel might vary considerably between suppliers, methods of payment or the type of product (see p18 on new products);
- **payment methods** – be careful when looking at figures provided by suppliers themselves. Some advertised savings are calculated not only on the basis that you switch supplier but also that you change to a different method of payment – eg, from quarterly cash payments to direct debit. You might be able to get the same benefit with your existing supplier by switching to a different payment method;
- **penalty on default** – suppliers have always had the power to penalise customers who do not pay their bills by disconnecting them (see Chapter 8), but at least one supplier has tried introducing extra penalties. If you have difficulty with meeting all your bills on time, avoid such terms if possible. See the section on unfair terms on p18;
- **supplier flexibility** – you might want to change your method of payment or some other aspect of your supply. For example, if you are on a prepayment meter, your current supplier might not allow you to change to a quarterly credit meter, whereas a new supplier might be more flexible. Ask different suppliers for this information.

Some suppliers offer dual-fuel supply deals (see p17) which are only available if you take both gas and electricity from them. Consider whether this would be the best for you. In particular, the convenience of a single supplier might outweigh any price disadvantages for some people.

When deciding whether or not to switch to a new fuel supplier and, if so, which one, it is best to have all the information on prices, terms and conditions so you can compare them and find the deal that best suits you. Note that suppliers are not allowed to enter into contracts through agents who require advance payments – you do not need an agent to get you a new contract and you should not use one. Full lists of all electricity and gas suppliers are available free from Ofgem. All suppliers must publish their standard terms and conditions.

Comparing prices

Ofgem provides practical information to help you change supplier, but does not recommend particular services or companies which provide this information. Consumer Focus goes further, and lists a number of price comparison websites accredited with its Confidence Code.[4] Check that any website you use has the Consumer Focus Confidence Code logo.

Confidence Code accredited websites

UKPower.co.uk	Confused.com
uSwitch.com	Energylinx
SimplySwitch	Fuelswitch.com
TheEnergyShop.com	Which? Switch
beatthatquote.com	energyhelpline.com
MoneySupermarket.com	switchelectricandgas.com
Unravelit	

The Confidence Code requires the service provider to be independent of any gas or electricity supplier. The service provider must be a company which runs its own website and uses its own tariff database and calculating system, not merely hosting those of another service provider, and must list at least five of the cheapest suppliers. The service provider may take commission from energy suppliers, but this must not influence the information given.

Requirement seven of the guidance imposes standards of accuracy and requires calculations to be based on certain assumptions. These include:

- discounts for paying by a certain method – eg, direct debit;
- dual-fuel supply discounts;
- fixed charges.

Introductory offers which provide initial discounts should not be included in the calculations.

To make a meaningful price comparison, you will need to collect information about your current supplier, payment method, annual usage and bills for the last 12 months, and then use the 'ready reckoner' comparison tables which provide a broad overview. A number of services exist allowing you to compare the price.

The potential savings available to you will depend on where you live (as prices vary in different parts of the country), whether you want to switch gas or electricity supplier or both, the payment method (both gas and electricity) and whether you have Economy 7 (electricity). Not all suppliers operate in all parts of the country. For details of payment methods, see Chapter 4.

Other issues to consider before switching supplier

Although the price offered by a new supplier may suit you, the other terms and conditions might not and you should check them carefully (see p18 for other terms and conditions to consider).

Before changing supplier, consider the performance and complaint handling record of the new company. Consumer Focus produces quarterly figures relating to the company performance of the 'big 6' energy suppliers.[5] Its complaint league table shows the ranking of each supplier in terms of complaints received (via Citizens Advice consumer service, Consumer Focus and the Energy Ombudsman), seriousness of the complaint, and the length of time taken to resolve the matter. Five stars indicate the best performing companies and zero stars indicate the worst performing companies.

You may be entitled to a Warm Home Discount (see p49 for eligibility). Before switching, check that your new supplier offers the discount and if you will be eligible under its criteria.

When speaking with a potential new supplier, be aware of the use of 'propositions' as sales tools. A proposition, or 'prop', is an offer used to induce a new customer into a contract. Some offer vouchers for transferring and further incentives for remaining with the company for a fixed period of time. It is important to remember that the unit price and standing charge may be more expensive than your current supplier and will therefore cost you more in the long run.

Changing supplier with existing debts

How easy it is to change might depend on whether you owe your existing supplier any money. If you have owed any money for less than 28 days (eg, you have not yet paid a recent bill), then are normally able to change supplier in the usual way, and the debt will be transferred to the new supplier.

Changing supplier while in debt is subject to provisions contained in a protocol agreed between Ofgem and energy suppliers. Under these arrangements, if you have a prepayment meter you may be able to switch supplier and transfer a debt of up to £500 (see p78).[6]

If you do not have a prepayment meter and you have a debt, your supplier can stop you from switching to a new supplier until you pay off your debt – this is sometimes called 'debt-blocking'. If your supplier blocks your request to switch, it must give you advice on the best tariff for you, managing your debt and energy efficiency.[7]

2. **Marketing and sales**

Marketing standards

There is a condition in the licences of all suppliers which requires them to meet certain standards in their marketing activities.[8] If a supplier fails to meet those standards, Ofgem can take action (see Chapter 14). Ofgem has guidance notes which explain in more detail what it expects of suppliers and the circumstances in which it would take action.

The Code of Practice for Face-to-face Marketing of Energy Supply covers all forms of marketing including direct selling, door-to-door visits and telemarketing. The 'big 6' energy companies are members of the Code and all sales agents working for them have to adhere to it. The Code also imposes standards of selection and training on sales agents, the checking of references for staff and criminal convictions relevant to their role. Energy UK says that since the Code was introduced in 2002, complaints have dropped by 99 per cent. Details of the scheme, including a PDF version of the Code, can be found at www.energy-uk.org.uk.[9]

The standards set by the licence conditions and the Code of Practice include the following.

- All advertising and promotion must not give false or misleading information.
- Members, their agencies/contractors and sales agents must comply with all applicable licence and legislative obligations.
- The timing of calls should be convenient for the consumer, including no calls outside the hours of 9am to 8pm, and in sheltered housing the warden should be contacted first.
- Callers must identify themselves by producing an ID without being asked and leaving a phone number by which you can verify their credentials (see Chapter 10 for the standards suppliers must meet when their representatives come to your home).
- The sales agent must withdraw voluntarily if you indicate that the approach is unwelcome, inconvenient or inappropriate.
- If you refuse to sign a contract, the salesperson must not persist in persuading you against your wishes.
- The principal terms and conditions of the contract must be made clear before you sign (see p13 for your right to cancel the contract up to seven days after you sign).
- You must be given a copy of any contract you sign.
- If you sign a contract, you must be given the opportunity to refuse receipt of future advertising and promotional material – ie, junk mail.

Information on charges

For both gas and electricity, the supplier or its representative must provide you with 'an estimate of the total annual charges for the supply of electricity which would be payable' under the offered contract. The details must be in writing or by way of an electronic display. A written copy must also be supplied for your own records if you subsequently enter the contract.

Compensation for mis-selling

Compensation may be payable in some cases of mis-selling. Standard Licence Condition (SLC) 25.7 outlines the types of practices which constitute mis-selling, however there is no statutory requirement within the current SLCs for suppliers to award compensation for mis-selling and Ofgem does not currently have the same statutory powers as other regulators (eg, the Financial Services Authority), to seek redress on your behalf. Instead, the *Code of Practice for the Face-to-Face*

Marketing of Energy Supply leaves it up to individual suppliers to decide the amount of compensation.[10]

There have been recent calls for Ofgem to be given greater regulatory powers in respect of mis-selling with a number of high profile cases making the news. In May 2011, Scottish and Southern Energy were successfully prosecuted by Surrey County Council and fined £1.25 million at Guildford Magistrates Court for mis-selling during door-to-door sales.

In March 2012, EDF agreed to enter into a dialogue with Ofgem regarding potential breaches of its licencing conditions. As a result of negotiations, EDF offered, on a voluntary basis, to make a £4.5 million package available to assist vulnerable customers.

In light of these cases, the Department of Energy and Climate Change has agreed to consider the possibility of giving Ofgem stronger and more clearly defined powers of redress in mis-selling cases in the future.

See Chapter 14 for a discussion of the remedies available if any of your rights have been breached. If you want to complain about a possible breach of a licence condition or the Code of Practice, complain first to the supplier, preferably in writing. If you need to, you can then take it further with Energy UK, Citizens Advice consumer service or your local authority trading standards department.

Cancelling a contract

Following the recent case involving Scottish and Southern Energy (see above), the 'big 6' fuel suppliers have now largely stopped using doorstep sales methods to encourage customers to switch supplier. However, the cooling-off period described here also applies to contracts signed away from the trader's normal place of business, such as a trade fair or shopping centre.

The normal rule in contract law is that if you sign a contract you are bound by the terms and conditions in the contract, even if you have not read it.[11] However, extra protection is given to people who sign contracts at home in response to a visit by a sales representative. If you sign a contract for the supply of gas and/or electricity after an unsolicited visit from a supplier's representative, that supplier must give you a 'cooling-off period' of at least seven days.[12] This means you can cancel any contract up to seven days after you signed it (or longer if the supplier says so). Ask the representative how long the cooling-off period is if s/he does not mention it her/himself. If you cancel a contract within the relevant period you must be given back any money already paid.[13] Also, at the time you sign the contract, the sales representative must give you written notice of your right to cancel. If s/he fails to do so, the contract is not enforceable against you, whether you cancel within seven days or not.[14]

If a contract for the supply of electricity also includes providing goods or services (eg, energy efficiency measures), the charges for each must be separately identified, in keeping with requirements of fair treatment of customers when selling.[15]

Misrepresentation

In addition to the right to bring a complaint to Citizens Advice consumer service about misrepresentation, you also have civil law remedies.

A signed contract may be set aside for misrepresentation at common law. This means that where you are led to enter into a contract because of a false statement of fact (not opinion or law) and the statement is untrue, you are entitled to have the contract set aside (the legal term for this is 'rescinded'). A misstatement of fact may be deliberate, negligent or innocent, but if the statement is untrue and induces you to enter a contract, then a remedy will exist in law. A court can order that a contract is rescinded and may also award damages where there has been financial loss. In practice, a supplier may be prepared to cancel a contract if there has been a misrepresentation rather than face legal proceedings. In most cases, the sums involved will be £5,000 or below, the level for the small claims court procedure (see Chapter 14).

A similar rule applies to written contracts where the terms of the contract you are presented with by the seller are false or misleading. If a signature is obtained from you because the nature or contents of the agreement are wrongly described, then it is not considered binding.

Forging of signatures

Forging of signatures is a criminal offence,[16] and compensation will be payable in a case where forgery can be shown. The police or trading standards could take action in a case of forgery. If it is established that a sales representative has forged a signature to transfer you to her/his company, £250 compensation is available.[17] For all other forms of complaint, the supplier will apply its individual company compensation policy.[18]

---

3. **Contracts**

Electricity

Supply contracts

A **'supply contract'** is an agreement for the supply of electricity to domestic premises. A supplier must not supply electricity to such premises except under a supply contract. Electricity suppliers' licences place conditions on what they are allowed to put in supply contracts (eg, terms regarding security deposits) – these are dealt with where appropriate throughout this book. This means that, when offering you a contract and supplying you with electricity, a supplier must conform to its licence conditions or face action from Ofgem (see Chapter 14).

Supply contracts are governed by Standard Licence Conditions (SLCs) 22 and 23. Contracts must be in a standard form, although there can be different forms for different areas, cases and circumstances. They must set out all the terms and conditions on which the supplier will rely on. If the contract is for goods and services as well as the supply of electricity, the charges for each must be separately identified. The cost of any credit element must also be shown separately.

Copies of each kind of supply contract used by a supplier must be published in a manner to secure adequate publicity. Copies must be sent to Ofgem and be available on request under SLC 22.8. The contract should be provided 'within a reasonable period of time after receiving the request'. You should also be able to get information from the supplier summarising the terms of its supply contracts, with details of anything likely to influence you when deciding whether or not to take up a contract. Such information must be adequately publicised and the supplier must provide copies to Ofgem. Consumer Focus also has jurisdiction to deal with complaints involving energy suppliers and problems in switching supplier.

Deemed contracts

A deemed contract may arise with respect to a supply of electricity from a supplier where a contract has ended without being formally renewed. Deemed contracts may also arise where there are new occupiers who do not formally arrange a new supply contract. **'Deemed contracts'** for electricity are governed by Schedule 4 paragraph 3 of the Utilities Act 2000, Schedule 6 of the Electricity Act 1989 and SLC 7, and apply to situations where the supply of electricity to domestic premises continues but the original contract is no longer in force. In such cases, you remain under an obligation to pay and the supplier is expected to behave reasonably with respect to terms and conditions and charges. Under SLC 7.8, the electricity supplier must provide a copy of the terms of its deemed contract on request. Suppliers are also under a duty to use 'reasonable endeavours' to inform you of the terms, act reasonably towards you, and must not impose onerous terms.

A deemed contract will continue until such time as a new contract is agreed between you and the supplier or you end the contract by leaving the premises. Paragraph 3(1) of Schedule 6 of the Electricity Act 1989 and Schedule 4 paragraph 3 of the Utilities Act 2000 also state:

'Where an electricity supplier supplies electricity to any premises otherwise than in pursuance of a contract, the supplier shall be deemed to have contracted with the occupier (or the owner if the premises are unoccupied) for the supply of electricity as from the time…when he began to supply electricity.'

Gas

Supply contracts

Gas suppliers supply domestic customers with gas under the terms of a contract or a 'deemed contract' (see below).[19] Suppliers must have a 'scheme' setting out the principal terms of contracts. The principal terms will include details of the prices to be charged for gas and will state if there may be any fluctuation in the amount of the bill due to variations in the amount charged by transporters to suppliers for transporting gas to your premises.

Details of the principal terms must be published in a way which is likely to bring them to the attention of the customers concerned. Ofgem must be kept informed of the suppliers' principal terms and of any variation. You are entitled to a copy of the principal terms on request and the supplier must send one within a reasonable time of receiving a request.[20] Supply contracts are required to be in writing.[21]

The terms of contracts may vary between different types of customer and between different areas, but not so that there is undue preference or discrimination between customers.[22] SLC 27.2, as from 1 October 2010, requires that any difference in terms and conditions offered to customers on different payment methods must reflect actual cost differences. However, individual suppliers increasingly set prices on a national basis with less local variation than with electricity. Ofgem and the industry talk openly about the need for **'cost-reflective pricing'**. This means that groups of customers who are cheaper to supply may be offered discounts on the rates offered to other groups of customers.

A contract may be for an indefinite period of time, known as a 'rolling contract', or for a fixed term. Where a contract is due to come to an end, the supplier must offer you a new contract and inform you of the terms of the 'deemed contract' (see below) which would apply if no new contract is agreed. A supplier may not enter into a contract with you if another person has a contract with a different supplier for the supply of gas to the same premises,[23] unless that contract will have expired, or have been breached or have been terminated before you require a supply.

Contracts for other services

Gas suppliers can offer contracts for the supply of gas together with other services, including the provision of service pipes or the provision of energy efficiency goods or services. Such contracts must clearly and separately identify the charges made for the supply of gas and the other services. These contracts may have different terms and conditions to contracts offered under published 'principal terms'.[24]

Deemed contracts

Where your contract comes to an end and no contract was agreed for a further supply of gas, your gas supplier may charge you for any gas used under the terms of a deemed contract, with details being sent to you in writing 'on or about 30 days' before the contract expires.[25] However, most suppliers have auto-renewal provisions or allow for ongoing 'rolling' contracts which require a positive act to terminate. Particular provision is made for a deemed contract to apply where a supply to a previous owner or occupier has come to an end because that person is no longer the owner or occupier, and a new owner or occupier has used the gas supply without arranging with the existing supplier to do so.

Suppliers must set up a scheme for determining the terms and conditions which are to be incorporated into deemed contracts. As with supply contracts, deemed contracts may vary between different customers or groups of customers. Details of the scheme and of any changes must be published and a copy of the scheme and any changes must be sent to Ofgem. A supplier should provide you with the principal terms of the deemed contract; and give notice that contracts, with terms that may be different from the terms of deemed contracts, may be available and of how information about such contracts may be obtained.[26] Suppliers must also provide copies of deemed contracts on request 'within a reasonable time'.[27]

Dual-fuel supply contracts

Some suppliers offer both gas and electricity – this is called dual-fuel supply. There are obvious potential advantages of convenience for you if you take a dual supply. Sometimes there may also be discounts for taking a dual supply. But check whether you will actually get a discount or other advantages – eg, you may have to deal with separate arms of the same company for your gas and electricity, which might feel little different from being supplied by two different companies. Apart from convenience, there are no other automatic benefits of having a dual supply, and you should check the terms of your contract in the same way as for any other fuel contract. Of course, dual-fuel supply contracts will have to comply with both sets of provisions for gas and electricity.

If you are paying one company a single amount for both your gas and electricity, be aware of how your payment is treated. Normally, the charges for gas and electricity should be separately specified in a bill. If you make only one payment towards the cost of both gas and electricity and do not specify which fuel you are paying for, the supplier can decide which to put the payment towards. For example, if you owe £10 for gas and another £10 for electricity and then pay £10 to the supplier, the supplier can choose whether to put this towards paying off your gas bill or your electricity bill. On the other hand, if you say clearly before you pay that you are paying the £10 specifically for, say, gas, the supplier will normally be bound by your decision. If you have a dispute over this, refer the matter to Consumer Focus in the first instance, who may refer the matter on to the Energy Ombudsman (see Chapter 14) or take legal advice on an action in the county court in England and Wales or the Sheriff Court in Scotland (see Chapter 14).

Contractual terms

- **Period.** A contract is either for a fixed term of weeks, months or years or it is indefinite. The latter is known as a 'rolling contract'. All contracts can be terminated on 28 days' notice, but there may be a financial penalty if you terminate a fixed-term contract early. Check with the supplier whether there would be a penalty for early termination and how much it would be. In some cases a supplier may be prepared to exercise its discretion and drop a penalty which might otherwise be imposed for early termination. Early termination is covered by SLC 24. If you want to terminate your contract after receiving notice of a unilateral change to your contract terms, such as a price increase, and switch to another supplier, your old supplier must terminate your contract within 15 days of receiving confirmation that you now have a contract with your new supplier. For more information on this process, see Chapter 5.

- **Special services.** Some contracts may be offered together with other services, such as improving the energy efficiency of your home. The costs of the supply and the services should be listed separately, including any credit element, so you can compare prices with other suppliers.

- **New products.** Some electricity suppliers offer special products. For example, for a premium (eg, a 10 per cent higher charge) some suppliers will guarantee to buy enough electricity from environmentally renewable sources or from coal-generated sources to supply your needs. Other suppliers may offer a variety of combined deals. You need to do some careful research and detailed calculations to ensure that a decision to switch supplier is based on your own circumstances, usage, location and payment method.

Unfair terms

Compared with most other businesses, gas and electricity are heavily regulated (see Chapter 14). Therefore, there should be less chance of contracts containing unfair terms and if you come across a term which might be unfair, you can complain, initially to the Citizens Advice consumer service.

However, regulation is not a guarantee. You may still need to assert your rights against unfair terms. Even better, you can try to avoid unfair terms by checking over a contract before you sign it. All terms are approved by the Department for Business, Innovation and Skills and reviewed by Ofgem. The scope or power of consumers to negotiate different terms (by objecting to specific terms or supplying counter terms and conditions) has yet to be tested in law in the context of consumer fuel contracts.

An **'unfair term'** is one which causes a significant imbalance in the parties' rights and obligations under the contract to the detriment of the consumer – ie, if a contractual term goes too far in favour of the supplier, it is unfair. An unfair term is not binding on you. Unfair terms are governed by The Unfair Terms in

Consumer Contracts Regulations 1999,[28] which are enforced by the Director of Ofgem and the directors of other selected agencies.

Regulation 5(1) provides: 'A contractual term which has not been individually negotiated shall be regarded as unfair if, contrary to the requirement of good faith, it causes a significant imbalance in the parties' rights and obligations arising under the contract, to the detriment of the consumer.' The regulations apply to any term in a contract which has not been individually negotiated, which will be the bulk of most supply contracts.[29] This will apply to any of a supplier's standard terms and conditions,[30] and it is particularly relevant where, in the absence of any actual agreement, a contract is deemed to exist for either gas or electricity (see p16).

Gas and electricity supply contracts often contain terms which are meant to incorporate or reflect provisions in the relevant statute, regulations or licence conditions. If such a term accurately incorporates or reflects the relevant provision, then the regulations do not apply to it,[31] but if such terms try to go beyond the relevant provision, the regulations do apply.

Contractual terms must be written in plain, intelligible language.[32] If there is any doubt as to the meaning of a particular term, the interpretation most favourable to you should be used.[33] If you come across possibly unfair terms or unintelligible language, you can refer the contract to the Director General of Fair Trading, Consumer Focus or Ofgem (see p229). The civil courts can also grant a remedy known as a 'declaration' to establish the legal effect or meaning of a term. Sales representatives from gas and electricity suppliers should now be trained about these regulations and act in accordance with them. For further details, see Chapter 14.

Penalties

In some cases, a supplier will demand payment of a fee or penalty for early termination on a contract, but a number of restrictions are placed on any power to impose such penalties.

SLC 24 for electricity provides that a termination fee shall not be demanded in the case of a contract of indefinite length (ie, a rolling contract, not a fixed-term contract) or where the customer has notified the supplier of an intention to terminate where the supplier has unilaterally changed or intends to change the contract. Other situations where a supplier may not impose a fee or penalty include where a property is sold or the customer moves out or where a contract of supply is for more than 12 months or is for an initial fixed-term period.

A supplier may be prepared to waive a penalty in certain circumstances at its discretion – eg, where a contract has to be ended because the consumer has gone into care or has died. The supplier may also accept a lesser sum in full and final settlement of any claim for the penalty as a way of settling legal proceedings (see p107).

There may also be an argument that a supplier is under a duty to mitigate its loss (ie, take steps to reduce any loss) from early termination of the contract. The duty to mitigate is imposed at common law in a case of breach of contract. A supplier cannot just demand any sum in compensation or damages it sees fit simply because the contract has been broken in some way by the consumer. The duty to mitigate losses should be referred to in correspondence to settle such a dispute.

Terminating a contract

Some gas and electricity contracts can be terminated on 28 days' notice. If you feel you made a mistake in changing to a particular supplier, you can give 28 days' notice and either go back to your original supplier or sign a contract with a new one. However, always check your contract – if it was for a fixed-period, there may be a penalty for early termination. Some suppliers also offer long-term contracts which make provision for a 'reasonable' termination payment. It is possible that energy companies may offer three-, four- or five-year contracts with consumers in the future, subject to Ofgem approval, with the longer term being in exchange for particular energy services. Changes in the Standard Licence Conditions allow companies to offer fixed-term, long-term contracts without the need for extra services.

Notes

1. Suppliers

1 Available at
www.energymadeclear.co.uk
2 Condition 23 SLC
3 http://
energyapps.consumerfocus.org.uk/
price/fact_sheets
4 Consumer Focus, *The Confidence Code: A
voluntary code of practice for online
domestic price comparison services*, 2010

2. Marketing and sales

5 see http://
energyapps.consumerfocus.org.uk/
performance/
6 Ofgem debt assignment protocol for
prepayment meter customers letter 24
September 2012 (www.ofgem.gov.uk/
Sustainability/SocAction/Publications/
Documents1/Debt Assignment Protocol
Review.pdf)
7 Consumer Focus leaflet, *Switching
energy suppliers when in debt to your
current supplier*
8 Condition 25 SLC
9 www.energy-uk.org.uk/customers/
energy-industry-codes/energysure-code
10 clause 11.2, *Code of Practice for the Face-
to-Face Marketing of Energy Supply*
11 See *L'Estrange v Graucob* [1934] 2 KB
394
12 CP(CCCBP) Regs
13 Reg 5 CP(CCCBP) Regs
14 Reg 4 CP(CCCBP) Regs
15 Conditions 22 and 25 SLC
16 Forgery Act 1981
17 Clause 11.1 *Code of Practice for the Face-
to-Face Marketing of Energy Supply*
18 Clause 11.4 *Code of Practice for the Face-
to-Face Marketing of Energy Supply*

3. Contracts

19 Condition 22.1 SLC
20 Condition 22.7 SLC
21 Condition 22.4 SLC
22 Condition 25A.2 SLC
23 Condition 14 SLC
24 Condition 22.4 (a) SLC
25 Condition 23.2 SLC; Sch 6 para 3 EA
1989 as amended by UA 2000

26 Condition 7.7 SLC
27 Condition 7.8 SLC
28 SI 1999 No.2083
29 Reg 5(2) UTCC Regs
30 Reg 5(2) UTCC Regs will cover standard
supply contracts
31 Sch 1 UTCC Regs; Conditions SLC 46
and 47; *Goh Kim Hai Edward v Pacific Can
Investments Holdings Ltd* [1996] 2 SLR
109; *Brace v Calder* (1895) 2 QB 253
32 Reg 7(1) UTCC Regs
33 Reg 7(2) UTCC Regs

3

Chapter 3

The right to a supply

This chapter covers:
1. Who is entitled to a supply (below)
2. Squatters (p26)
3. Travellers (p27)
4. Mobile home and caravan sites (p28)
5. When you can be refused a supply of electricity (see p28)
6. Getting your supply connected: electricity (p30)
7. Conditions of supply: electricity (p31)
8. Tariff customers and customers with special agreements: electricity (p31)
9. Charges for connecting a supply: electricity (p32)
10. When you can be refused a supply of gas (p33)
11. Getting your supply connected: gas (p35)
12. Charges for connecting a supply: gas (p37)
13. Security deposits (p38)
14. Alternatives to security deposits (p43)
15. Disruption of power supply (p43)

This chapter assumes that you are legally responsible ('liable') for your fuel supply. Check Chapter 5 to ensure that you are in fact responsible for the supply.

1. Who is entitled to a supply

Electricity

Contract suppliers have a duty to offer a contract when they receive a 'request from a domestic customer'[1] and will supply electricity to you if the contract is accepted. Normally it is quite clear that you are requesting a supply but, to ensure it is treated as valid, your request should include:
- details of the premises to be supplied;
- the day on which the supply should commence;
- maximum power to be supplied, if this differs from that normally required by an ordinary domestic customer;
- the minimum period for supply;

- any reference to a continuing supply already established at the premises (where relevant).

Under Standard Licence Condition (SLC) 22, the supplier must offer to enter into a domestic supply contract with you as soon as is reasonably practical. The duty to provide a supply is only enforceable by Ofgem because it is contained in the supplier's licence, not in the Electricity Act (see Chapter 14). The contract must be in a standard form containing all the terms and conditions, including the price and your right to terminate the contract (see p13).

If you accept the offer of a contract, the supplier must provide, and continue to provide, a supply of electricity until the contract is properly terminated, subject to exceptions which are dealt with below. If the supplier fails to fulfil its obligations in the contract, this will be a breach of contract which may give rise to legal remedies, including a right to compensation.

It is worth noting that the SLCs for contract suppliers make no mention of 'occupier' (see below) or anything else connected with your right to occupy the place where you want a supply of electricity. This means that squatters are probably not excluded from the supplier's duty to offer a contract (see p28). Tariff suppliers and contract suppliers are covered by different legal provisions (see p31 for the difference between tariff and contract suppliers). Tariff suppliers' duties to supply are set out in the Electricity Act 1989, whereas contract suppliers' duties are set out in the licence granted to them by Ofgem. Tariff suppliers have a statutory duty to supply you if:

- you are an owner or occupier of the premises; *and*
- you request a supply by giving notice in writing.[2]

In practice, most domestic supplies are by way of contract and reference may be made to the SLCs. An **'occupier'** is a person who occupies any premises legally, whether paying rent or some other charge, or paying nothing (see p26 for squatters).[3] Relatively few customers remain who are subject to tariff arrangements.

Guaranteed standards of performance

Electricity distribution companies are subject to guaranteed standards in accordance with the Electricity (Connection Standards of Performance) Regulations 2010 as amended.

If the distributor fails to meet the standards laid down, you are entitled to receive a payment. The size of the payment varies on the situation and the length of delay.[4] For example, if a quotation for a connection is not provided within five working days, the supplier is liable to pay you £10 for each day, including the day on which the quotation is provided.[5] (Various sums may become payable where a supplier fails to provide a schedule of works and starting times for different types of connection, within various time periods.)

Disputes as to whether compensation is payable in a particular case may be referred to Ofgem.[6]

These payments can be made direct to you or via your electricity company.

Gas

If you want a supply of gas, you have rights and obligations in a similar fashion as you do for electricity.

You have the right to be connected to the gas network by a gas transporter (see Chapter 1). Gas mains and service pipes are owned by gas transporters. There are a number of gas transporters, but National Grid Gas (previously Transco) is the main one. A gas transporter has a statutory duty to connect your premises to the gas mains if:

- you are the owner or occupier (an **'occupier'** is a person who occupies any premises legally, whether or not s/he pays rent or some other charge); *and*
- the premises are within 23 metres of the nearest gas main.

Where there is an existing domestic supply you obtain a contract by contacting the gas supplier. Under SLC 22 a gas supplier must offer to enter into a gas supply contract with you after receiving a request. The offer must be made 'within a reasonable time' of receiving the request.

From 10 November 2011 a domestic supply contract or a deemed contract must include:[7]

- the identity and address of the supplier;
- the services provided (including any maintenance services) and any service quality levels to be met;
- if a connection is required, when that connection will take place;
- the means by which up to date information on all applicable tariffs and any maintenance charges may be obtained;
- any conditions for renewal of the contract.

If there is no existing supply, you must inform the transporter in writing that you require a supply of gas at the premises concerned (there will normally be a standard form). You will be charged for the costs of connecting your premises to the network (see p37) unless you choose to have independent contractors do the work for you (see p37).[8]

All gas suppliers are under an obligation to supply gas under a contract to new customers (ie, owners or occupiers who request a supply) whose premises are already connected to the gas mains either directly or by a service pipe. The 'obligation to supply' is a condition of each supplier's licence. You cannot enforce the obligation to supply without the help of Ofgem because it is contained in the supplier's licence rather than in legislation. All gas suppliers must publish the principal terms of the contracts available from them and bring them to the attention of customers.[9] These cover the terms and conditions under which gas will be supplied and are regulated by conditions within the supplier's licence.

If you have been supplied under the terms of a contract initially, the supplier must continue to supply you until either the contract comes to an end or it is terminated. A gas supplier will continue to supply gas under the terms of a deemed contract if your contract has come to an end (see p15).[10] The supplier must invite you to enter into a further contract to run immediately following the expiry or termination of your existing contract.

Obligation on a gas supplier to supply you with gas under the terms of a deemed contract could also arise if a supplier were ordered to do so by Ofgem. Ofgem has the power to suspend or revoke a supplier's licence. If this happens, or if a supplier is unable to continue to supply gas (eg, if the company goes into liquidation), Ofgem can order an alternative supplier to supply you instead.

There are minimum standards for supply and distribution for gas, under the Gas (Standards of Performance) Regulations 2005.

Obligation to complete a supply transfer within three weeks

Where you are seeking to transfer your supply of gas or electricity special rules apply whereby the transfer must be completed within 21 days.

Under SLC 14A.1, the licensee must include a term in every contract made with a customer on or after 10 November 2011 requiring that the supplier complete the supply transfer within 21 days.[11] Exceptions to this duty arise where:

- you request that the supply is completed at a later date; *or*
- you cancel the supply contract and notify the supplier that you do not wish the supply transfer to take place; *or*
- an existing supplier is entitled to block the transfer because of an unpaid debt; *or*
- the supplier does not have all of the information it requires to complete the transfer having taken reasonable steps to obtain the information and it cannot readily obtain that information from another source; *or*
- you are currently taking a supply of electricity through an exempt distribution system.

Exceptions

There are situations where a supplier/transporter does not have a duty to supply, or continue to supply, electricity or gas. A supplier/transporter is entitled to refuse to connect a supply or to disconnect a supply which has already been given in certain circumstances – see p28 for electricity and p33 for gas.

From 1 September 2012 squatters fall into a separate category as they may no longer be considered to be 'occupiers' and, therefore, are not entitled to a supply if the relevant test remains occupation (see p26).

Exceptions to the minimum standards of performance

In a number of situations the minimum standards of performance do not apply. These include where:

- you inform the relevant supplier or operator that you do not wish any action to be taken;
- you agree another course of action with the supplier or operator;
- you supply information to a supplier or operator at the wrong address or outside reasonable hours which the supplier or operator has specified;
- it is not reasonably practicable for the supplier or operator to act in a prescribed time owing to severe weather conditions, an industrial dispute or the action of a third party;
- the supplier or operator has been unable to gain access to premises;
- action may be in contravention of the law;
- you have failed to pay the relevant charge after receiving a notice or where you have committed a criminal offence;
- there are exceptional circumstances beyond the control of the supplier or operator.

2. **Squatters**

Previous editions of this guide recognised that squatters were entitled to a supply of gas or electricity under contract and that anyone who was a squatter should indicate that s/he is willing to meet the obligations under a contract and state that residency may be on a short-term basis, in order to rebut any allegation that s/he is dishonestly using gas or electricity (see Chapter 9).

However, this position has now changed by the effect of the criminalisation of squatting in residential buildings from 1 September 2012 under section 144 of the Legal Aid, Sentencing and Punishment of Offenders Act 2012.

Consequently the position in England and Wales has been brought in line with that in Scotland (where squatting has never been legal) as respects the use of residential buildings by trespassers when they are deemed to be living in the building. Suppliers are entitled to refuse to supply gas or electricity to anyone who is committing the offence created under section 144. Furthermore, an arrangement of a supply by a trespasser might be taken as evidence that an offence under the Act is being committed by demonstrating an intention to live in the building.

However, it is important to note that the offence is only committed where a person is deemed to be 'living' in the residential building and does not affect squatted premises which involve non-residential activities – eg, where a residential building is used other than for living purposes such as the storage of goods, commercial purposes, for holding art exhibitions or cultural purposes such as concerts.

The precise scope of law has yet to be clarified on such matters as temporary occupation in cases where a person may have a settled home elsewhere or cases of mistake.

It is also postulate other situations where a supply may be possible without involving a person living in the building – eg, where a trespasser occupies a garden or yard or is living in a non-domestic part of a building such as a garage.

Persons holding over from a temporary previous lease or licence are specifically excluded from the offence of squatting[12] and remain entitled to a supply of gas or electricity.

If you were a squatter before 1 September 2012, it is unclear what the impact on supply of power will be and how Ofgem or the courts may interpret any rights to the supply of fuel after this date in the case of pre-existing contract.

Although squatting has been made an offence, the provision of gas or electricity to a squatter under contract is not illegal and a refusal to supply and terminate an agreement might potentially give rise to a breach of contract by the supplier, depending on how 'living' is interpreted by the courts. The legislation considers 'living' as meaning residing for any period of time, but much will depend upon how courts approach cases on their facts, as living at an address is not simply determined by the amount of time spent at a property.[13] Cases will be complicated where a person may use two or more addresses and argues that s/he is actually staying for the purposes of living at more another address. Everything will depend upon how Ofgem and the courts may interpret the terms of a supply contract in such situations.

3. **Travellers**

Local councils in England and Wales are provided with guidance on practical aspects of site provision and management by the Department of Communities and Local Government or the Welsh government. The guidance contains the standards for the supply of electricity, gas and water to sites.[14]

Standards vary according to the type of site provided.

- There are no provisions requiring the supply of electricity to transit or short-stay sites or to residential sites which have not yet been developed into permanent sites.
- On permanent sites for long-term residential use, every family should have the use of a pitch provided with electricity.

The local council as landlord is responsible for the supply and is entitled to resell electricity, although its charges cannot exceed the maximum re-sale price for electricity (see p204).

4. **Mobile home and caravan sites**

Sites for mobile homes are licensed by local councils under the Caravan Sites and Control of Development Act 1960. Model standards for the provision of electricity and water are issued to local councils. Local councils can decide what conditions, if any, to attach to caravan site licences. Guidance to local councils is in very broad terms and suggests that sites should be provided with an electricity supply sufficient to meet all reasonable demands of the caravans situated on them. There is no guidance for the supply of gas.

Always look at the provisions in the caravan site licence to determine if your site owner is obliged to provide a supply of electricity to your site. Site owners may resell electricity to you, but cannot charge more than the maximum re-sale price (see p204).

If there is no provision for electricity on your site, there is nothing to stop you from applying for a supply to be connected if you are the owner or occupier of a mobile home or caravan. However, note the possibility of significant connection charges.

Contact the National Association of Caravan Owners (www.nacoservices.com) for further advice.

5. **When you can be refused a supply of electricity**

Electricity suppliers may refuse to supply electricity, refuse to connect a supply to new premises, disconnect an existing supply, or refuse to reconnect a supply which has been disconnected. Disconnection for arrears is dealt with fully in Chapter 8.

You may be refused a supply for a number of reasons. Some of these reasons applying to tariff suppliers were set out in the Electricity Act 1989, but grounds for refusal are now set out in the Standard Licence Conditions for contract suppliers. All of the following reasons apply.

- You refuse to take a supply on the terms offered.
- You have not paid your bill for any electricity supplied, standing charges, meters and any connection charges within 20 working days of the date of the bill (see p96). You are entitled to two working days' notice of disconnection. Your supply may only be disconnected in relation to the premises where the debt arose under the Utilities Act 2000 Schedule 4 paragraph 2(1). Every supplier is required by its licence to have a code of practice on payment of bills, including procedures to deal with customers who have difficulty paying (see p97).[15] The terms of your supplier's code could protect you from disconnection by setting out alternatives.

- You did not pay your bill for any of the above charges at your previous address. The supplier may refuse to connect a supply at your new address. The supplier is not entitled to payment of your arrears from the next occupier of your previous address. Similarly, you cannot be held liable for debts left by previous occupiers of your new address.
- You have not paid a security deposit within seven days of being sent a notice requiring you to do so (see p41) and the requirement of a security deposit is reasonable in the circumstances.
- You refuse to accept a supply under a 'special agreement' under the Electricity Act 1989.
- Your premises are already being supplied by another electricity supplier under arrangements which have not expired or been terminated.
- Supplying you with electricity would, or might be, unsafe – eg, because your wiring is in a dangerous condition.
- You refuse to take your supply through a meter.
- There has been damage or tampering to a meter and the matter has not been remedied (see Chapter 9).
- The supplier is prevented from supplying you by circumstances outside its control – eg, if it has been prevented from laying cables because of extreme weather conditions or a civil disturbance.
- It is not reasonable in all the circumstances. This is a 'catch-all' provision. Most disconnections or refusals to supply will be on one or more of the grounds above, but this provision might be used if those grounds no longer apply – eg, you are no longer in arrears but the supplier is insisting that you can only be supplied through a prepayment meter for future consumption. If you refuse to accept a prepayment meter, the supplier will need to demonstrate that disconnection was the only reasonable alternative. The supplier cannot use this catch-all provision unless it first gives you seven days' notice of the intention to disconnect.

Suppliers are not entitled to disconnect for alleged non-payment if the amount is genuinely in dispute (see p121).

Notice of planned supply interruption

If the distributor needs to switch off a supply of power on the network, it should normally give you a minimum of two days' notice. The requirement to give notice includes any interruption by a distributor which affects a supply from another distributor. This notice should give the date of the interruption in supply.

Where a distributor fails to give at least two days' notice, stating the date on which supply is to be interrupted or where the distributor interrupts supply on a different date, the distributor must pay you £22. You must make your claim within one month.

6. **Getting your supply connected: electricity**

Notice

To obtain a supply of electricity you must contact the supplier with your request. You can do this by writing a letter or by completing the supplier's standard application form. However, most suppliers will not always require written notice and will connect your supply if you phone to request a supply or if you call into a customer service centre. You may wish to safeguard your rights by making your request in writing or by following up your phone request in writing. Keep a copy of your letter in the event of any dispute arising.

Most application forms contain all the necessary details. If you are writing a letter but are not sure what maximum power is required, it should be sufficient to make clear that you want an ordinary domestic supply. If you have a preference, also specify what type of meter you would like and how you wish to pay for your supply (see Chapter 4).

If you choose not to give information about yourself (eg, about your previous address or creditworthiness), you may be asked for a security deposit. You do not have to give information about other people living in your home, but note that liability for the bill may be decided on who signs the application form or letter (see Chapter 5).

If your requirements on the application form are acceptable (ie, if the supplier is prepared to supply you on your choice of meter, method of payment or other terms and conditions), a contract supplier will offer you a contract which you can accept or reject.

When your supply be connected

The connection is carried out by the supplier (see Chapter 1), which is governed by the following standards of performance (see Appendix 2).

- If your premises were previously supplied with electricity, you should be given an appointment within two working days for your supply to be connected and a meter installed. If the appointment is not made within the specified time, you are entitled to automatic compensation of £22. If the appointment is made and not kept, you are entitled to automatic compensation of £22.

- If your premises have never previously had a supply of electricity, and you make a written request for an estimate of the charges of connection, this should be sent within five working days if the work is simple, or within 15 working days if the work is complicated. You are entitled to a compensation payment of £44 if the estimate is not sent within these time limits. For a contract supplier, connection times will depend on how quickly you respond to its offer of a contract.

If you experience unreasonable delays in getting your supply connected, contact Citizens Advice consumer service for advice or consider getting a court order (see Chapter 14).

7. **Conditions of supply: electricity**

Standard Licensing Conditions (SLCs) apply to all suppliers of electricity. Under SLCs which apply from January 2013, a supplier is under a duty to offer a contract to a domestic consumer. When suppliers supply by contract, they can only supply under contracts which contain standard terms and conditions that comply with their licence conditions. SLC 22.1 provides that electricity will not be supplied unless it is done so under a domestic supply contract or a deemed contract. Once you sign a contract, you are legally bound by its terms, but if you think any are unfair or unreasonable, Ofgem has the power to stop a supplier enforcing any term which is incompatible with its licence conditions. See p14 for contractual terms and Chapter 14 for details about unfair terms.

8. **Tariff customers and customers with special agreements: electricity**

In the event that there are still a small number of people who are 'tariff customers', or there remain historic debts not subject to standard contracts with suppliers, the following note is included on former tariff customers. **'Tariff customers'** are customers of tariff suppliers who are or were supplied under legislative provisions, not contracts (see p3) and should be distinguished from persons who benefit from special supplier tariffs under contract. Former tariff customers fall into the category of having their electricity supplied in accordance with the relevant legislation, namely the Electricity Act 1989 and regulations made under it.

There is, however, provision for an alternative status for tariff customers. This is known as a 'special agreement' under section 22 of the Electricity Act 1989. The terms and conditions which bind both you and the tariff supplier would be the terms of the agreement rather than those under the Act. Under a tariff supplier's licence, a special agreement is referred to as a 'contract', so that a special agreement must be a designated supply contract and must conform with the licence conditions covering the form and content of designated supply contracts (see p3).

There are two sets of circumstances in which the question of a special agreement might arise.

- A supplier has the discretion to grant you a special agreement if you ask for one when you give notice requiring a supply.

- You could be required to enter into a special agreement by the supplier if it was 'reasonable in all the circumstances'.

In the case of a claim for a debt from the past, it is important to remember that the Limitation Act 1980 places a six-year limit on the recovery of debts owed under contract. The six-year limit applies from the date that the debt fell due or from which a written promise to pay was extracted from the debtor.

In the past, tariff suppliers attempted to impose special agreements only in exceptional circumstances and usually only when disconnection was considered to be the only alternative. These provisions have now been overtaken by the schemes for special tariffs which suppliers are now offering to customers.

9. **Charges for connecting a supply: electricity**

Connecting an electricity supply will be carried out by a distribution network operator (DNO) which is licensed to distribute electricity through cables and provide connections to premises. Distributors are not responsible for meter-reading or billing – your energy supplier does this.

A DNO is obliged to provide and install assets necessary to connect a customer to a distribution network and will own the electricity wires and cables which provide the supply.

You may be charged for the connection of a supply. Details of connection charges are available from each DNO. Each has a website with connection charge details and a phone number for help and assistance.

To obtain a connection, you need to notify the DNO within a reasonable time of the details of the premises to be connected, the time the connection is required and (to the best of your knowledge) the maximum power to be supplied.

A DNO should provide you with a quotation for connection to its distribution system, but will not normally fit a meter until instructed to do so by your chosen electricity supplier. When providing a quotation, the DNO will normally specify that you need to nominate a supplier before connection takes place, and preferably before accepting the quotation. It is advisable to appoint and sign a contract with an electricity supplier at least 28 days before the date you want the electricity to flow.

When accepting a connection from the DNO, you or your supplier will be obliged to enter into a connection agreement. A connection agreement outlines the rights and obligations associated with the connection.

On connection, the DNO is obliged to maintain the connection for as long as required and to repair or replace any electrical lines or plants when necessary (except when you may be responsible for any damage to the equipment).

If you are dissatisfied with any aspects of connection, complain in the first instance to the company concerned. If the problem cannot be resolved, contact one of the consumer bodies detailed in Chapter 14 direct. In certain cases, it may also be appropriate for Ofgem to intervene.

Independent electrical engineers may be employed to carry out certain electrical connection work. A list of independent electrical engineering companies can be obtained from a local DNO. Lloyd's Register operates the National Electricity Registration Scheme (NERS) and a list of companies registered as competent for electrical connection work can be found at www.lloydsregister.co.uk/ners in its section on UK utilities and industries.

The NERS scheme covers the following services in respect of connection:
- designs;
- project management;
- cable laying;
- cable jointing;
- overhead lines wooden pole and/or steel tower (up to 132kV);
- substation installations;
- all associated civil engineering works and operations including excavation, cable laying and backfilling.

Cables and wires running between your meter to your electrical appliances are not covered by any connection agreement with the DNO and the electricity supplier – a qualified electrician would have to install them for you. Customer protection equipment such as fuse boxes and switches are also not covered by the connection agreement.

10. **When you can be refused a supply of gas**

A gas supplier may refuse to connect a gas supply to a new address, may cut off an existing supply or refuse to reconnect a supply which has been disconnected. A gas transporter may refuse to connect your premises to the gas supply network and may also disconnect your supply in a number of circumstances. Disconnection for arrears is dealt with fully in Chapter 8.

A **gas supplier** may cut off your supply in the following circumstances.
- You do not pay your bill within the 28 days following the date of the bill. You are entitled to a minimum of seven days' notice of the supplier's intention to disconnect. Note that there is no right to disconnect when the bill is genuinely in dispute. You may be protected from disconnection by conditions contained in your supplier's licence.[16]
- You change your supplier and you owe money to your previous supplier, in which case the previous supplier can assign some of your debt to your new supplier.[17] The new supplier cannot refuse debt assignment and will collect the

debt through a prepayment meter. However, the new supplier is unlikely to cut off the supply. What is termed 'debt blocking' – the refusal to take on a debtor with a prepayment meter as a customer by a new supplier – should not take place if the debt is £500 or less, following the debt assignment protocol (see p78).[18] You are entitled to a minimum of seven days' notice of the new supplier's intention to disconnect. The new supplier may also refuse to connect in these circumstances if your previous supplier cut off your supply and is still entitled to keep your supply cut off. The relevant debt does not include any sums for which you had already been billed by the previous supplier by the date you transferred to the new supplier and which you had failed to pay within 28 days. It does include any subsequent amounts for which you are billed by the previous supplier, providing you have failed to pay within 40 days. The previous supplier is only entitled to assign the debt if it has given you 14 days' notice of its intention to do so. If you are a credit meter consumer, you can ask for debt assignment, which is at the discretion of suppliers. If the debt is assigned, disconnection may arise from non-payment. There is no right to disconnect when the bill is genuinely in dispute. You may be protected from disconnection by conditions in your supplier's licence (see p126).

- You do not pay a reasonable security deposit or agree to accept a prepayment meter within the seven days following the supplier's request for a deposit. A supplier's right to request a security deposit is a condition of the supplier's licence. The Gas Act 1986 contains a provision enabling a gas transporter to request security for the initial connection of the supply.
- You fail to take your supply through a meter.
- You fail to keep a meter belonging to you or to someone other than the gas supplier or transporter in proper order.
- You intentionally damage or interfere with gas fittings, service pipes or meters (see Chapter 9).
- You do not/no longer require a supply of gas.
- You do not/no longer require the use of meters or other gas fittings belonging to the supplier/transporter. You are entitled to 24 hours' notice.
- Your supply has been reconnected without the consent of the supplier.
- Supplying you with gas would, or might, involve danger to the public.
- A gas transporter or another gas supplier has disconnected your supply and is under no obligation to reconnect your supply.
- A gas shipper has prevented the transfer of gas to your premises.
- A supplier's ability to supply its customers would be significantly prejudiced if it were to offer you a supply.
- There are circumstances beyond the supplier's control.[19]

A **gas transporter** may refuse to connect your premises to, or may disconnect your premises from, the gas supply network in the following circumstances.
- Your premises are not within the transporter's authorised area.

- Your premises are not close enough to a gas main – ie, the premises are not within 23 metres/25 yards of the transporter's gas main or could not be connected by a service pipe to a transporter's gas main.
- A transporter asks you to install a meter as near as possible to its main and you refuse. This applies when:
  - gas was not previously supplied to your premises by the transporter; *or*
  - a new/substituted pipe is required; *or*
  - the meter is to be moved.

  Note that the transporter may permit you to install a meter in alternative accommodation or in an external meter house, but this discretion lies with the transporter.
- You use gas improperly or deal with gas so as to interfere with the efficient conveyance of gas.
- The transporter is concerned to prevent the escape of gas or it suspects there may be an escape of gas. Note that the transporter has a duty to prevent gas escaping immediately after being informed of a gas leak. It is a criminal offence if a transporter fails to act within 12 hours. The transporter will have a defence if it can show that it was not reasonably practicable for the gas leak to be made safe within the 12 hours and that the leak was made safe as soon as reasonably practicable.
- You fail to take your supply through a meter.
- You fail to keep a meter belonging to you or to someone other than the gas supplier or transporter in proper order.
- You intentionally damage or interfere with gas fittings, service pipes or meters (see Chapter 9).
- You do not/no longer require a supply of gas. You are entitled to 24 hours' notice.
- You do not/no longer require the use of meters or other gas fittings belonging to the transporter. You are entitled to 24 hours' notice.
- The transporter is prevented from connecting you or maintaining your connection by circumstances not within its control.
- Supplying you would, or might, endanger the public.
- A pipe laid by the owner or occupier of the premises is not fit for the purpose.

11. Getting your supply connected: gas

Full competition exists for the supply of gas in the UK, and you are entitled to buy gas from any gas supply company licensed to sell gas within Britain.

If you move into a home which is not physically connected to the gas mains network, you will need to arrange a supply. There are three ways to get connected to a gas supply.

- Using a gas transporter who is licensed to supply gas through pipes and is under a duty to provide a gas connection where it is economical to do so. There will be a charge for the connection costs (see p37). There will also be a charge if you ask the transporter to lay any pipes which are needed. In addition, you may be asked to pay a security deposit to the transporter.
- Through a licensed gas supplier who can arrange for pipes to be laid by either the local gas transporter or an independent contractor. The gas supplier can pass on the charge for providing the connection and the pipework. This charge may include an arrangement fee.
- Through a qualified independent engineer installing pipes between a meter and a gas appliance. Once your home is physically connected to the supply network, the gas transporter will become responsible for the maintenance of the pipe. Ownership of the pipe concerned will be transferred to the transporter.

If your home is already connected to the gas mains network, you will need to enter into a contract with a gas supplier for your supply of gas. You do not have to use the supplier who was previously supplying the premises, although you may be deemed to have a contract with it if you do nothing about it (see Chapter 5). If you do not know who the current supplier to your premises is, you can find out through the M number (see p7) helpline (tel: 0870 6081 524), which can tell you the gas shipper for your address. Normally, the shipper and the supplier are the same company. If not, you will be referred to the shipper, who can tell you who the supplier is. See also Chapter 2 for details on contracts for the supply of gas.

When your supply be connected

In practice, the gas supply often remains connected after the previous occupier moves out, so there is often no interruption to the supply. If the supply of gas has been disconnected, the gas supplier which you have chosen will arrange a date to reconnect. It must do this as soon as reasonably practicable. If the meter has been removed, the supplier will arrange with the transporter for a meter to be installed or may itself provide you with a meter. If there is already a meter in place, the supplier will make arrangements with the owner of the meter (usually National Grid) for the existing meter to remain in place. This will not apply when the meter in place is not suitable.

National Grid and British Gas (or, in Scotland, Scottish Gas) are subject to various service standards which they previously agreed with Ofgas (the gas regulator prior to Ofgem). This is because they will be dominant in the gas market for some time to come, and it was felt that they needed extra regulation to ensure fairness for consumers. These standards include ones dealing with the connection of premises to the gas supply network.

The relevant key standards state that when a customer requests a gas supply:

- if a survey visit is required, contact will be made within two working days to arrange an appointment which will be within three working days, or later if requested by the customer;
- following such a visit, a quotation for providing a supply will be despatched within five working days of the visit where the property to be supplied is adjacent to a public highway in which there is a suitable gas main, or otherwise within 20 working days;
- if no visit is required, a quotation will be dispatched within five working days of receipt of the enquiry.

In the event of an unreasonable delay, take the matter up with Ofgem as a possible enforcement matter. You may be able to obtain an injunction or, in Scotland, an order of declarator and specific implement (see Chapter 14). You may need to seek legal advice.

12. **Charges for connecting a supply: gas**

Normally you should not be charged for the connection of a gas supply when you are taking over the supply at premises which are already connected to the gas network. An exception is where the connection has been capped for over 12 months and a new connection would be needed.

A gas transporter will make a charge for connecting your premises to the gas network for the first time. You may be charged for all work done on your premises and land and for any pipe which has to be laid, although the first 10 metres of the pipe which is not on your property or premises will be covered by the gas transporter. For domestic premises within 23 metres of a relevant gas main, a transporter is obliged to connect premises and provide and install the necessary assets for connecting the premises.[20]

Gas transporters are subject to different obligations in respect of:

- infills – where existing premises in an area are connected to a new main laid under regulations, allowing the gas transporter to determine connection charges at the start and to apply a similar charge to all connection requests in respect of the main for a maximum of 20 years;
- supplemental connection charge areas – where the gas transporter has been authorised by Ofgem to recover the cost of connecting premises in a specified area from gas shippers to those premises, over a fixed period of time, rather than directly from owners or occupiers of the premises.

For premises further than 23 metres from a main or consuming more than 2,196,000 kWh, the gas transporter will quote a price for connecting premises. All work to connect this type of premises will be chargeable.

Potential customers may face high connection charges, particularly if a new supply is required some distance away from the gas mains network or if costs cannot be shared between a number of new customers. Information and quotations can be obtained from National Grid. Any charges should be checked closely to see if the expenditure is reasonably incurred; it may be possible to contest some charges.

Charges are based on National Grid recovering the cost of laying new mains within a five-year period, less a discount reflecting the anticipated revenue from the new customers. This was considered acceptable by an earlier regulator, Ofgas, which held that this approach was consistent with the relevant regulations.[21]

You may be charged if your gas main is less than five years old at the time that you ask for a gas supply. You may be asked to finish paying for the costs of having the supply put in, but the extra charge will only apply if:

- the amount of the charge is no more than anyone previously supplied from the main has been charged; *and*
- the transporter has not yet recovered the full cost of the main; *and*
- the transporter has supplied you with any information you reasonably requested concerning the cost of the main, the date it was laid and how much has been paid by previous consumers.

This charge will not apply if you are an owner or occupier who has paid contractors to connect the supply.

Ofgem has a duty to resolve disputes concerning connection charges. In the event of a dispute, you may wish to ask it to make an independent decision. See Chapter 14 for more about disputes.

13. **Security deposits**

What is a security deposit

A 'Security deposit' is a sum of money requested by electricity or gas suppliers as a condition of providing a supply. Gas transporters can also ask for a security deposit as a condition of connecting your premises to the mains network.

Deposits are held separately from customers' normal accounts and are used to offset costs for the supply of electricity or gas, usually following a disconnection. Deposits should not be regarded as a credit payment towards future bills. Note, however, that the licence conditions for gas suppliers appear to allow the possibility that a supplier may use some or all of your deposit to reduce your gas bill. See p41 for the return of a deposit.

When you can be asked to pay a security deposit

Electricity

Rules for security deposits are the same for all electricity suppliers and details are set out in Standard Licence Condition (SLC) 27.

Electricity suppliers may ask for a security deposit if:

- you refuse to take a supply through a prepayment meter; *or*
- it is not practicable to install a prepayment meter; *and*
- it is reasonable in all the circumstances to do so (a tariff supplier's power is expressed as the right to ask for reasonable security, which amounts to the same thing).

When a contract supplier asks for a security deposit, it must inform you of when it will be returned (see p41) and of the power of Consumer Focus/Ofgem to determine any dispute about the deposit. As an alternative, action through the county court can be used to recover a deposit which is owed to you and which a supplier refuses to refund. In Scotland, small claims of up to £3,000 go to the Sheriff Court and may be pursued as a summary cause if between £3,000 and £5,000.

If you are a new customer, you may be routinely asked for a security deposit by electricity suppliers, particularly if:

- you refuse to provide information about previous addresses, or you cannot demonstrate a satisfactory payment history at a previous address and you do not otherwise provide sufficient information about your creditworthiness; *or*
- you have been assessed as having a poor credit rating as a result of credit vetting by a supplier; *or*
- you are in short-term accommodation. You should not be treated as being in short-term accommodation if you are a secure or assured tenant.

Electricity suppliers cannot insist on both a prepayment meter and a security deposit (see p43).

Electricity suppliers should include an explicit statement of their policies on security against the non-payment of future bills within their codes of practice on the payment of bills. The code should also state if and how policy differs for new and existing customers and what, if any, credit vetting procedures are used. It should further indicate the steps you would need to take to improve your creditworthiness or to ensure that security is no longer needed.

Security deposits may also be required from existing customers if:

- your payment plan has broken down. You will almost always be able to have a prepayment meter as an alternative – see p43. Remember that the requirement for a security deposit must be reasonable. If the reason your payment plan broke down was that you could not afford it, you may be able to negotiate another payment plan instead of either having to pay a security deposit or having a prepayment meter installed (see Chapter 7); *or*
- theft, tampering or damage to meters/equipment has occurred (see Chapter 9).

If a particular group of consumers is always asked for a security deposit (eg, because they happen to live on a particular estate), Consumer Focus should be asked to intervene. It is unlawful for a supplier to discriminate unduly in how it supplies customers, including in respect of security deposits. Contracts are individual agreements and a supplier should avoid discriminating against any particular class of customer. If the supplier is also part of the Ombudsman scheme, a complaint may also be made to the Ombudsman.

Gas

Gas suppliers can, under the terms of their licence, incorporate demands for security deposits in their contracts and 'deemed contracts' (see p16). Deposits may be cash deposits, or a secure method of payment such as a direct debit or a prepayment meter. Conditions in the supplier's licence will limit the circumstances and amounts of deposits which may be requested. Suppliers cannot ask for a security deposit if you agree to a prepayment meter, unless your conduct makes it reasonable to ask for a deposit.

Under SLC 27.3A(b) a gas supplier must not require payment of a deposit where 'it is unreasonable in all the circumstances of the case to require that customer to pay a security deposit.' The wording indicates that the supplier is required to consider the individual circumstances of a customer and cannot apply a blanket policy of imposing deposits upon particular classes or customers or certain areas.[22]

The code of practice of your supplier on the payment of bills will provide a statement of its policies. All suppliers are subject to the same obligations in respect of security deposits. If you do not provide the security requested, the supplier may refuse to connect your supply, if you are a new customer, or disconnect your supply, if you are an existing customer. Security can mean:

- you pay a cash deposit; *or*
- you join a gas payment plan; *or*
- a prepayment meter is fitted for you.

Suppliers may ask for security if:

- you live in short-term accommodation. You should not be treated as being in short-term accommodation if you are a secure or assured tenant; *or*
- you have a poor payment record at your present or last address; *or*
- you are a new customer and you do not give proof of your identity or your last address.

A gas transporter is also entitled to ask for a security deposit if connecting premises to the gas pipe network where the premises are no more than 23 metres from the gas main and it will be laying the pipes needed for the connection. The transporter may refuse to supply and lay the pipe if you fail to pay the security requested.

Amount of deposit

Electricity

Electricity suppliers are subject to the same rules on the amount of deposit. For a contract supplier, it should be 1.5 times the value of the average quarterly consumption of electricity reasonably expected at the premises. The amount can only be more than this if that is reasonable in all the circumstances.[23] The amount of deposit required may be increased if the existing security has become invalid or insufficient. The amounts actually requested will vary between suppliers.

Gas

Gas suppliers' licence conditions state that the amount of a deposit must not exceed a reasonable amount.[24] If you consider the amount unreasonable, the amount should be referred to Consumer Focus or Ofgem to look at all the circumstances of the case. What is reasonable will require a consideration of all relevant facts, including your income and capital and personal factors such as disability and previous payment record. Previously, it was considered that gas suppliers should only request a deposit of a maximum 1.5 times the value expected in quarterly consumption.

Disconnection if you do not pay a security deposit

An electricity supplier, gas supplier or gas transporter may refuse to connect, or may disconnect, your supply if you fail to pay the requested deposit within seven days of being billed. Your supply may remain disconnected for as long as you refuse to pay the amount requested.

If you cannot afford to pay a reasonable security deposit for a gas supply straight away, your supply will only be disconnected if no financial assistance or counselling is available from the Department for Work and Pensions, another agency, or if a prepayment meter cannot be installed or is refused.

A gas supplier is not entitled to withhold the supply or threaten to disconnect for any amount of security deposit which is genuinely in dispute. This would apply if you dispute the amount of, or the need for, a security deposit. See Chapter 14 for more about disputes.

Return of security deposits

Electricity

Contract suppliers must repay any deposit:

- within 14 days where, in the previous 12 months, you have paid all charges for electricity within 28 days of each bill being sent to you; *or*
- as soon as reasonably practicable, and in any event within one month, where you have stopped taking a supply from that particular supplier and have paid all outstanding charges.

Where there is a failure to return a deposit, a small claim could be commenced through the civil courts, as the deposit will be under £5,000. In Scotland, a small claims action can be brought in the Sheriff Court for sums up to £3,000 or as summary claims for sums between £3,000 and £5,000.

Gas

Security deposits held by a gas supplier under the terms of a contract or deemed contract must be returned to you if, for a continuous period of 12 months, you:

- pay your bills within 28 days of their being issued; *or*
- otherwise comply with the terms in respect of payment under the terms of your contract.

The deposit must be returned within two months of this period, unless it is reasonable for the deposit to be retained due to your conduct.

If you have stopped taking a supply within a period of 12 months and paid all dues, check the terms of your contract in relation to the deposit.

Interest on security deposits

Electricity

Interest is payable at simple interest rates on every sum held for more than one month by an electricity supplier. The rate of interest is the base rate of Barclays.[25]

Gas

The provision that gas suppliers should pay simple interest on any deposit held for more than one month is not included in SLC 27. To pursue a claim for interest would require court action on a claim for the return of the deposit.[26]

Disconnection and reconnection costs

A gas supplier may demand the expenses of disconnection and reconnection if it has disconnected for failure to pay a deposit. The supplier is not entitled to payment where the amount of a deposit is genuinely in dispute.

Electricity suppliers may demand the reasonable expenses of both disconnection and reconnection as well as payment of a security deposit prior to reconnecting the supply.

Disputes

The Energy Ombudsman, consumer advice services and Ofgem may all consider and resolve disputes over security deposits.

A relevant dispute could include whether it is reasonable for the supplier to provide a prepayment meter or a payment plan as an alternative to a security deposit, and the matter may also be taken to the county court in England and Wales where the customer has a case in law.

14. **Alternatives to security deposits**

Payment plans and guarantors

Both electricity and gas suppliers routinely accept direct debit payments and payment plans as acceptable alternatives to cash security deposits.

Some electricity suppliers will accept guarantors as an alternative to a security deposit. Potential guarantors should be aware that if the bill is not paid, they would be liable for the debt and could be pursued for the debt through the courts. Guarantors of an electricity supply who own or occupy the premises to which the bill relates could have their supply disconnected either at that premises, or at any other premises which they occupy.

Before acting as a guarantor for anyone, it is important to establish the facts and circumstances of the proposed fuel supply and to obtain an estimate as to the likely size of any bill.

Prepayment meters

Electricity

Electricity suppliers are not entitled to a security deposit if you are prepared to have a prepayment meter and it is reasonably practical for the supplier to provide one. Suppliers are entitled to take into consideration the risk of loss or damage to a meter in deciding whether a prepayment meter can be offered.

Some suppliers are particularly keen to impose prepayment meters on low-income customers, using the argument that this type of payment method gives them the security they need to safeguard payment. This raises the question of choice of payment method for low-income customers.

Gas

Gas suppliers are not usually entitled to a security deposit if you agree to have a prepayment meter instead. You may be asked to pay a security deposit and have a prepayment meter if this is reasonable as a result of your conduct – eg, if there is evidence that you may damage your meter. If the supplier thinks that you can afford the deposit, but will not pay, you might be refused a prepayment meter and be required to pay the security deposit instead.

15. **Disruption of power supply**

Suppliers may be liable to pay compensation for any disruption in the supply of electricity or gas. Such disruption can arise in many ways such as severe weather, equipment failure and vandalism.

Various options are open to you if you suffer a loss of power, including a claim for compensation under the Electricity (Standards of Performance) Regulations 2010 or a civil action for damages through the courts. In many cases, the claim will lie against the electricity distribution network owner (DNO).

There are 14 major electricity distribution networks in Great Britain, each covering a geographical area and operated by a licensed company. The 14 DNO businesses are monopolies owned by seven corporate groups.

DNOs have to meet guaranteed standards of performance for restoring supplies to customers. The basic principle is that a payment will be paid where a supply to your premises is interrupted as a result of a failure of fault in or damage to a distributor's system and not restored within a set time period. Further payments will be payable for each subsequent 12-hour period in which power is not restored.

If your electricity supply fails during normal weather conditions because of a problem with the distribution system the DNO should restore it within 18 hours of first becoming aware of the problem. If the DNO fails to restore supply within 18 hours and you make a valid claim within three months of the date the supply is restored, you are entitled to receive £54 and a further £27 for each additional 12 hours you are without supply.[27]

For larger scale interruptions of power, affecting large numbers of customers a longer period applies. If the incident involves 5,000 customers or more, the DNO is required to restore supply within 24 hours of first becoming aware of the problem. If the DNO fails to restore power within 24 hours and you make a valid claim, you are entitled to receive £54 and a further payment of £27 for each additional 12-hour period that you are off supply up to a maximum of £216.[28]

If your electricity supply fails because of a problem on the distribution system due to severe weather, generally, if a supply is not restored within 24 hours, you are entitled to receive £27 and a further £27 for each additional 12 hours you are without supply to a maximum payment of £216.[29]

The scheme does not apply to the Highlands and Islands in Scotland.[30]

Ofgem will look into cases of power cuts. Advice on how the complaint process works is available at www.ofgem.gov.uk/Consumers/Pages/Consumer.aspx.

A claim can be started by writing directly to the supplier with details of the disruption to supply. The letter is the key document to begin the process and should set out details of the dates and times when the loss of power occurred (so far as it can be identified) and any particular consequences it has had on members of the household concerned. A reasonable time limit of 14 days should be given to the supplier to respond. It is advisable to contact Ofgem about a claim for sums payable under the regulations arising from disruption of supply if the company concerned has already offered a payment, particularly if the payment (known as an ex gratia payment) is lower than the sum suggested by the regulations. Equally, amounts may be higher where there has been special damage which has arisen from the loss of power.

Energy Ombudsman

The Energy Ombudsman (see p245) can act in claims arising out of power cuts. It can ask the company to take practical action to resolve a dispute and, in some cases, make a financial award.

Court action

As an alternative to seeking compensation from a supplier, if you have lost either electricity supply or gas under contract, you may bring a claim under contract or negligence through the civil courts (known as 'delict' in Scotland).

Claims may be brought in relation to the terms of the contract or with reference to section 14 of the Supply of Goods and Services Act 1982, which puts an implied term into every consumer contract for services that the service will be provided with a reasonable degree of competence and skill. Where there is a failure in the service, the provider may be liable to pay compensation for breach of this implied term.

Sums awarded by a court for nuisance and inconvenience arising from disruption of supply are likely to reflect those set out in the regulations. In addition, any losses which flow directly from the breach of supply and which are reasonably foreseeable as a result of power loss may also be recoverable. For example, these might include the cost of spoiled food in a freezer where power supply has been lost or where damage has been caused to a computer hard drive by a loss of power.

If a failure to supply power results in serious loss or damage or personal injury, legal advice should be taken on a claim. There may be a possibility if a claim for negligence is brought against a power company. Claims in negligence will arise independently from any contract and you need not be a party to a supply contract to claim. Under the Unfair Contract Terms Act 1977, it is not possible to exclude liability for personal injury or death by way of a term in a contract.

It is possible that in extreme weather cases, power companies will claim the benefit of a common law defence known as 'Act of God'. If such a claim is raised, specialist advice should preferably be sought. Such a claim will normally be begun in the county court or the Sheriff Court in Scotland; where the claim is £5,000 or less, this will go through the small claims court in England and Wales, or the Sheriff Court in Scotland where the sum is below £3,000 (see Chapter 14).

Self-help

Some consumers may adopt self-help remedies with respect to disruption of supply by withholding payment for part of their bill for the period affected. Such a self-help remedy is unlikely to be endorsed by Ofgem, Consumer Focus or Citizens Advice consumer service, but lawyers have considered it unlikely that suppliers will take action where the amount withheld corresponds with the amount of compensation available for disruption of supply, since this would force them to disclose details of practice and procedures in respect of supply disruption and require officers to answer questions in court.[31] Costs of this will exceed the compensation concerned. Self-help should always be backed up by a formal complaint in writing. Keep a record in writing of all actions taken by yourself and the supplier.

Note that if you withhold payment you might lose a prompt payment discount and disconnection might be a possibility (although the argument could be raised at the disconnection hearing – see Chapter 10). Evidence suggests that suppliers will add sums that are withheld to future bills or try to pursue them as a debt.

It may be possible to negotiate a settlement of a lesser sum. Such agreements should be in writing (see Chapter 7).

Preferably, seek legal advice before adopting a self-help measure; further information on legal proceedings is found in Chapter 14.

As an alternative you could approach the distribution network operator for payment for a failure to supply or for hardship caused as a result of the interruption.

Liability for damage arising from faulty connection

If damage arises from a faulty connection (or re-connection), the power company and/or its sub-contractor are liable. A power company is liable for the negligence of its sub-contractor under a principle known as 'vicarious liability'. In the event that a legal claim is made, both the supplier and its sub-contractor could be treated as defendants in any claim, pleading the negligence of the sub-contractor and negligence on the part of the supplier in selecting an unsuitable sub-contractor. Legal advice should be obtained if the claim is substantial or personal injury has been caused.

Consumer redress orders

The Energy Bill 2012/13 introduces a consumer redress order (CRO) scheme for breaches of licence conditions by suppliers. Clause 117 and Schedule 14 of the Bill require energy companies which breach licence conditions or other relevant regulatory requirements to provide redress to direct consumers who suffer loss, damage or inconvenience as a result of the breach. Amendments will be made to both the Gas Act 1986 and the Electricity Act 1989, allowing Ofgem to issue CROs which can order a supplier to pay compensation directly to consumers. CROs will also allow Ofgem to terminate a supply contracts to consumers. The Bill proposes that individual consumers will also be given an enforceable right in the civil courts to take action against contract suppliers where Ofgem has issued a CRO. However, the right of action will not apply to any breach of a licence condition which occurred before the Energy Act 2013 becomes law.

Notes

1. Who is entitled to a supply

1. Condition 22 SLC
2. ss16 and 64 EA 1989
3. *Woodcock v South Western Electricity Board* [1975] 2 All ER 545
4. Sch 1 E(CSP) Regs
5. Reg 5(2) and Sch 1 E(CSP) Regs
6. Sch 2 E(CSP) Regs
7. Electricity and Gas (Internal Markets) Regulations 2011
8. s10(1)(b) GA 1986, as amended by GA 1995; see also SLC 4B Gas Transporters Licence Conditions, March 2009
9. Gas SLC 23.1
10. Gas SLC 23.2

2. Squatters

11. Sch 7 Part 3 and Sch 8 Part 4 Electricity and Gas (Internal Markets) Regulations 2011 No. 2704; SLC 14A for gas and electricity
12. s144(2) Legal Aid, Sentencing and Punishment of Offenders Act 2012
13. *Doncaster Borough Council v Stark and Another* [1997] CO/2763/96 5 November 1997, Potts, J ; *Frost (Inspector of Taxes) v Feltham* [1981] 1 WLR

3. Travellers

14. *Designing Gypsy and Traveller Sites: Good Practice Guide,* Department of Communities and Local Government, May 2008

5. When you can be refused a supply of electricity

15. Condition 27.5 SLC

10. When you can be refused a supply of gas

16. Gas SLC 27
17. Condition 14 SLC
18. Ofgem debt assignment protocol for prepayment meter customers letter 24 September 2012 (www.ofgem.gov.uk/ Sustainability/SocAction/Publications/ Documents1/Debt Assignment Protocol Review.pdf)
19. Condition 22.5 SLC

11. Getting your supply connected: gas

20. Condition 4B Gas Transporters Standard Licence Conditions 28 August 2012
21. Ofgas *Annual Report* 1993, p28

13. Security deposits

22. Condition 27.3A(b) SLC
23. Condition 27 SLC
24. Condition 27.4 SLC
25. Condition 27 SLC
26. s69 County Court Act 1984

15. Disruption of power supply

27. Reg 5(2)(a) and (b) and Schedule 1 E(SP) Regs
28. Reg 6 E(SP) Regs
29. Reg 7 E(SP) Regs
30. Reg 9 E(SP) Regs
31. Opinion of Richard Colbey, barrister, in 'Storm is brewing over customer cut-offs', *The Guardian*, 16 November 2002

Chapter 4

Meters and methods of payment

This chapter covers:
1. Standing charges and special tariffs (below)
2. Types of meters (p50)
3. Payment methods (p53)
4. Fuel Direct (p57)
5. Choosing how to pay (p58)

For more information on reading your meter, see Appendix 3.

1. Standing charges and special tariffs

Standing charges

'Standing charges' are fixed charges which must be paid regardless of how much fuel you use. Suppliers are entitled to make these charges to cover costs such as billing, meter reading, customer services, servicing meters and so on. Standing charges are often higher for variable rate meters (such as Economy 7). However, different deals are available and it is worth shopping around. Some suppliers offer tariffs which do not impose standing charges at all. The advantage of this is that you only pay for the energy you use. It is important to remember that 'no standing charge' tariffs often have a two tier pricing structure, where the first quota of gas or electricity units consumed are charged at a higher rate with the remaining units charged at a lower rate. It is always worth checking what tariff you are being billed on and if you will save money by changing tariff, payment method or supplier.

Historically, people using prepayment meters paid more for their energy than direct debit customers. Since 2009,[1] there have been active steps to try and reduce discrimination in the cost of fuel, particularly between those customers who have prepayment meters and those who pay by direct debit or e-billing. This is now included in Standard Licence Condition 25A which provides that suppliers must ensure that in supplying or offering electricity they do not discriminate between groups of domestic customers.[2]

Following a European Directive in 2004,[3] UK gas and electricity suppliers have had to offer a wide choice of payment methods and not impose higher rates for certain types of payment method. In essence, the suppliers are not allowed to profit from using different payment methods, as it is normally those who must pay by cheque, prepayment meter, or cash, that are normally the hardest hit by fuel costs and administrative costs, and those most likely to fall within the definition of fuel poverty.

Warm Home Discount

Until recently, suppliers offered customers in, or at risk of, fuel poverty a 'social tariff' which was a low cost tariff equal to, or lower than, the lowest tariff offered to customers in their area, including online deals. Social tariffs are no longer offered to new customers. They have been replaced with the Warm Home Discount.

The Warm Home Discount is a four-year scheme running from April 2011 to March 2015 to help low-income and vulnerable households meet their energy costs. This is a mandatory scheme, funded by the major fuel suppliers.

There are two main groups within the scheme.

- **Core group.** A yearly discount, ranging from £120 in year one to £140 in year four, is made to the winter electricity bill of each eligible customer. Eligibility alters each year, but is targeted at customers over pension credit (PC) age. In 2012/13, you are considered if, at the qualifying date, you are aged under 80 and receiving only the guarantee credit of PC (no savings credit) or aged 80 or over and receiving the guarantee credit of PC (even if you get the savings credit as well). The Department for Work and Pensions data-matches its records with participating energy suppliers so, if you are eligible, you receive the discount automatically.
- **Broader group.** Participating energy suppliers have discretion over the eligibility criteria for the broader group, but they are still required to target those in, or at risk of, fuel poverty. The eligibility criteria is subject to approval from Ofgem. The annual electricity discount for the broader group is also between £120 in year one to £140 in year four. There is no data-matching exercise with this group so, if you think you are eligible, contact your energy supplier direct. The discount is awarded on a first-come-first-served basis.

Special tariffs

Some suppliers offer special tariffs, aimed at certain customers. E.ON's Staywarm scheme is aimed at customers over 60, offering a fixed price commercial tariff for energy, regardless of actual usage. Ebico offers regional tariffs which charge the same regardless of payment method.

2. **Types of meters**

Meters are owned by meter operator companies contracted by suppliers to provide metering services to their customers. In many cases, meters are owned, checked and read by National Grid and the privatised electricity suppliers (see p7) even if the fuel is supplied by another company, but more meter operator companies are being established. Metering remains the responsibility of the supplier, which is liable for the acts and omissions of its sub-contracting meter operator company.

The main types of gas and electricity meters supplied are: standard credit, variable rate credit, prepayment and smart.

Standard credit meter

Most customers have credit meters, with fuel supplied in advance of payment. Credit meters record consumption and are read periodically – usually twice yearly, quarterly and in some cases every two months. There is no requirement under the standards of performance to read all meters regularly, but meters must be read at least once every two years under the supplier's licence. Estimated bills are sent for the rest of the year, with a customer reading correction facility available by phone or online.

Estimated bills are a frequent source of complaint. A succession of estimates can result in inaccurate billing, with you paying too much or not enough. This often leads to problems with arrears and the threat of disconnection. If you have problems with arrears as the result of a succession of estimated bills, see Chapter 7.

A bill is sent at the end of each billing period, after the meter has either been read, or was due to be read, or estimated. The price per unit of fuel does not vary according to the time of day or night the fuel is used when you use a standard credit meter. Appendix 3 describes how to read your own credit meter.

If you are of pensionable age or disabled, you could use the special meter reading facility under the Priority Service Register. Quarterly readings can be arranged for you and a special password service is available as protection against bogus callers. If you are disabled and it is difficult for you to reach or read your meter your supplier may reposition it to a more convenient location free of charge. Free safety checks on all gas appliances are also offered. Contact your supplier for information about Priority Service Register services in your area.

Variable rate credit meter

Variable, or off-peak, electricity credit meters record different rates or 'tariffs' at different times of day or night. Night-time electricity usage is generally cheaper than on-peak day usage. The most common type of variable rate credit meter is known as Economy 7 in England and Wales and sometimes referred to as white meter in Scotland (see p51).

Suppliers offer different systems, depending on your supply area, and these may change from time to time. Ask your supplier for information on the type of system it operates.

Economy 7/white meter

Economy 7/white meter is a scheme allowing you to pay for your electricity at two different rates or 'tariffs'. You need a special meter, usually an Economy 7 credit meter, but in some areas Economy 7 prepayment meters are available as well. A white meter is a similar type of meter which preceded Economy 7 meters. They are still very common in Scotland, but are being phased out elsewhere.

Electricity is charged for at two different rates per unit, with a lower rate at night. The daytime rate is charged at a higher rate than the standard rate for credit meters. The standing charge is often higher than for credit meters. The amount of the charges varies from supplier to supplier.

Consider changing to Economy 7/white meter if you use electricity to heat your home and to heat water overnight. You may also be able to make savings in your fuel costs if you run electrical appliances (such as washing machines and tumble dryers) overnight, usually by using a timer to ensure the appliances operate within the optimum time band.

The higher standing charge and higher daytime rate may counterbalance any savings made if your night-time use of electricity is not large enough. Look carefully at the amount of electricity you use during the day and night, and at the rates, to establish if an Economy 7/white meter would save you money. Suppliers should have specialist staff to advise you.

Smart meter

Under a European Union Directive,[4] the UK is required to ensure that gas and electricity customers are provided with accurate meters which 'provide information on actual time of use' as far as is technically feasible. The Directive became law through the Energy Act 2008 which set the mandate for installing smart meters.[5] The government's aim is for every household to have a smart meter by 2019.[6] The government has placed responsibility on energy suppliers to replace over 53 million gas and electricity meters, involving visits to 30 million homes and small businesses. Although several hundred thousand households have already received a new meter through small trials and pilot projects, the majority of customers will receive their smart meter during the mass roll-out, expected to start in early 2014 and be completed by the end of 2019.

It is hoped that the introduction of smart meters will help Britain attain a low-carbon economy and help meet some of the longer-term challenges in ensuring an affordable, secure and sustainable energy supply.

The term 'smart meter' relates to the services and benefits obtained from such a meter rather than a specific type of technology. Smart meters measure your exact fuel usage and send the information electronically to your supplier without the need for meter readings to be taken.

For a useful guide to smart metering as it develops, see Consumer Focus' *Go smart, get smart* questions and answers.[7]

Advantages of smart meters

- There will be no need for estimated bills, with suppliers able to read meters remotely via two-way communications technology. This should dramatically reduce the number of inaccurate bills issued – currently the biggest source of consumer complaints about energy companies.
- You will be able to be better judge your consumption of energy. You will have real time information to help control and manage your energy use, save money and reduce emissions. You will be able to compare the amount of electricity and gas you use today against what you used the day before, the week before, the month before and even the year before.
- It will herald the end of inaccessible meters under the stairs and in cupboards. The information on your energy use will be provided through a hand-held display device (which can be displayed on your kitchen worktop or living room table), via the internet or even through a mobile phone.
- Smart meters will provide more detailed, user-friendly information on your energy consumption. The display will show you how much gas and electricity you are using and roughly how much it is costing you in pounds and pence. It is hoped that by knowing how much you are using, and how much your appliances cost to run, you may be able to reduce your energy consumption and save money.
- According to the season and time of day, you can be rewarded for off-peak consumption. There is also the hope that these meters will allow consumers to automatically respond to fluctuations in price by using gas and electricity when it is at its cheapest.
- Power outages can be communicated to suppliers and fixed remotely before even being reported. Also, unauthorised usage such as that of squatters or energy theft by neighbours could be terminated remotely, helping to save customers money.
- If you have a prepayment meter, it should be easier to top-up your meter. Cash payment will always be accepted, but suppliers will also offer more convenient ways to top up, such as over the phone, internet or with a special mobile phone app.

Disadvantages of smart meters

- Remote disconnection of your gas or electricity supply in the event of non-payment, or an error creating an assumption of non-payment. This removes the protection afforded by most suppliers with the previous system – that suppliers could not disconnect your supply in the first instance without being given access to your property to perform the disconnection, or to fit a prepayment meter. With smart meters, entry is not necessary for disconnection. Ofgem has, however, introduced new rules to ensure that suppliers treat disconnection as a last resort. Suppliers must ensure that vulnerable households are not disconnected. If you have an energy debt, discuss repayment options with your supplier.

- From 2014, suppliers will be able to remotely switch the meter between credit mode and prepayment mode and do not have to physically visit the property to change meters. Ofgem guidance states that suppliers must first ensure that it is safe and reasonably practical for a customer to use a prepayment meter.[8]
- Concerns have been raised regarding purported health issues associated with the wireless technology used by smart meters to transmit information between supplier and meter.[9] The government is expected to confirm which communications technology will be used in smart metering during 2013, and is constantly reviewing the scientific evidence on this subject.

3. **Payment methods**

Your choice of payment method will depend on the type of meter you have. You may wish to change your meter to allow you to use a particular payment method. If your circumstances change, you may be able to change to a more suitable payment method.

Each gas and electricity supplier publishes a code of practice on the payment of bills, outlining the various options available. Many also publish additional detailed information about the costs of the different options.

Credit meter payment methods

Payment can be made on receipt of a **quarterly bill** – either in cash at a customer service centre, by posting a cheque or giro, using a credit or debit card or paying directly into the supplier's account at a post office, PayPoint or through internet banking. A service charge may be applied if you pay at the post office. Using a credit card could be a very expensive way of obtaining credit because of the interest charged on balances. If you are in financial difficulty, consider the other budget options available.

Quarterly billing is currently the most expensive way to pay for your gas and electricity. Switching to direct debit will save you money. Furthermore, a succession of estimated bills can result in inaccurate billing, with you either paying too much or not enough. This can lead to a debt accumulating.

Direct debit is usually the cheapest way to pay for your gas and electricity. Your estimated annual costs are spread over 12 monthly payments (or four quarterly payments), which are deducted direct from your bank account.

Payments should be enough to cover your annual consumption. If the direct debit payments are set too low you will accumulate arrears. Suppliers are able to adjust the direct debit amount but must inform you when this is the case.

Setting up an **online account** with your fuel supplier and paying by direct debit attracts a discount of around seven per cent and is usually the cheapest way to pay for your energy. This 'paperless billing' process enables you to view your bills online and submit regular meter readings.

Standing order is similar to direct debit with monthly or quarterly payments deducted direct from your bank account. The main difference is that you have to instruct the bank of any changes to the debited amount. Standing orders do not attract the same level of discount as direct debits. Remember to take into consideration the extra costs of becoming overdrawn if you are considering standing orders or direct debits.

There is a range of **budget schemes** which allow you to pay for your fuel on a weekly, fortnightly or monthly basis. This gives flexibility and helps you to budget, but is not the cheapest payment method. This is a useful way to pay if you do not have a bank account.

A **flexible payment scheme** enables you to pay any amount at any time at customer service centres, at a bank or by post. The amount paid is credited towards your next bill, which must then be settled each quarter. This is useful if you have a variable income.

PayPoint is a free national bill payment network aimed at households who prefer to pay utility bills in cash on a weekly, fortnightly, monthly or quarterly basis. Retail outlets at convenient locations offer this free bill payment service. Locations of PayPoint outlets can be found at www.paypoint.co.uk/paypointlocator.

Internet banking allows you to make payments to your fuel account from most banks accounts.

Prepayment meters

A substantial number of people have a **prepayment meter** – in excess of 3.7 million electricity meters and 2.5 million gas meters. Over 70 per cent of these meters were installed to recover a fuel debt.[10] Frequently marketed as a 'pay-as-you-go' budgeting method, there are several types of prepayment meters, including card and key meters. Some electricity prepayment meters can operate with Economy 7 and other variable rate tariffs.

Token and card meters

Note: token/card meters are have almost all been phased out and replaced with newer key prepayment meters.

Electronically coded payment cards or tokens, usually available in units of £5, can be purchased from local shops, post offices, petrol stations or customer service centres. Your account is credited every time you purchase a token/card from a reputable source. When the token or card is inserted into the meter it will record the amount of fuel purchased and will then automatically cancel the token/card. Your annual statement should show a near zero balance – with fuel consumption equalling token/cards purchased.

Token meters need to be manually adjusted after every price rise and you are at risk of continuing to buy top-ups unaware that you are no longer paying the correct cost for fuel. If there is a substantial delay in recalibrating the meter to reflect the price increase, a large debt may accumulate on your account. Your supplier should give you at least 30 days notice of a price increase and should take steps to recalibrate your meter as soon as possible.

Key meters

These operate in the same way as token/card meters. The difference is that you are provided with a rechargeable 'key' when the meter is installed. The key can only be used in your meter. You need to charge the key by paying at a charging point (eg, at a PayPoint outlet) or you may be able to top-up at home using the internet and a device provided by your supplier (eg, ScottishPower's PowerPod). Your key is electronically encoded at the charging point with the amount you have paid. When the key is inserted into the meter, the amount of fuel you have bought is registered and the key is cancelled. A certain amount of emergency credit is usually available on these meters. Your key may be able to read your meter and pass on the reading when you charge it. Key meters do not need to be manually updated after a price rise.

Quantum meters

The gas Quantum meter is an electronic card prepayment meter. It is charged by an electronically coded 'Gascard'. The card is encoded with your reference number and the meter's serial number and cannot be used to purchase gas for anyone else. The card reads the meter and passes the reading on to the charging point when you next purchase credit.

Collecting arrears

All types of prepayment meter can be set to collect a fuel debt. They allow you to pay for your supply of fuel, a daily standing charge and extra for any arrears you owe. It is important to note that the settings for these charges will operate on a regular, usually weekly, basis. This means that an absence from home will result in the deduction of the pre-set charges for the number of weeks' absence. If you are due to spend time away from your home (on holiday or a short hospital stay), ensure that your meter is 'topped-up' with enough credit to cover these charges. Gas Quantum meters are usually set to recover an agreed weekly figure. The agreed sum is deducted from the gas purchased when inserting the card on a fixed day once a week. The meter is programmed to ensure that you always receive 30 per cent of your credit as an actual supply of gas. This means that even if you have been absent from your home, the meter will allow you some supply.

Emergency credit

If your fuel runs out, you can use an emergency button on the meter to obtain a small amount of credit (typically worth £5). The next time you top up, the credit is used to pay for the emergency fuel – no more fuel will be available until this has been paid.

Self-disconnection

With insufficient funds in a prepayment meter, you effectively disconnect yourself, rather than the energy supplier having to take steps to enforce any debt.

Information displayed on prepayment meters

Prepayment meters have a liquid crystal display which displays a range of information about how the meter has been set. For instance, it will inform you of how much credit remains, the total outstanding debt remaining or the amount of emergency credit you have used.

Gas Quantum meter displays will warn you to ensure that all your gas appliances are turned off before you turn the supply back on again.

Advantages of prepayment meters

- They can be useful as a budgeting aid, as they restrict your use of fuel according to your means. You are forced to become aware of your fuel consumption. This can be useful if your budget is limited, but you should also consider the risk of self-disconnection. Many customers choose to retain their prepayment meter as a budgeting aid even after arrears have been paid off.
- Ease of adjustment – the smart card or key reads your meter and conveys the information from your supplier. If your supplier agrees to change the setting, there is no need for a visit, as the card/key adjusts the setting of the meter the next time you charge it up and use it.
- Meters can be reset to pay off arrears as an alternative to disconnection.

Disadvantages of prepayment meters

- These meters should never be installed if you are at risk of leaving appliances turned on after the money has run out, or are incapable of operating the meter to obtain credit or emergency credit. They also should not be installed if you cannot obtain the tokens, cards or keys to operate them.
- There are hidden costs. If you cannot afford to buy much fuel at any one time, you will need to make frequent journeys to the nearest charging point. The extra cost of travel is effectively part of your fuel cost.
- You cannot spread the cost of large winter bills over the whole year if you pay for your fuel in advance week by week. A payment plan might be preferable if

you could not afford to pay for your heaviest weeks' consumption from your weekly income.

- 'Self-disconnection' is a problem if you cannot afford to top up your meter and you may face intermittent or extended periods of disconnection. Fuel costs may take up too high a proportion of your income, particularly if you live in a property that is hard to heat or if your income is low.

- Paying back arrears and emergency credit can result in hardship. If a meter is set to collect arrears, a supply of fuel may not be available until the arrears charge has been paid. With some types of meters if you are away from home or cannot afford to charge the meter for a week, you will have to insert two weeks' arrears before you will obtain a supply. With most types of prepayment meter, if you have used your emergency credit, you will also have to pay the amount of the emergency credit before obtaining a supply. In some situations (eg, if you come out of hospital) you may be able to persuade the supplier to reset your meter. But check first that this will not involve any extra cost.

- Your repayment of arrears may be highest when you can least afford it if you use the crude mechanical gas prepayment meters. These operate by overcharging for each unit of gas used, so the more gas you use, the more you pay towards your arrears. This means there is no problem if you are absent from your home for any period of time – you will always get gas for every top up.

- Using the meters can be difficult, particularly if you have visual problems or disabilities. Note, however, that meters can often be re-sited free of charge to make them easier to use (see p50).

- Obtaining top-ups may present problems. Frequent journeys to buy them may present particular difficulties if you are caring for small children, are disabled or have limited mobility, or are in full-time work. It may be difficult to obtain top-ups outside shopping hours. Vending machines have had problems with jamming, vandalism and becoming full. Consider also the safety aspects of trying to obtain cards out of hours. Be sure to keep your receipts when charging keys/cards so that you have a record of payments.

- Keys can be easily lost or mislaid. If you lose your key, ask the supplier to replace it.

- You may be denied the option of changing to Fuel Direct (see below) to pay your arrears if you already have a prepayment meter that has been reset to recover arrears.

- See p143 for the problems associated with illegally cloned keys.

4. Fuel Direct

Access to Fuel Direct, or the Department for Work and Pension's (DWP) 'third party deduction system', requires that you are in debt for gas or electricity and in receipt of income support, income-based jobseeker's allowance, income-related employment allowance, pension credit or, from October 2013, universal credit.[11] Payment for fuel arrears plus on-going consumption, or for fuel arrears only (if you have a prepayment meter), is deducted directly from benefit. Deductions are made on a weekly basis from benefit payments, but are only paid to the supplier once every 13 weeks.

There is a maximum weekly debt recovery rate per fuel, set at £3.60 (during 2013/14). The total fuel debt owed must not be less than the rate of personal allowance for a single person aged 25 or over (£71.70 in 2013/14).

For a Fuel Direct arrangement to be set up, it is necessary to secure the agreement of both the DWP and the energy supplier. An application for the Fuel Direct scheme can be made by either you or the supplier.

If the supplier refuses to set up Fuel Direct on your behalf, see Chapter 11. Some DWP offices may also try to discourage use of the scheme. If you are refused access to the scheme, you can appeal to the First-tier Tribunal. Full details of the Fuel Direct scheme are in Chapter 11.

5. **Choosing how to pay**

The legal provisions affecting your choice are broadly similar for both gas and electricity. An assessment is made of your creditworthiness in general and of your ability to pay for gas/electricity in particular. If you cannot show creditworthiness in general, provisions relating to the requirement for security come into play. If you cannot show an ability to manage your gas/electricity account, both provisions relating to security and policies for debt management come into play. It is important to note that an existing fuel debt is no longer an automatic bar to changing to a supplier who may offer a different type of payment method. If you have a debt of up to £500 and use a prepayment meter, you may be able to switch to another supplier, taking the debt with you (see p78).[12]

If you can show that a request for any kind of security from you would be unreasonable (ie, you can prove your identity, show that you are creditworthy and have a good record of paying your gas/electricity bills on time, live in settled accommodation and are not in arrears with your bill), there would be no reason for a supplier to attempt to restrict your choice of meter or method of payment. You should be allowed to pay using the method of your choice.

A supplier can restrict the choices available to you if it can demonstrate that it is reasonable to regard you as not creditworthy, even though you may not necessarily be in arrears with your gas/electricity bill. If it is reasonable for the supplier to require some form of security from you, your choices will be restricted so that you are not allowed to accrue charges in the same way as customers paying quarterly in arrears. Payment to the supplier will be required at least monthly, and possibly fortnightly or weekly, under the terms of the various budget schemes available.

Payment in advance of receiving a supply, or prepayment, is at the other end of the scale. Suppliers claim it is costly for them, but actually it is the consumer who pays. This method of payment is the ultimate in security for the suppliers. No money – no fuel.

A prepayment meter may be your only option if the supplier has established a right to disconnect your supply, if you are in arrears and you cannot manage a payment plan. Similarly, if the supplier can demonstrate that a requirement for security is reasonable, and you cannot pay a deposit or arrange an alternative form of security, such as direct debit, a prepayment meter will be the only alternative to disconnection.

Supplier discretion in switching with a debt

There is nothing to prevent a company allowing you to switch with debts in excess of £200. The decision to take on a customer with an existing debt is at the discretion of the company, and a number of suppliers appear willing to take on consumers who may have been previous customers and who have had good payment records. Switching supplier will also be an effective method of preventing disconnection from another supplier to whom a debt may be owed.

From 1 November 2012, if you have a prepayment meter you may be able to switch supplier if you have a fuel debt of up to £500 (see p78).[13]

Legal provisions: gas

The main provisions affecting your choice of meter or method of payment for gas as described above are:
- condition 27.5–9 and 27.11–12 of the Standard Conditions of Gas Suppliers' Licences – this sets out the steps to be taken by a supplier when a bill is unpaid;
- condition 27.3–4 of the Standard Licence Conditions (SLCs) – this enables gas suppliers to require reasonable security from customers.

Prepayment meters and credit meters have been put very much on an equal footing by the Gas Act 1995 and the way in which the suppliers' licences have been drafted. Under the terms of its original authorisation, British Gas was required to offer customers in arrears a payment plan as a way of repaying arrears. A prepayment meter could only be offered if this failed. This is no longer the case. Under the terms of the new suppliers' licence, prepayment meters are no longer seen as a last resort option, but simply as an alternative method of payment.

Legal provisions: electricity

The main provisions affecting your choice of meter or method of payment for electricity as described above are:

- condition 27 of the Private Electricity Supply Licence – this sets out the steps to be taken by a supplier when a bill is unpaid;
- SLC 27.3-4 – provides for security deposits, although no security deposit is needed for prepayment meters;
- your supplier's code of practice, approved by Ofgem, on the payment of bills – this sets out your supplier's policy on the treatment of customers in arrears and for requesting security deposits;
- section 20 of the Electricity Act 1989 – this allows distributors to request reasonable security (although there is no express power for contract suppliers to request reasonable security, it is clear from their licence conditions that they have such a power).

If a supplier unreasonably requires some form of security, reference should be made to its code of practice. In the event of an on-going dispute, contact Citizen's Advice consumer service.

Notes

1. Standing charges and special tariffs

1 Ofgem Licence Modification Notice 7 August 2009
2 SLC 25A consolidated 1 October 2010
3 paragraph (d) of Annexe A to EU Directives 54/2003 and 55/2003

2. Types of meters

4 2006/32/EU Energy Services Directive on Energy End Use and Energy Services
5 ss88-91 Energy Act 2008
6 DECC, *Smart Metering Implementation Programme, Programme update,* April 2012
7 Available at www.consumerfocus.org.uk/files/2012/05/FAQ-Go-smart-get-smart2.pdf
8 For suppliers' obligations, see *Energy Safety Net* at www.energy-uk.org.uk/publication/finish/30-disconnection/308-era-safety-net
9 Advisory Group on Non-ionising Radiation, *Health Effects from Radiofrequency Electromagnetic Fields – RCE 20,* April 2012

3. Payment methods

10 Consumer Focus, *Cutting back, cutting down, cutting off – self-disconnection among prepayment meter users,* 2010

4. Fuel Direct

11 Sch 5 para 7 Universal Credit, Personal Independence Payment and Working-age Benefits (Claims and Payments) Regulations 2012 DRAFT
12 Ofgem debt assignment protocol for prepayment meter customers letter 24 September 2012 (www.ofgem.gov.uk/Sustainability/SocAction/Publications/Documents1/Debt Assignment Protocol Review.pdf)
13 Ofgem debt assignment protocol for prepayment meter customers letter 24 September 2012 (www.ofgem.gov.uk/Sustainability/SocAction/Publications/Documents1/Debt Assignment Protocol Review.pdf)

Chapter 5

Responsibility for the bill

This chapter covers:
1. Introduction (below)
2. When you are liable for an electricity bill (p62)
3. When you are liable for a gas bill (p66)
4. Common problems (p73)

1. Introduction

It is always worth checking whether you are legally responsible for a bill, particularly when you are in dispute with a gas or electricity supplier about arrears. It may be that you should not be held liable for all, or some, of the bill – perhaps because the bill was in the name of a partner who has left, a flat-sharer, your landlord or someone who has died. Electricity and gas suppliers may attempt to recover these sums from you – but they will not always be entitled to do so.

Be careful when taking over a supply of gas or electricity through a prepayment meter. These meters may be set to recover arrears from the previous occupier. If you do not inform the supplier that you have taken over responsibility for the supply, you may end up paying the last person's bill in addition to your own.

Deciding who is liable to pay the supplier for gas or electricity really ought to be straightforward and based on clear and easily understood principles. Unfortunately, this is not always the case. Often energy company staff who you initially communicate with (usually by phone) have little or no training in the law of contract and may find it difficult to understand the legal principles involved. In the case of a dispute, speak to the legal department or solicitor for the company (if it has one).

Electricity

Suppliers use contracts under which liability is determined by long-standing rules of the law of contract. The person who signs a contract is the person who is liable to pay under that contract.

Electricity suppliers – or debt collecting companies to whom they assign the right to collect debts – may attempt to secure payment from people who have used the electricity supplied rather than chase the people actually legally liable. Previous suppliers may also assign the right to recover debts from new suppliers where the consumer has switched supplier. One example is where, on the breakdown of a relationship, if the bill was in the sole name of the partner who has left, the remaining partner is asked to pay the arrears.

The present law on liability for electricity is governed by contractual principles. Any remaining tariff suppliers require their customers to complete an application form for the supply of electricity. Some contract suppliers will accept you as a customer without you actually having signed a contract. A county court case covering the pre-1989 law suggests that it does not matter if you actually apply in writing or sign a contract, so long as it is clear who asked for the supply. While this case is helpful in establishing the liability to pay for customers who have requested a supply, whether in writing or not, it does not deal with the situation where nobody has requested a supply. Normally, once you move in you are responsible for any consumption, but only from the date that you moved in. For this reason, it is important that you take a meter reading as soon as you move into a new property.

In practice, suppliers are unlikely to pursue you once you have left a property either owing arrears or where there is an outstanding argument over liability. However, note that a failure to pay outstanding fuel bills may affect creditworthiness for up to six years after the fuel debt fell due.

Gas

The Gas Act 1995, as amended by the Utilities Act 2000, allows gas to be supplied by gas suppliers under the terms of contracts and 'deemed contracts'. If the details of contracts are clearly confirmed in writing, disputes about liability are less likely. However, the provision for deemed contracts (see p16) in many situations enables gas suppliers to hold owners or occupiers liable to pay a gas bill where they are the 'person supplied with gas'. The formulation is the same as that applied to 'tariff customers' under the pre-1995 law. If you are faced with this situation, consult Ofgem. Suppliers may be prepared to reach an agreement and settle an argument over liability by the part-payment of a bill in return for a new, signed contract being established.

2. **When you are liable for an electricity bill**

In this section, all references to 'the bill' refer only to 'charges due' for the supply of electricity and do not include other charges such as credit sales charges for appliances. See p123 for more information about 'charges due'.

Your liability for the bill will depend on how, or whether, you contacted the supplier to say you required a supply of electricity.

Your liability when you have signed for the supply

You are liable to pay an electricity bill to a contract supplier if you signed a contract.

Your liability for the bill will begin from the date you stated you wanted the supply to begin, providing your supply was actually connected on that date, or from the date you signed the contract.

You are solely liable for the bill if you alone signed for the supply, regardless of whether you live alone or with other adults. You are jointly responsible for the bill if you and one or more others also signed for the supply.

Your liability will end:

- where you give at least two working days' written notice that you will no longer be an owner or occupier of the premises, on the day that you cease to be the owner or leave, as the case may be;
- where you did not give at least two working days' written notice that you were leaving, the earlier of any of the following three events:
  - two working days after you actually give written notice of ceasing to be an owner or occupier; *or*
  - on the next date that the meter is due to be read; *or*
  - when any subsequent occupier gives notice requiring a supply or signs a contract for a supply to the same premises.

If you have a contract, you can also end your liability by terminating the contract in accordance with any provision for termination contained in the contract. You must give at least 28 days' notice of termination of a contract. You will continue to be liable to the original supplier until another supplier takes over the supply to your home or until the supply is cut off altogether.[1]

Your liability in the case of former tariff suppliers

A very small number of consumers might still be liable for tariff supply arrangements that existed before contracts. The situation was slightly different for tariff suppliers from that of contract suppliers (see Chapter 2).

You were liable to pay an electricity bill to a tariff supplier if:

- you were an owner or occupier of premises; *and*
- you gave written notice that you required a supply of electricity; *and*
- the supplier had a statutory duty to supply you (see p22).

You would also have been liable to pay a tariff supplier if you entered into a 'special agreement' with it (see p31). Liability under special agreements was determined in the same way as for contracts (see above).

You remain liable for such a debt for up to six years from the last day of supply.

Your liability when you contacted the supplier by phone

Many electricity suppliers will connect your electricity supply without asking you to sign anything at all to confirm that you require a supply or that you accept liability to pay for any electricity supplied. Many will operate a system where you negotiate with them by phone to obtain your supply. In these situations, it is often clear exactly who is requesting the supply. Usually, payment is requested from the person who made the phone call.

In the law of contract, a verbal contract is as good as a written one, so what matters is not whether you signed a formal document but whether it can be shown that you were the person who asked for the supply and entered into the contract.

There is a danger that someone can contact the supplier over the phone to say that you want the supply to be in your name, but you have no knowledge of this and do not consent to it. In one case, a gas supplier attempted to obtain payment from a tenant. The tenant did not contact the supplier to request the supply in his own name and, in fact, paid his landlord for gas in with the rent. One bill was paid in the tenant's name, but there was no evidence that the tenant had made this payment. It was held that the tenant was not liable to pay for the gas consumed.[2] Although this case relates to gas, the principles apply equally to electricity.

Establishing joint liability for a supply may be problematic if you contact the supplier by phone. In practice, it will be straightforward to ask the supplier to include someone else's name on the bill as well as your own, but what if that person denies s/he had an agreement to be jointly liable with you? It is best in these circumstances if everyone who requires the supply in her/his name signs for the supply. Your liability to pay will start from the date you ask for the supply to be put in your name. It will end on the basis of the rules given above (see p63). Always arrange a final reading of the meter, and take a meter reading yourself to check your final bill.

Your liability when no one has contacted the supplier

You may be liable to pay the supplier if:
- there is no tariff customer and no one has a contract; *or*
- the liability of the tariff customer or contract holder has come to an end (see above); *and*
- you have, in practice, been supplied with electricity.

This situation often occurs when people move into new premises where the supply is already connected, or where the bill was in the name of another joint occupier but that person has left. There is nothing illegal about continuing to use the supply in another person's name, or where the bill is addressed to 'The Occupier', so long as you intend to pay for it. Anyone who uses fuel without intending to pay could be prosecuted for theft (see Chapter 9). The suppliers could rely on the law relating to 'unjust enrichment' to ensure payment in these circumstances. This applies when someone unjustly obtains benefit at someone else's expense. In England and Wales, the idea of unjust enrichment arises in the law of restitution; in Scotland, the equivalent is found in the law of recompense. However, if it can be shown that the supplier continued to provide fuel or power in spite of a request to disconnect or terminate a contract then the doctrine of unjust enrichment and the requirement of restitution will not apply.

Establishing who should pay the bill depends on the facts in each case. For example, if you are a sole occupier and you never asked for a supply because it was already connected and you receive bills addressed to 'The Occupier', you could be held liable for the bill from the date you moved in, based simply on the facts.

In situations where there is more than one occupier, establishing who is liable is often more difficult. Facts which might be relevant in establishing who is liable include:

- your status as an occupier;
- the extent of control you have over the use of fuel;
- your actual use of fuel;
- the degree of control you have over income within your household;
- the date you moved in;
- where the bill was previously in the name of another joint occupier, her/his status as an occupier and the date s/he left, whether you are registered at the dwelling for council tax purposes or for other utility bills.

A technical problem existed with the law relating to tariff suppliers. Strictly speaking, if no one gave notice requiring a supply of electricity, there was no 'tariff customer' (see p31 for who is a 'tariff customer'), and any claim is now likely to be caught by the Limitation Act 1980 (see below).

It is advisable to give the supplier notice that you are leaving to avoid disputes about the end of your period of liability and supply a meter reading.

Your liability when someone else has been responsible for the supply

You are not liable to pay the supplier for the electricity bill if:

- you have not entered into a contract; *and*
- someone else is liable for the supply under contract and that person's liability for the supply has not come to an end (see above).

You should also not be held liable for the supply when it is clear that someone else took responsibility for it, perhaps as a result of phone contact with the supplier. In one case, the court held that the wife of a deceased man should not be held liable for an electricity bill accrued by him in his name. She was only liable to pay for the supply following his death. The supplier had tried to argue that the woman should be held jointly liable for the debt, as she had benefited from the use of the supply – the 'beneficial user argument'. The judge declined to follow the county court case cited by the supplier in support of its argument.[3]

Sending the bill to another person

If you are of pensionable age, disabled or chronically sick, the supplier may send the bill to another person to deal with. Standard Licence Condition 26 for gas and electricity suppliers requires this to be done 'where reasonably practical'.

Privity of contract

In some cases, a legal principle known as 'privity of contract' may be helpful in establishing liability. Basically, the principle states that only the two parties who have made and established the contract will be subject to binding rights and obligations under it. If one party breaks the contract, the other party is the only person entitled to seek a remedy. Action cannot be taken against a third party who is a stranger to the contract.

For example, where a supplier has provided fuel to a house occupied by students and an energy bill has gone unpaid, a supplier cannot approach the parents of any of the students and demand payment of the bill. The parent is not liable for the debts of her/his student child, since no contract was made with the parent. Under the doctrine of privity of contract, the supplier is only entitled to pursue the party with whom the contract is made, namely the student concerned. Liability cannot be imposed on a third party in the absence of any agreement or guarantee given by another. Similarly, when a person moves into a new property where previous occupiers have failed to pay an energy bill, the new occupier cannot be held liable for the bills left behind.

The doctrine of privity of contract is of importance where a house is in multiple occupation and residents are transient. In many cases, it will be arguable that the long-term occupiers or the landlord are those who are liable under the supply contract, since these will be the individuals who have actually reached a binding agreement with the supplier, either in writing, orally or by conduct.

3. **When you are liable for a gas bill**

The Gas Act 1995

Since 1 March 1996, gas has been supplied to existing customers of British Gas under the terms of a 'deemed contract'. From this date, new customers who request a supply from any supplier, including British Gas, are supplied under the terms of a contract. Any new customers who receive a supply of gas from a gas supplier without first entering into a contract are supplied under the terms of a deemed contract instead. Contracts and deemed contracts are discussed in detail in Chapter 2.

You are liable for a gas bill if:

- you were a tariff customer of British Gas on 31 January 1996. You will have had a deemed contract with British Gas from 1 March 1996. You will be liable to pay for your supply under the terms of the deemed contract which applies to you;
- you entered into a contract with any supplier from 1 March 1996. You are liable to pay for your supply under the terms of the contract;
- you have a deemed contract with a supplier which started after 1 March 1996.

Former 'tariff customers' under the Gas Act 1986

If you were a tariff customer of British Gas immediately before 1 March 1996, you will have automatically become a customer with a deemed contract. You can be held liable to pay the bill under the terms of a deemed contract if you were the tariff customer under the provisions of the Gas Act 1986, before it was amended by the Gas Act 1995. This question can only be decided under the terms of the law that applied at that time. A **'tariff customer'** was defined as 'a person supplied with gas' under the Gas Act 1986;[4] and should not be confused with customers under special tariff schemes run by individual power companies.

It can be argued that the pre-1995 legislation for gas provided some straightforward principles for deciding liability in individual cases. These principles will help you to assess if you should be classified as the tariff customer immediately prior to 1 March 1996 and hence if you should be regarded as liable for the bill from that date under the terms of a deemed contract.

These principles were discussed in greater detail in the 9th edition of this *Handbook*, but are summarised here for ease of reference.

You will have been liable to pay the supplier for a gas bill if:

- you were an owner or occupier of premises; *and*
- you gave British Gas notice in writing that you required a supply of gas; *and*
- British Gas had a statutory duty to supply you.

You will have been solely liable for the bill if you alone gave notice in writing requiring the supply, regardless of whether you lived alone or with other adults.

You will have been jointly responsible for the bill if you and one or more others gave notice requiring a supply. Your liability for the bill started on the date that you required the supply.

Your liability for the supply will have continued until:

- where you gave at least 24 hours' written notice that you intended to leave the premises, the day you left;
- where you did not give at least 24 hours' written notice that you were leaving, the earliest of:
  - 28 days after you actually gave written notice you were leaving; *or*

- on the next day when the meter should have been read; *or*
- on the day when any subsequent occupier of the premises required a supply.

If your liability for the supply ended prior to 1 March 1996 as described above, you cannot subsequently be held liable for the supply at the premises concerned under the terms of a deemed contract.

You may have been liable to pay the gas bill if:

- the liability of the person(s) who gave notice had come to an end (see above); *and*
- you were, in practice, supplied with gas.

The Limitation Act 1980

It is not unknown for some energy companies to attempt to pursue debts more than six years after the sum fell due. A six-year recovery limit is placed on sums due under contract (actual or deemed) by the Limitation Act 1980. The Act applies to a contract to supply energy in the same way that it applies to other contracts. This means that if you have not acknowledged the debt for six years then the energy company cannot take court action to recover the money claimed. Making a payment to the energy company for the sum claimed would constitute acknowledgment, as would writing to it about the debt. It is not usually possible to acknowledge a debt verbally – eg, over the telephone. You should exercise caution about your contact with the energy company if the debt is nearing the six year limit, as acknowledging the debt can start the clock running again. In Scotland, the limitation period is five years.[5]

If the supplier has obtained a county court judgment within the relevant limitation period, then in theory there is no limit on the amount of time that the energy company can pursue you for the balance due under the judgement. However, if the judgment is over six years old the creditor may need to obtain the permission of the Court to enforce the debt.

Customers with contracts

Your liability for the bill

To be eligible to enter into a contract, you must be the owner or occupier of the premises where the gas supply is needed. You must request a supply, though your request need not be in writing.[6]

A supplier may not enter into a contract with you if someone else has a contract for the supply of gas with another supplier for the same premises,[7] unless that contract will have expired or terminated before you require a supply. In practice, you do not have to terminate your existing contract formally before entering a new one – if you sign up to a new contract, the changeover should be handled by the two suppliers.

You will need to agree the terms of your contract with your supplier. Terms of contracts are not individually negotiated. Your supplier will have set up a 'scheme' setting out the 'principal terms' of the various contracts on offer. The scheme will have been approved by Ofgem. Details are published by the supplier. You are entitled to a copy of the principal terms on request.[8]

Contracts may be for various periods of time and can vary from supplier to supplier. The period of the contract may be for an indefinite period (known as a 'rolling contract') or a fixed period. Where a contract is due to come to an end, the supplier must offer you a new contract and inform you of the terms of the deemed contract (see p16) that would apply if no new contract is agreed. The terms of contracts are restricted by provisions within a supplier's licence and regulated by Ofgem. Licence provisions relating to a customer ending a contract are discussed below.

Ending your liability for the bill

You are liable to pay for the supply under the terms of the contract until:

- **Your contract comes to an end**. If a contract for a specified period is due to come to an end, the supplier must offer you a new contract and inform you of the terms of the deemed contract (see p71) which would apply if no new contract is agreed. This should normally be done 30 days before the contract is due to end.[9]
- **You terminate your contract while you are still an owner/occupier of the premises**. A contract for a fixed period may be ended at any time during that period if you give the supplier notice according to the contract and pay the supplier any termination fee referred to in the contract, unless either of the following conditions apply.
- **Your contract is of an indefinite length of time.** This also applies where an initial fixed-term contract has expired and you have continued to receive a supply from the company on a rolling contract.[10]
- **Your supplier has unilaterally varied a term in your contract.** The most obvious example is an increase in the charges being made for supply. However, any other change made to your terms which would significantly disadvantage you also applies here.[11]

To avoid the termination fee on the basis that your supplier has made a unilateral variation, you must have notified your current supplier on or before the date of the relevant variation taking effect of your intention to switch supplier. This notification does not have to be in writing. If you notify your supplier orally, make a note of the date and the name of the person you spoke to. You do not have to actually switch supplier or switch within a particular timeframe to avoid the termination fees.

If a termination fee is charged, the amount of the fee must be reasonable in the particular circumstances. What is reasonable may be determined by a court and it may be noted that if a supplier claims that you are in breach of contract, the supplier is still under a duty to mitigate its loss (if any). The supplier may be prepared to reach an agreement to waive any termination fee if you fall into a vulnerable category. In other cases, your notice period will not start until you have paid the fee. If you do not pay the fee, you will not be able to end your contract.

You may want to terminate your contract with your existing supplier because you want to switch to another supplier. See Chapter 2 and below for more information about this process. You do not have to pay a termination fee if you want to switch suppliers because your supplier has changed the terms of your contract – eg, by increasing the charges.

You must have notified your current supplier on or before the date of the relevant variation taking effect of your intention to switch supplier. This notification does not have to be in writing. If you notify your supplier orally, make a note of the date and the name of the person you spoke to. You do not have to actually switch supplier or switch within a particular timeframe to avoid the termination fees.

If you have arrears with your current supplier you can still in theory change supplier, but you must clear the arrears within 30 days.

If you have a prepayment meter, your supplier can only block you from switching to another supplier if you owe more than £500.[12]

Contact Citizens Advice consumer service if you want to terminate your liability and switch supplier and you believe that your current supplier is being obstructive.

- **You no longer occupy the premises.** The supplier must include a term that the supply contract ends two days after you have told the supplier of the dates on which you stop owning or occupying premises. If you do not give notice, the contract must end at either:
  - the end of the second working day after you have notified the licensee that you have stopped owning or occupying the premises; *or*
  - the date on which any other person begins to own or occupy the premises and takes a supply of electricity at those premises.

Where a contract is brought to an end in this way, you remain liable for the supply of gas to the property until the date on which that contract ends.

If you give your supplier a minimum of two working days' notice, or if your supplier agrees to accept a shorter period of notice before you leave, your contract will end on the day you leave.

If you do not give your supplier notice that you are leaving, your contract will not terminate, and you will continue to be liable to pay for the supply of gas until the earlier of the following two events:

- two days after you have told the supplier you have left; *or*
- the date when another person requires a supply from either the same or a different supplier.

It will always be in your interest to inform the supplier that you are leaving/have left. Make sure you arrange for the supplier to take a final meter reading and also read the meter yourself so you can check your final bill. Suppliers may be contacted by post, phone or email. It is advisable to back up any communication by phone or email with a hard copy.

Keep a copy of your letter or communication. Without such evidence, if someone else uses the supply, it may be difficult for you to provide evidence of when s/he started to use the supply if s/he has not informed the supplier themselves.

- **The supplier varies the terms of your contract.** If your supplier increases the charges made under the terms of your contract or varies other terms of your contract and the variations will significantly disadvantage you, the supplier must inform you in writing of the changes made. Note that Ofgem has ruled that suppliers must give customers 30 days notice of a price rise or any other change to billing which will leave them worse off.[13] The supplier must also notify you that you have the option to change supplier, and direct you to a source of free and impartial advice about this process. If you decide to terminate your contract after receiving a price increase notice, and switch to another supplier, your old supplier must terminate your contract within 15 days of receiving confirmation that you now have a contract with your new supplier. Your old supplier cannot apply the price rise to your bill for the remainder of your contract with it.

- **The supplier's licence is revoked by Ofgem.** If this happens, your contract with that supplier is terminated. Ofgem will require another supplier to continue to supply you with gas under terms directed by Ofgem for up to six months.[14] You would then become liable to pay the new supplier under those terms. If you choose to enter into a contract with the new supplier, the terms of the contract apply from the date you enter into the contract. The same applies if you choose to be supplied by a different supplier.

Customers with deemed contracts

Your liability for the bill

You are supplied with gas under the terms of a deemed contract if you are a consumer (see p72) at the premises supplied with gas and:

- you were a tariff customer (see p72) of British Gas immediately prior to 1 March 1996 and your liability for the supply did not come to an end before that date; *or*

- you are the remaining owner or occupier of the premises supplied with gas, and the liability for the supply of the former tariff customer (see p67) has come to an end or been terminated; *or*

- you became the new owner or occupier of the premises on or after 1 March 1996 and you have not entered into a contract with a supplier for a supply of gas; *or*
- your contract for the supply of gas has come to an end or been terminated and you continue to receive a supply of gas from the supplier; *or*
- you are being supplied with gas by another supplier because your supplier's licence has been revoked by Ofgem.[15]

A '**consumer**' is defined as 'a person who is supplied with gas conveyed to a particular premises by a gas transporter'. For practical purposes, this is an identical definition to that of a 'tariff customer', updated to reflect the new structure of the gas industry.

The terms and conditions of a deemed contract is determined in accordance with a scheme set up by the relevant supplier. They may include terms and conditions enabling the supplier to determine the amount of gas supplied to you where a meter reading has not been taken at the start of the deemed contract. Your liability is assessed under these terms until the earliest of the following three events:

- the date of the first meter reading; *or*
- the time the supplier ceases to supply you with gas; *or*
- the date you cease to take a supply of gas.

Disputes over the rate of gas consumption

In some cases, there may be a dispute over the amount of gas consumption, particularly where appliances have broken down or have not been used. In such a case, a supplier providing a gas supply under a deemed contract is required by Standard Licence Condition 7.9 to act reasonably and take into account relevant consumption data for the premises. For more on high bills, see Chapter 6.

Ending your liability for the bill

Your liability under the terms of a deemed contract will continue until:

- **You enter into a contract while you are still an owner or occupier of the premises.** You continue to be liable under the terms of a deemed contract until your new contract takes effect.

You may terminate a deemed contract at any time by giving the supplier seven days' notice. The notice period may be shorter if the supplier agrees. If you have not arranged to enter into a contract with the same supplier at the end of the notice period, your supply will continue under the terms of a further deemed contract.

If you intend to transfer to an alternative supplier, you must give your existing supplier at least 28 days' notice, unless the supplier agrees to accept a shorter notice period.

You may not bring a deemed contract to an end without the agreement of the supplier, if you are being supplied by an alternative supplier because your supplier's licence was revoked by the regulator. You will only be able to bring such a deemed contract to an end:
– with the agreement of the supplier (which will be given if you accept a contract with that supplier); *or*
– by transferring to another supplier; *or*
– by ceasing to take a supply of gas at the premises.

- **You cease to occupy the premises.** If you give your supplier a minimum of two working days' notice, or if your supplier agrees to accept a shorter period of notice before you leave, your deemed contract will end on the day you leave. If you do not give your supplier notice that you are leaving, your deemed contract will not terminate and you will continue to be liable to pay for the supply of gas until the earliest of:
– 28 days after you inform the supplier you have left;
– the next date the meter is due to be read;
– the date when another person requires a supply from either the same supplier or a different supplier.

4. Common problems

Your liability when your name is on the bill

Electricity
The person named on a bill is not always liable to pay. Sometimes only one person is actually named on a bill, disguising the fact that several people signed the notice requiring a supply or the contract or that no one signed anything. For example, suppliers often ask outgoing occupiers the names of the next occupiers. You may find that your name is on a bill without your ever having had any contact with the supplier. A person who is named on the bill has sole liability for the bill if s/he alone gave written notice requiring a supply or s/he alone made a phone request for the supply. Otherwise, the name on the bill is only evidence of who might be liable.

Gas
If you have been a customer of British Gas continuously since before 1 March 1996, you have a deemed contract with British Gas (see p66). You will need to check that you are liable under the provisions for deciding who becomes a customer with a deemed contract (see p71).

If you have entered into a contract with British Gas (or an alternative supplier), your name is on the bill and you are liable under the terms of the contract (see p16).

Your liability when no one is named on the bill

Electricity

When no one is named on the bill, liability depends on the facts.

Gas

If no one is named on the bill, you may be liable for the bill under the terms of a deemed contract (see p71).

Moving in: becoming liable for the supply

It is in your interest to have some evidence of when your liability begins. When moving to a new address, make a note of the meter reading and preferably agree the reading with the last occupier(s). Arrange to have the meter read by the supplier, and inform it that you require a supply. Check your first bill to ensure that it does not include the previous occupiers' charges. Incoming occupiers cannot be held responsible for the previous occupiers' arrears of electricity or gas.

Electricity

If an electricity supplier does not routinely use application forms for giving notice, consider whether you should give notice in writing (see p30). One person can give notice if that person wants to take responsibility. If you are a joint occupier who wants to share liability, ensure that everyone signs the application form, letter or contract. Some suppliers have application forms that suggest you can apply on behalf of another person who is named as an occupier on the form. This appears to allow the possibility of another person making you liable for the supply without your consent or knowledge. It is the author's opinion that you cannot be made liable for a supply in this way.

If one joint occupier moves out and you move in to take her/his place, there is nothing to prevent you from giving notice specifying that you are replacing a joint occupier or arranging a new contract. Liability will depend on who signs the new arrangement on the principles discussed above.

Gas

If you do not inform a supplier that you have moved in, the last supplier to supply gas at the premises is entitled to charge you for any gas you have used under the terms of a deemed contract. It is in your interests to contact the supplier to obtain a supply. You will initially be liable under the terms of a deemed contract, until you enter directly into a contract with the supplier.

Moving out: ending liability for the supply

If you are an occupier and you give a supplier proper notice that you are leaving, you will be protected from being held liable for the fuel used after you have left.

Electricity

In the absence of notice, ending liability will depend on the terms of your contract with the supplier.

Gas

There are provisions in both the Gas Act 1986, as amended by the Gas Act 1995, and in suppliers' licence conditions which set out when your liability for gas ends under contracts (see p68) and deemed contracts (see p71).

You remain liable for six years after the date on which a bill for gas or electricity fell due in England and Wales; five years in Scotland. Thus, if you change supplier but have an outstanding debt to a previous supplier, the previous supplier has a right to bring legal action against you for up to six years. Thereafter, the debt becomes irrecoverable under the Limitation Act 1980. In Scotland, the limitation period is five years.[16]

Who is liable when the person named on the bill has left

Sole liability

Electricity

A person who is named on the bill will have had sole liability for the bill if s/he alone became the tariff customer by giving written notice requiring a supply or entered into a contract. Her/his liability will have ended either when s/he left if s/he gave notice of leaving or with the passing of time (see p63). As a joint occupier, spouse or co-habitee, you cannot be held liable for her/his bill if you have not given notice requiring a supply or entered into a contract (see p65).

Gas

If you alone entered into a contract for the supply of gas, your responsibility for that supply ends either on your terminating the contract (see p72) or with the passing of time (see p72). One or more remaining occupiers may subsequently have responsibility for the supply under the terms of a deemed contract (see p71).

If you are liable under the terms of a deemed contract, your liability will end either with the termination of that deemed contract or with the passing of time (see p72). The liability of the remaining occupiers is also under the terms of a deemed contract.

Shared liability

Electricity

If the person who left gave written notice or entered into a contract to obtain the electricity supply, her/his liability ends either when s/he informs the supplier s/he is leaving or with the passing of time (see p63). Any remaining occupiers who originally gave notice in writing or entered into the contract are liable for the arrears along with the person who has left.

In situations where nobody gave notice or signed a contract, liability for the arrears depends on the facts. You could still be held liable for all of the arrears, but may be able to negotiate a compromise with the supplier (look at the supplier's code of practice on payment of bills, which may contain useful guidance on the supplier's attitude).

As a joint occupier or sharer, you could ask for the amount of the arrears to be apportioned between the people responsible for the bill, particularly if the supplier knows the whereabouts of all the parties. Electricity suppliers are entitled to refuse to supply an occupier who owes arrears[17] and, in any event, could pursue each debtor separately through the courts. In one case, Ofgas (the gas regulator prior to Ofgem) persuaded British Gas to pursue four previous occupants for their share of a bill where arrears had accrued because of a series of estimated bills. British Gas accepted that the fifth (still current) occupant should only pay one-fifth of the total bill.[18] Although the case relates to gas, the principles apply equally to electricity.

If the occupier who left was your spouse or co-habitee, and you had little or no control over the income of the household (eg, only your partner had a wage or received benefits), you could argue that you should not be held responsible for any arrears that accrued while your partner was present and ask the supplier to pursue your partner for the arrears.

In other circumstances, it might be appropriate to ask the supplier to apportion the arrears. In the event of a dispute, contact Citizens Advice consumer service. In a case of vulnerability Consumer Focus's Extra Help Unit may be prepared to intervene (see p223).

Gas

If you were jointly supplied under the terms of a contract, the terms of the contract apply. There may be scope for you to argue that any arrears should be apportioned between the parties to the contract. When the previous joint occupier leaves, make sure you inform the supplier of the meter reading and/or apply for a new contract/deemed contract in your own name so the arrears relating to the joint occupancy are clearly established.

Where a joint deemed contract comes to an end because one of the occupiers has left, it will also be in your interests to inform the supplier and establish any arrears relating to the period of joint occupancy.

The former regulator Ofgas acknowledged that the strict application of its legal position on liability for a bill[19] created problems for many customers with children left with large arrears after a spouse/partner had left. British Gas agreed with Ofgas to treat these situations sensitively, taking into account the individual circumstances of each case. It also agreed to take into consideration the existence of legal agreements between the parties concerned for responsibility for household expenses, including gas.

When a consumer dies

When a consumer dies, the supplier may attempt to secure payment from someone who was living with her/him. In these circumstances, the situation is as outlined above. Where no one else is liable for the bill, any bills outstanding can be charged to the deceased's estate. This means that outstanding bills must be paid for out of money belonging to the deceased, or out of the proceeds of the sale of any belongings. Electricity and gas debts compete on an equal footing along with all other debts. They do not take priority. If the person left nothing, the bill lapses and the supplier bears the loss. If you have paid the bill of a person who has died, in the mistaken belief that you were responsible for doing so, the supplier can usually be persuaded either to credit your own account or refund the money. If the supplier refuses to do so, seek legal advice and seek to recover through the small claims court (see Chapter 14).

Priority between debts

If a consumer dies and leaves some money, but not enough to pay all outstanding debts, then the cost of the funeral and any costs involved in dealing with the estate take priority over all other debts except 'realised securities' such as a mortgaged property. So, if a consumer dies with an outstanding mortgage and the house is sold to meet this debt, anything left will go first to pay for the funeral and administration costs; any outstanding fuel bills will be a lower priority. See CPAG's *Debt Advice Handbook* for more on the priority of debts.

Assignment of outstanding charges

In some cases, you might become liable for an old energy bill where the supplier has assigned the outstanding debt to your new supplier. If you failed to pay the old supplier within 28 days of the charges being due, the first supplier may assign the debt to the new supplier. If your new supplier agrees, it can take over the debt where:

- it has become due to the first supplier;
- it had been demanded in writing; *and*
- you were notified that the charges might be assigned.

However, it is more likely that the transfer will be blocked by a supplier within the framework laid down by Standard Licence Condition (SLC) 14.

Domestic customer transfer blocking

Under SLC 14, the supplier may ask or allow the relevant gas shipper to prevent a proposed supplier transfer in relation to a domestic customer at a domestic premises where there are outstanding charges or where the transfer has been begun in error, or where the terms of the contract prevent a transfer (eg, where the contract does not end until a fixed date in the future).

A supply transfer cannot be prevented where gas is supplied by a prepayment meter and you have agreed to pay the existing charges. Nor can a transfer be stopped where the supplier has increased charges but has not re-set the prepayment meter within a reasonable period, and the outstanding charges only relate to the period since a price increase.

Switching supplier when you have fuel debts

Where there is an unpaid bill, a supplier may block a transfer to another energy provider. However, if you have a prepayment meter, where there are outstanding charges of amounts up to £200, these may be assigned to a new supplier. From 1 November 2012, the 'big six' fuel suppliers have made a voluntary undertaking not to block transfers where there are arrears on a prepayment meter of up to £500. This will be formalised by a change to the standard licence conditions as soon as practicable.[20] Within this boundary your existing supplier cannot block a transfer, although this effectively discriminates against customers who have arrears but do not have prepayment meters.

Similarly, if you have a disputed debt of £500 or less transferred onto a prepayment meter, the supplier cannot block a transfer where charges are disputed in their entirety or there is supplier error. The precise scope of this condition has yet to be tested by the courts or by the regulators.

One such situation may be where you have offered and paid a lesser sum in full and final settlement for an existing debt and accepted the imposition of a prepayment meter.

Suppliers are required to:
- keep evidence of that request and of the reasons for it for at least 12 months after the request is made; *and*
- inform the proposed new gas supplier:
  - that the objection has been raised at your request; *and*
  - of the reason given you for making the request,

as soon as reasonably practicable after the licensee asks the relevant gas supplier.

Normally, within 90 days of taking over a supply, the new supplier is given a notice by the previous supplier to assign the charges. The new supplier must then pay the outstanding charges to your previous supplier. Your new supplier may then seek to recover the money from you. If the old supplier fails to act within prescribed time limits, the right of assignment may be lost.

SLC 49, which formerly applied for gas, provided that the domestic customer in question shall not be regarded as having failed to pay any charges for the supply of gas:
- if the supply is genuinely in dispute and the dispute does not relate to the volume of gas which was shown on the register of the gas meter through which the supply was taken when the first supplier ceased to supply gas; *or*
- where charges are in relation to the provision of a gas meter.

Similar provisions applied for electricity. Contact Citizens Advice consumer service for advice on the position with charges and difficulties with a supplier; it may also be worth involving the Energy Ombudsman (see Chapter 14).

Ultimately, it is the county court in England and Wales and the Sheriff Court in Scotland which could be called upon to determine the matter (see Chapter 14). A debt which has been assigned is not enforceable if there is a dispute which you are prepared to raise as a defence. Only when the dispute has been resolved against you and a judgment given will any debt be legally enforceable. Alternatively, your new supplier also has discretion to waive charges or collect a lesser sum.

Harassment by suppliers and debt collectors

In some cases, a supplier may wrongly attempt to pursue a claim against you long after any supply and any liability has ended. Such acts may constitute harassment if the supplier persists despite you establishing the true position.

In extreme cases, sending demands for payment accompanied by threats of disconnection or referral to credit reference agencies may constitute harassment both in civil and criminal law.[21]

As a result you may have claims in civil and criminal law against the supplier for harassment (see Chapter 14).

In other cases, an old debt may be assigned by the energy company to a firm of debt collectors. Basically, the energy supplier gives up on trying to recover the debt and sells it to another company to seek to recover what it can. Debt collecting companies may buy up old energy debts from suppliers and then seek to recover the money owed themselves. These companies specialise in sending out letters by computer demanding payment. Often they are based far from where you live and have no intention of issuing any sort of legal proceedings or visiting you, despite claims in the letter that they will do so. In many cases, the cost of beginning legal proceedings would exceed the amount of the debt or any sum that could be recovered (see Chapter 14).

If you deal with these companies, do so in writing rather than by telephone and contact an advice agency which is used to dealing with these debts and before responding.

Any such claim should be closely examined to ensure that there has not been a mistake. If contacting a debt collecting company, request copies of all the alleged paper work on which the claim is based.

If the debt is more than six years old, it will not be recoverable under the Limitation Act 1980. In Scotland, the limitation period is five years.[22]

Debt collectors have no right to force entry to your home. If they make threats or commit acts of harassment they may be prosecuted under section 40 of the Administration of Justice Act 1970 which makes it a criminal offence to harass a debtor. Civil and criminal liability may also lie for acts amounting to harassment under the Protection from Harassment Act 1997 (see Chapter 14).

Notes

2. When you are liable for an electricity bill

1 Condition 24 SLC covers termination of contracts
2 *British Gas plc v Mitchell* (unreported) Pontefract County Court, May 1994
3 *Faulkner v Yorkshire Electricity Group plc* [1994] Legal Action, February 1995, p23

3. When you are liable for a gas or electricity bill

4 s14(5) GA 1986, repealed by GA 1995
5 Prescription and Limitation (Scotland) Act 1973
6 Condition 22.2 SLC
7 Condition 22 SLC
8 Condition 22 SLC
9 Conditions 22 and 23 SLC
10 Condition 24.3 SLC
11 Condition 24.4 SLC
12 Ofgem debt assignment protocol for prepayment meter customers, letter 24 September 2012 (www.ofgem.gov.uk/Sustainability/SocAction/Publications/Documents1/Debt Assignment Protocol Review.pdf)
13 Condition 23.4.a SLC
14 Condition 8.2(b) SLC
15 Conditions 7 and 22 SLC set out the obligations of a supplier under deemed contracts

4. Common problems

16 Prescription and Limitation (Scotland) Act 1973
17 Condition 22 SLC
18 Ofgas *Annual Report* 1990, p40
19 Ofgas *Annual Report* 1990, p29
20 Ofgem debt assignment protocol for prepayment meter customers, letter 24 September 2012 (www.ofgem.gov.uk/Sustainability/SocAction/Publications/Documents1/Debt Assignment Protocol Review.pdf)
21 *Ferguson v British Gas Trading Ltd* [2009] EWCA Civ 46
22 Prescription and Limitation (Scotland) Act 1973

Chapter 6

High bills

This chapter covers:
1. Amount of the bill (below)
2. Accuracy of the bill (p83)
3. Accuracy of the meter (p87)
4. Circuit and installation faults and faulty appliances (p92)
5. Overcharging by prepayment meters (p94)

This chapter looks at ways of checking whether you are paying the correct amount for your gas and electricity. If your bills are correct, see Chapter 4 for help in deciding how to pay; Chapters 11 and 12 for financial and other help with paying them; and Chapters 7 and 8 if you are in arrears and/or facing disconnection. Chapter 14 suggests remedies for when a supplier charges you the wrong amount.

1. Amount of the bill

Check consumption

If a fuel bill seems to be too high, check whether consumption has actually increased by comparing the units consumed with those used during the same period in previous years. You can do this by looking at bills for previous years.

Helpfully, Ofgem has introduced new standards of conduct for suppliers contained within Standard Licence Condition (SLC) 31(A)2 requiring that the information on your bill must include more detail, making it easier for you to compare previous consumption with current levels of consumption.

You should have started receiving these more detailed bills since December 2010. Each bill should include the following information:
- your current tariff;
- your current consumption for the last 12 months in kwh, unless you have been a customer for less than 12 months;
- a cost estimate in pounds per year of your supply for the next 12 months, assuming that you stay on the same tariff, at the same rate, using the same amount of electricity or gas.

Ofgem has ruled that suppliers must give you 30 days notice of a price rise or any other change to billing which will leave you worse off. This change is effective from May 2011 and can be found at SLC 23. Previously, suppliers only had to notify you 65 working days after the increase had taken place.

If you do not receive regular bills (eg, because you have a prepayment meter), your supplier must send you an annual statement which contains the information set out above.

If you feel that your consumption for a period is unusually high, use statements received from previous periods as a point of comparison. Suppliers must now provide you with details of your last 12 months consumption, which you examine to spot unusually high consumption or to challenge unreasonably high monthly direct debit payments. Bear in mind that consumption can fluctuate seasonally, so you are likely to consume more fuel in cold winter months than you are in the summer.

You can also use the information on your annual statement for comparing your current tariff against other suppliers' tariffs. Simply calculate your average annual cost using your current unit rates, then substitute your rates for those of another supplier (remembering to include any discounts and ensuring that you factor in VAT). This will show you whether or not you could get a better deal by switching to another supplier.

If you have not kept previous bills, ask the supplier for copies. Some suppliers may charge for these. If the charge seems unreasonably high, contact Citizens Advice consumer service for guidance; Consumer Focus may act where groups of consumers who are vulnerable are affected (see Chapter 14).

Exceptional reasons for a high bill

Check whether consumption is higher than usual because of exceptional reasons – eg, because of:

* an emergency, such as a flood;
* a new heating system which you are not used to operating or which might be defective;
* a period of exceptionally cold weather;
* someone in the household being ill, leading to higher heating costs.

If you think the bill is accurate after taking any exceptional circumstances into account, see Chapters 4, 11 and 12 for help on how to pay.

Other charges in the bill

Bills may also be high because they contain items other than the cost of fuel and standing charges. The supplier may also include charges for disconnection or reconnection, and for replacing meters. Check to see if these have been lawfully charged by reading Chapter 3 on supply and charges for connecting supply, and Chapter 8 on disconnection for arrears.

Obtaining information under the Data Protection Act

Suppliers are likely to hold a large amount of information about their customers electronically. This may include details of previous bills and consumption, credit ratings, and prosecutions. If a supplier refuses to provide information voluntarily, you may still be able to get hold of this information by using your rights under the Data Protection Act.

To exercise your rights, write to the supplier. It will send you an application form and a list of categories of information that the supplier has registered on the Data Protection Register. You can look at a copy of the Register itself at your local main public library. You then select the appropriate category from which you want your records, and return the form. You have to pay a fee of not more than £10 and fill out a separate form for each category. The supplier will then provide the information.

As well as the right to be supplied with copies of information, you have the right to:

- have inaccurate information corrected;
- claim compensation for loss caused by inaccurate information;
- complain to the Information Commissioner's Office if the supplier fails to provide the information, to correct inaccuracies, or to obtain and process information fairly and lawfully.

2. **Accuracy of the bill**

Always check that the supplier has got its sums right. If the units consumed are correctly recorded, check that the cost has been correctly calculated. Arithmetic error is rare but does happen.

If disconnection is threatened but you think the bill is inaccurate, tell the supplier. A supplier cannot disconnect in respect of that part of a bill that is genuinely in dispute.[1] However, you cannot avoid paying for gas or electricity used simply on the basis of a mistake generating an inaccurate bill – the supplier has the legal right to make you pay for what you have used, even if it initially made an error on the bill.[2] In particular, you should pay for that part of the electricity bill that you do not dispute, or you could be disconnected in respect of that alone (see Chapter 7).

If you experience difficulty in dealing with a supplier, particularly if staff at call centres prove unable to help, request to speak to the company solicitors, and be prepared to lodge a complaint. This will usually result in reaching a more senior member of staff to deal with the issue.

Suppliers are committed to Codes of Practice for Accurate Bills for domestic customers, including back billing, suppliers' commitment to bill you regularly and accurately, and impose limitations on the circumstances where you can be billed for previously unbilled energy that is more than 12 months old.

These principles are set out in the Codes of Practice for Accurate Bills which has been developed by the Energy Retail Association (ERA) with British Gas, E.ON, EDF Energy, npower and Scottish Power; these companies all support the independently audited Code of Practice and are committed to the Code as a minimum standard of service for customers. Scottish and Southern Energy has a Domestic Customer Charter which includes similar standards of service in relation to billing and back billing.

Under these codes, companies who have through their error failed to issue bills will not be permitted to bill for any amount which dates back for longer than a year. This is known as back billing. You must be able to show that you have not avoided payment – eg, by refusing to cooperate with attempts to read the meter or to resolve queries. You must also be able to show that you have made a reasonable attempt to contact a supplier to make or arrange payment.

Where a supplier issues a bill which has these principles applied, it will credit your account with the value of the unbilled energy consumed over 12 months ago, taking into consideration any payments already made by you or credits applied to the account, so that you are not required to pay any additional sums towards this previously unbilled energy consumption.

The clause relating to back billing within the ERA Code of Practice applies to domestic credit customers, as defined in the supplier licence agreement. It does not apply to customers whose express terms and conditions exclude them from receiving bills or statements.

Although prepayment customers are not explicitly covered by this clause, the ERA states that suppliers will apply similar principles in relation to debt over 12 months old.

Billing delays

You may find that the supplier has billed you for a longer period of time than normal and, when you finally receive the account, it covers that whole period. Suppliers are not obliged to bill you at any particular interval, although they will normally send bills every three months or six months. If you have a prepayment meter, statements are usually sent to you at least once a year. If regular bills have not been sent, or are late, point out to the supplier that the high level of debt is partly its own fault by making it difficult for you to monitor or modify consumption. It should be possible to negotiate time to pay. In any such negotiation, use anything in the supplier's code of practice or Standard Licence Conditions that supports your case.

Bills sent after a long time should be examined with care: the charges or the rate of VAT may have changed since the previous bill. If the prices have gone up, check to ensure that the supplier has not charged all, or too many, of the units at the higher rate. If it has, the bill should be reduced appropriately. Also check that the supplier has complied with the requirement at SLC 23 to give you 30 days' notice of any changes to the cost of your supply.

There have been cases of bills being sent out late by months or even years (old bills are sometimes served when a person applies and obtains a mortgage). Unless fraud is involved (see Chapter 9), charges cannot be recovered where:

- in England and Wales, if the electricity or gas was used more than six years ago;[3] *or*
- in Scotland, if the supplier has not raised legal proceedings against you for them and you have not acknowledged the charges for five years.[4]

Otherwise, you must pay for the gas or electricity that was supplied to you (see Chapter 5). With a bill that is very late, much of the bill may be estimated (see below). The longer the delay, the better the chances of having part or all of the bill written off, or being given time to pay. Be prepared to negotiate and place proposals in writing, setting out your circumstances as necessary. Citizens Advice consumer service can advise and Consumer Focus or the Energy Ombudsman could apply pressure on the supplier to settle on a reasonable solution as appropriate (see Chapter 14).

Estimates

Check to see whether the bill has been estimated. If it has, there will be an 'E' ('estimated') next to the figure in the 'present meter reading' column. Note that one supplier uses a 'C' instead of an 'E' to represent an estimate. An 'A' ('assessed') will be there if the reading is based on an accurate figure taken by a meter reader or by you. Note that in some regions 'A' means 'actual'. Any letter symbols should be explained on the bill – check this if in doubt.

If practical, take your own reading (see Appendix 3). Do this as soon as possible after receiving the estimated bill and make an allowance for units consumed since the date of the bill so that the comparison is as accurate as possible. You can calculate an average daily rate and deduct that amount for the appropriate number of days.

Alternatively, to decide if an estimate is unreasonable, compare the amount of fuel used over the same period in the previous year with the estimated consumption on the present bill. If a bill covering the same period is not available (eg, because you have recently moved), try making a reasonable estimate using any bill you do have, or by calculating how much would be used by the appliances you have and the frequency with which you use them.

If you do not think the estimate is accurate, notify the supplier. Call the number which should be on the bill, or record your own meter reading on the back of the bill and ask for a more accurate bill to be sent later. The bill may be paid and the supplier should work out the difference owed. It is advisable to back up a telephone request with a written request, keeping a copy of the letter. Meter readers sometimes leave a pre-paid postcard for you to complete and return with your own reading. If your own reading shows that the bill is an overestimate, the supplier must take all reasonable steps to reflect your meter reading in your new bill – in line with SLC 21B.

However, remember that if a bill has been underestimated, a higher bill will result from any complaint. Normally, it will be best to set the record straight as soon as possible because the bill will have to be paid at some time. Also, be aware of cases where a high bill is the result of a low estimate on a past bill followed by an accurate meter reading later. Experience has shown that this is one of the most common reasons for an extraordinarily high bill: several quarters' bills are significantly underestimated, followed by an actual meter reading by the supplier which brings the account back up to date. This results in a large bill, incorporating the usage not paid for in the previously low estimated bills. For this reason, it is crucial to give an accurate reading yourself whenever you receive an estimated bill. The points made in respect of billing delays above also apply here.

Errors in reading the meter

Although actual meter readings are likely to be correct, even the supplier's own meter readers can sometimes make mistakes. You can use the same methods discussed above to detect errors, but the supplier might want to take a second reading to check any reading which you have taken. If the supplier has made a mistake, the bill should be amended. In properties in multiple occupation, where meters are often grouped together, it is not unknown for readings to be attributed to the wrong meter.

Smart meters

The new generation of smart meters (see p51) allow your supplier to read your meter remotely, without the need to estimate bills or even to visit your home to take a manual meter reading.

The government aims to install smart meters in every UK household by 2019. Fuel companies are responsible for meeting the cost of installing the new meters. A nationwide roll out is anticipated to start in 2014, although many fuel companies have already started installing smart metres – eg, many new build properties will have a smart meter fitted as standard.

The Department of Energy and Climate Change anticipates that smart meters will offer you greater control over your fuel costs by allowing you to access detailed information about your usage levels and a greater choice of payment options. For example, some smart meters have a digital display screen showing not only the amount of energy being used, but the cost of this energy in pounds and pence.

3. **Accuracy of the meter**

Even if the details on the bill appear to be correct, the meter may be faulty. Meters must be approved and certified by meter examiners.[5] If, as is the normal situation, the meter belongs to the supplier (or gas transporter), it is responsible for keeping it in proper working order.[6] An electricity meter is deemed to be accurate if it does not vary more than +2 to -3.5 per cent from the correct reading. For gas meters the limits are +2 to -2 per cent.

Note also that if gas or electricity appliances are old and/or have not been serviced recently, they may no longer perform in accordance with their rating.

Checking your meter

Gas meters must be installed in a readily accessible position and, if situated in a box or compound, you must be given a key. Meters may be repositioned for free if you are disabled, and you should ask your supplier to do this for you. The Electricity Act 1989, states that 'Where an electricity supplier, for the purpose of meeting the needs of a disabled person – (a) alters the position of any electricity meter provided by him for a customer of his; or (b) replaces such a meter with one which has been specially adapted, the supplier shall not charge the customer for the alteration or replacement.'[7] The Gas Act 1986 has similar provision for the re-positioning of a gas meter.[8]

You can check your meter by using the following method.

- Switch off all appliances, including pilot lights.
- Read the meter (see Appendix 3).
- Turn on an appliance with a known rate of consumption and note the time (see note on p88).
- Leave the appliance on for a measured period of time, preferably in whole hours.
- Switch off the appliance and read the meter again.

If everything is working properly, the following formulae should work.

Electricity
Difference in readings = rating of appliance (kW) x time on (hours).

Example
If your electric fire has a one kilowatt (1kW) rating and is switched on for one hour the figures on each side of the '=' sign should both be '1'.

Where an electricity meter is faulty and its readings are outside the statutory margins of error, you fall within the standards regulations and may be entitled to bring a claim. For electricity, the margin of error is laid down by paragraph 13 of Schedule 7 of the Electricity Act 1989.

Gas

Difference in readings =

$$\text{(hundreds of cubic feet)} \times 3.6 = \frac{\text{appliance rating (kW)} \times \text{time on (hrs)}}{\text{(calorific value* for region)} \times 2.83}$$

*The amount of heat produced by burning a specific amount of gas

Example

The rating for an average gas fire is 2.5 kilowatts (kW), assuming that the fire is on full and all the elements are being used. If it is switched on for one hour in an area where gas has a calorific value of 38.2, then the figures on each side of the '=' sign should both be 0.023 – ie, the reading should be 2.3 cubic feet.

To find out the rating of an appliance, if it is not marked on the appliance itself, contact the manufacturer, the appliance supplier or the gas supplier. The calorific value for the area will be shown on your gas bill, or you can ask your supplier.

Where a reading falls outside a specified margin of error, there may be the basis of a claim under the Gas Standards Regulations. The relevant standards are those set out in the Gas (Meters) Regulations 1983.

Standards of performance – electricity meters other than prepayment meters

The Electricity (Minimum Standards of Performance Regulations) 2010 may apply where you consider that a meter may be inaccurate or where the supplier expects the meter is inaccurate.[9] These rules apply where the meter in question is **not** a prepayment meter.

On being notified of the situation, the supplier is normally required to offer to investigate the matter by visiting your home within seven working days[10] or to issue an explanation. If the supplier does not respond within the seven days, you are entitled to a £22 payment, unless there is an exception (see p26).

Where the supplier is unable to provide an explanation for the likely reason for the inaccuracy without visiting your home, it is expected to either arrange a visit or to supply an explanation for the probable reason for the inaccuracy. If the supplier does not arrange a visit within seven days or fails to provide an explanation of a probable reason within five days, you are entitled to a payment of £22.

Where an appointment is made, a supplier is also expected to keep to the standards on appointments (see Appendix 2).

Standards of performance – electricity prepayment meters

If you have a prepayment meter, regulation 18 of the Electricity (Standards of Performance) Regulations 2010 apply if the meter is inaccurate. This imposes a strict duty on your supplier to investigate and repair or replace your faulty meter if you notify that it is not operating properly or circumstances exist that suggest it is not operating correctly.

Notification should be by phone, fax or email – not by the post. Where you contact the supplier outside normal working hours, the communication is deemed to have been made and effective the next day or in the next working period.

When notified by you, the supplier should send a suitably qualified person to repair or replace the meter. Where the supplier fails to send a qualified person to investigate or examine your meter within three hours on a working day or four hours on a non-working day, the supplier is liable to pay the customer £22.

Circumstances in which you will not be entitled to a £22 payment are:
- that you requested the electricity supplier not to attend the premises;
- that you requested that the electricity supply should not be restored;
- where the prepayment meter is found to be working correctly;
- where one of the exceptions listed applies (see p26).

Where an appointment is made, the general standards on keeping appointments will apply.

Standards of performance – gas meters other than prepayment meters

If your gas meter is inaccurate, the Gas (Minimum Standards of Performance) Regulations 2005 oblige the supplier to investigate the situation. The regulations may apply where you consider that a meter may be inaccurate or the supplier suspects the meter is inaccurate.

On being notified of the situation, the gas supplier is normally required to offer to investigate the matter by visiting your home within seven working days.[11] If the supplier does not respond within the seven days, you are entitled to a £22 payment, unless there is an exception (see p26).

Where the gas supplier is unable to provide an explanation for the likely reason for the inaccuracy without visiting your home, the supplier is expected to either arrange a visit or to supply an explanation for the probable reason for the inaccuracy. If the supplier does not arrange a visit within seven days or fails to provide an explanation of a probable reason within five days, you are entitled to a payment of £22.

Standards of performance – gas prepayment meters

Where you are charged for your gas through a prepayment meter, regulation 5 of the Gas (Standards of Performance) Regulations 2005 applies if the meter is inaccurate. This imposes a strict duty on your supplier to investigate and repair or replace your faulty meters if you notify that the meter is not operating properly or circumstances exist that suggest it is not operating correctly.

Notification should be by phone, fax or email – not by the post. Where you contact the supplier outside normal working hours, the communication is deemed to have been made and effective the next day or in the next working period.

After being notified by you, the supplier should send a suitably qualified person to repair or replace the meter. If the supplier fails to send a qualified person to investigate or examine your meter within three hours on a working day or four hours on a non-working day, it is liable to pay you £22.

Circumstances in which you will not be entitled to a £22 payment are:
- that you requested the gas supplier not to attend the premises;
- that you requested that the gas supply should not be restored;
- where the prepayment meter is found to be working properly;
- where one of the exceptions listed applies (see p26).

The supplier is not obliged to respond if it considers the information sent by you to be frivolous or vexatious (eg, hoax calls) or where you have committed a criminal offence or failed to pay charges for services due after receiving a special notice.

Meter examiners

If you think that a meter is not functioning properly, complain first to the supplier (or gas transporter, as appropriate) who can check it.

The National Measurement Office reported that in 2011 1,288 domestic gas meters were submitted for independent inspection.[12] 11 per cent of these were found to be operating outside statutory limits.

It may try a simple test of the meter without moving it, such as putting a check meter to run alongside your meter for a week or two or undertake a meter test. If you are still not satisfied, refer the matter to a meter examiner. The supplier/transporter can also make the referral.

If a meter seems to be over-registering, you could pay the supplier for the amount of fuel you think you have definitely consumed, without waiting for the examiner's decision. This would help to avoid disconnection because only the outstanding amount would be in dispute and the dispute would be considered a genuine one (see p83).

If the meter is removed a substitute meter should be installed. There should be no charge for this.

Electricity

The electricity meter examiner's service is contracted out to the National Measurement Office, an Executive Agency of the Department for Business, Innovation and Skills. An examiner will test the meter and the supply at your premises. The supplier will be invited to send a representative. The meter may then be removed for further tests. An electricity meter examiner's services are free but the supplier is likely to charge. Take a note of the reading on the meter before it is taken away.

If a notice is served by you, the electricity supplier or anyone else interested in the matter, then no one can alter or remove the meter until the dispute is resolved or an electricity meter examiner has finished her/his examination.

The findings of an electricity meter examiner can be produced in court and are presumed to be correct unless proven otherwise.

Gas

Gas meter examiners are also contracted out to the National Measurement Office. They do not come to your premises but examine meters that are sent to them by the gas supplier. Make a note of the reading before it is taken away.

The supplier may charge you for the removal of the disputed meter, installing a replacement, transporting the disputed meter for testing and reinstalling the meter at your property. This charge will be refunded if the disputed meter is found to be operating inaccurately. The charges made for meter examining vary – check with your supplier.

On completion of the examination, a gas meter examiner issues a test certificate with details of her/his decision. The decision is final and binding as to whether the meter is working properly or not.

Results

If your meter is found not to be working properly, the supplier will have to make a refund or an extra charge to you. The amount of the refund or charge depends on how long and by how much the meter is thought to have been registering incorrectly.

For electricity, the meter examiner has a duty to give her/his opinion concerning for how long and by how much the meter has been operating outside the prescribed limits. For gas, the meter is deemed to have been registering incorrectly for the whole period since the last actual meter reading. You should argue that this should be resolved in your favour. This means that, if the gas meter was over-registering, you should receive the entire extra amount charged, but if the gas meter was under-registering, you should have to pay only that part which exceeds the 2 per cent limit of variation.

Older gas meters may run fast – ie, they may over-register the amount of gas consumed. This is because they use a leather diaphragm to measure the amount of gas used and this can dry out. Since 1 April 1981, gas suppliers have installed only meters with synthetic diaphragms, which are more reliable. If you have an older meter and you suspect it is recording inaccurately, you can refer it to a meter examiner. New meters may be distinguished from old ones as they have either a yellow label with a large 'S' on the meter casing or a reference number which begins or ends with an 'S'. Often the supplier will just simply replace the old meter since it is recognised that synthetic diaphragm meters may be prone to drift into over-reading after a substantial period of years. Note that if a meter is removed by the supplier because it has made an allegation that it has been tampered with (see Chapter 9), it is important that the meter is preserved so that it can be inspected after removal. Each supplier sets out in its relevant code of practice how long it will keep a meter in such circumstances before destroying it. Check that the code of practice is being followed.

Prepayment meters

It is important when moving into a new property with a prepayment meter that you ensure the supply is in your name from the date of moving in. Otherwise, you may find that what you pay for fuel is not credited to your account or (if the previous tenant accrued debt) that you are paying the fuel debt of the last occupant.

Contact the fuel supplier at your new property as soon as you move in. Do not use the previous occupants' payment card/key as you may find that you are inadvertently making payments to their account.

Ask your supplier to provide you with a new card or key in your name. Some suppliers can re-set a key or card remotely (see p86) but will still require you to provide them with a meter reading from the date that you moved in. In other cases, your supplier may need to visit your property to re-set the meter, depending on the age and type of device you have. Contact the supplier to establish the procedure for your meter.

To check whether a prepayment meter is registering correctly or to find out the rate of charge, see Appendix 3.

---

4. **Circuit and installation faults and faulty appliances**

Faulty circuits

To check whether a circuit or installation is faulty, turn off all appliances (including pilot lights) and see if the meter is still registering. If an electricity meter is still registering, there may be a short circuit or a leak to earth. If a gas meter is still registering, there may be a gas leak. Apart from the effect either of these situations can have on the level of the bill, they are both dangerous and should be dealt with immediately. Once everything is turned off and the meter has ceased to register, each appliance can be checked to make sure it is registering a reasonable level of consumption by using the formulae for checking the meter (see p87).

In rented accommodation, landlords are nearly always responsible for gas piping and electrical wiring. If you have told your landlord about defects in installations or in wiring/piping, you can ask her/him to fix the problem and to pay the difference between a high bill and the normal level of the bill, if the difference is down to the defects. Appliances themselves may be damaged by dampness or disrepair in the premises where they are being used and your landlord may be responsible for this (see Chapter 13).

Faulty appliances

If a fairly new appliance is faulty and uses more fuel than it should, you can claim some of the excessive bill from whoever supplied the appliance by using your rights under the Sale of Goods Act 1979 (as amended by the Sale of Goods Act 1994). Under this Act, there are a number of promises made by the supplier of the appliance incorporated into the contract between you and it, including that:
* the supplier has the legal right to sell you the goods; *and*
* if the supplier sells appliances as its business, the appliance is of satisfactory quality. The appliance is of **'satisfactory quality'** if a reasonable person would regard it as such, taking into account how it was described, its fitness for the purpose for which it is normally supplied, its appearance and finish, freedom from minor defects, and safety and durability.

Liability for breach of these Sale of Goods Act promises lies with the seller of the goods (ie, with whom you make the contract), not with the original manufacturer of the goods. The seller is liable for faults which are present at the time of sale, whether s/he knows about them at the time or not. However, manufacturers may also be liable on occasion where a manufacturer's guarantee is included with the sale contract or under the law of negligence where faults in the goods cause damage to either individuals or to property.

The Supply of Goods (Implied Terms) Act 1973 puts similar terms into a hire purchase agreement. If an installation (eg, central heating) is installed defectively, you can use your rights under the Supply of Goods and Services Act 1982. These provide that work must be undertaken with a reasonable degree of competence and skill. If it is not, the person providing the service is liable. There are also regulations covering the installation of gas fittings (such as meters and pipes) and gas appliances (such as for heating, cooking or lighting).[13] Any gas fitting installed must be soundly constructed and not made of lead or lead alloy.[14] No gas appliance can be installed unless it can be used without danger to anyone and this has been checked by the installer.[15]

If goods are bought on hire purchase or on credit for £100 or more, and the credit was supplied by a lender associated with the supplier (this includes credit cards), then the lender of the money is liable for faults as well as the supplier under the Consumer Credit Act 1974.[16] This means you can sue or threaten to sue the credit card company or other lender – this tactic can be used to put pressure on the supplier to settle any dispute or to get redress if the supplier has gone out of business.

If damage is caused by a faulty appliance, you may be able to claim compensation from the producer under the general law of negligence or under the Consumer Protection Act 1987. If the damage includes physical injury to someone, take legal advice.

Damage caused by voltage variations

A problem related to defective circuits and appliances (although not to high bills) is that of damage caused to electrical appliances by variations in the voltage of the electricity supply. Electricity should be supplied at 230 volts, although it is allowed to vary 10 per cent above or 6 per cent below that figure.[17] Voltage in excess of this may cause susceptible appliances, like televisions, computers and videos, to 'burn out'.

You may have a claim against the electricity supplier for such damage, but there are difficulties. In a claim for negligence, it will be difficult to establish that the supplier has actually been negligent, since it could be argued that the fault could not have been prevented. Alternatively, you could argue that the supplier is in breach of the statutory duty to supply electricity within the voltage limits – this faces the same problem as a claim of negligence and has never been tried before. It may be worth negotiating a settlement, as the supplier will want to avoid circumstances that would damage customer relations; it will also be uneconomic for a supplier to defend a civil claim in the county court for less than £5,000.

Under the electricity standards of performance regulations (see p228 and Appendix 2), if you complain about a possible variation in the voltage, the supplier must either give an explanation or offer to visit in order to investigate. Failure to do so, or failure to send an explanatory letter or to keep an appointment for a visit, means you are entitled to a payment of £22.[18]

5. Overcharging by prepayment meters

In 2008 Ofgem became concerned by the gap in prices being charged by energy companies for customers with prepayment meters and those paying by direct debit and quarterly billing. Ofgem maintained that the extra costs should not exceed £87 a year. However, according to the National Housing Federation, some prepayment customers paid £500 more for their energy than direct debit customers during 2008.

In April 2010 all the major suppliers removed premiums for prepayment meters to supply gas and electricity. Ofgem's 2010 report on energy prices confirmed that the difference between the amount paid by a customer using a prepayment meter and a customer paying for their fuel by direct debit was at the time of writing less than £87.

However, it is possible that any household with a prepayment meter has been charged too much at some point. You have, in theory, up to six years to seek a refund. Contact Citizens Advice consumer service for advice.

If you have been charged excessively by your supplier for paying by cheque or by cash, write and demand a repayment of the amount that you have been overcharged. Contact Citizens Advice consumer service in the first instance.

Adjustment of energy charges

The Energy Act 2010 builds on (to date unused) provisions in the Gas Act 1986 and Electricity Act 1989 enabling the Secretary of State to deal with situations where energy suppliers treat customers less favourably according to the type of energy supplied. Given that such power has not yet been used, it appears this may be intended to drive supplier behaviour, so the aim may not be to use the power but to force suppliers to comply before it is utilised.

Notes

2. Accuracy of the bill
1 Sch 6 para 1(9) EA 1989; Sch 2B para 7(5) GA 1986
2 *Maritime Electric Co Ltd v General Dairies Ltd* [1937] AC 610
3 Limitation Act 1980
4 s6 Prescription and Limitation (Scotland) Act 1973

3. Accuracy of the meter
5 Sch 7 EA 1989; s17 GA 1986
6 Sch 7 para 10(2) EA 1989; Sch 2B para 3(3) GA 1986
7 Sch 6 para 1 EA 1989
8 Sch 2B para 6 GA 1986
9 SI 2010 No.698
10 Reg 17 E(MSPR) Regs

11 Reg 4(2) G(MSP) Regs
12 The National Measurement Office, Gas Meters – *Disputed Meter Accuracy – Analysis of findings of Gas Meters disputed between 1 January and 31 December 2011*

4. Circuit and installation faults and faulty appliances
13 GS(IU) Regs
14 GS(IU) Regs
15 GS(IU) Regs
16 s75 Consumer Credit Act 1974
17 Reg 30 ES Regs
18 Reg 8 E(SP) Regs

7

Chapter 7

Arrears

This chapter covers:
1. What are arrears (below)
2. Legal protection when you are in arrears (p97)
3. Arrears in another person's name (p100)
4. Arrears as a result of estimated bills (p100)
5. Ways of paying your arrears (p101)
6. Choosing how to pay your arrears (p105)
7. Arranging to pay your arrears (p106)
8. Rate of repayment (p110)
9. Lump-sum repayments (p112)
10. Breakdown of repayment arrangement (p112)
11. Resisting a prepayment meter (p113)
12. Multiple debts (p114)

---

1. **What are arrears**

You are in **'arrears'** of electricity or gas if you are liable to pay a bill but have not paid it on demand. You risk disconnection of your:
- **electricity** supply if you do not pay within 28 working days of receiving your bill;
- **gas** supply if you do not pay within the 28 days following the date of your bill.

In practice, some suppliers may take action towards disconnecting your supply as early as 10 working days from the date of your bill. Provided you can pay for what you are using and something, however little, towards your arrears, you should not be disconnected.

The provisions discussed in this chapter only apply to arrears for charges due for the supply of electricity and gas, and not for any other purchases you have made from suppliers, for appliances or other services. You should check to ensure that you are liable for the arrears. If your bill is high, perhaps because of billing delays or incorrect reading of your meter, see Chapter 6. This chapter looks at the position where charges for the use of gas and electricity have been correctly incurred, but you have been unable to pay within 28 days.

2. **Legal protection when you are in arrears**

Electricity

The way that electricity suppliers deal with customers in arrears is regulated by conditions within the suppliers' licences. A supplier must have a licence to be allowed to operate. Electricity suppliers are regulated by Ofgem, which can enforce the licence conditions using its statutory powers (see Chapter 14).

Pensioners, the chronically sick and disabled

Under Standard Licence Condition (SLC) 26 provision is made for customers who are of pensionable age, chronically sick or disabled. If you fall into one of these categories, the following services may be available from suppliers:[1]

- a free password may be agreed with you so that you can safely identify any person representing the supplier who visits your home;
- your bill or statement of account for electricity supply may be sent to any other person whom you nominate to receive them;
- provide help with reading a meter each quarter if you need it;
- move a prepayment meter if you are infirm and cannot access it.

If you are blind, partially sighted, deaf or hearing-impaired (or someone acting on your behalf), the supplier must provide information on bills and charges that are accessible (eg, Braille) and provide facilities, free of charge, which enable you to ask or complain about any bill or statement of account relating to the electricity supply or any other service by the licensee.[2]

The Priority Services Register

Suppliers are obliged to establish and maintain a Priority Services Register listing domestic customers who are of pensionable age, disabled or chronically sick; and have requested to be added to the Priority Services Register.[3] Someone can ask on your behalf for you to added to it. Suppliers must inform all customers at least once a year of the existence of the Priority Services Register and of how they may be included on it. If you are on the register, you could get:

- free advice on using gas and electricity;
- password protection scheme – anyone calling at your home on behalf of the supplier will use the password to prove who they are;
- a prepayment meter moved to a more accessible location if it is safe to do so;
- free quarterly meter reading if you are unable to read your meter;
- bills sent to a friend, relative or carer so s/he can help to check it on your behalf;
- special help if a gas supply is disrupted if all adults living in your property are eligible for the Priority Services Register;
- advance notice if an electricity supply has to be interrupted;

- meter readings and bills provided in a suitable format: braille, large print, audio tape, textphone or typetalk.

In addition, you may be offered a free, annual gas safety check of appliances and other gas fittings if you are eligible for the Priority Service Register, own your home, receive an income-based benefit and:
- live alone; *or*
- live with other adults, all of whom are eligible; *or*
- live with others, at least one of whom is under five years old.

Standard Licence Condition 27

Condition 27 of the SLCs requires that electricity suppliers produce and publish codes of practice setting out their procedures for customers who have difficulty in paying. Electricity suppliers must provide copies of their codes of practice on request. It is essential to obtain an up-to-date copy of your supplier's code of practice, as they vary from one supplier to another.

The code of practice represents the stated policy of the supplier. It is not legally enforceable in individual cases, although a departure from the published code at policy level may be a breach of the relevant licence condition. Individual breaches should be reported to Ofgem or Consumer Focus, which should investigate to ensure that the supplier is not operating a policy which is in breach of the relevant licence condition (see Chapter 14).

The licence conditions state that suppliers must adopt methods for dealing with customers in arrears. In particular, they must provide protection for customers who 'can't pay' as a result of misfortune or inability to cope, as opposed to those who 'won't pay'. Further provisions offer protection from disconnection for vulnerable groups such as those over pensionable age, who should not be disconnected during the winter months. Suppliers will typically install prepayment meters instead of disconnecting supply, although this may result in consumers effectively disconnecting themselves if they lack the money to pay.

The supplier must offer a number of services when it becomes aware or has reason to believe that you are having *or will have difficulty* paying all or part of the charges for the supply of electricity.[4] The following circumstances could indicate that there is a need for such assistance:
- high consumption (over £500 per annum), especially if all electric;
- an increase in consumption beyond a certain threshold;
- a debt over a certain amount;
- payment by Fuel Direct or cash (prepayment or budget scheme);
- a history of struggling to pay or self-disconnection;
- a sudden increase in usage;
- you live in a target area as defined by the fuel poverty index or indices of social deprivation.

The wording of the licence condition requires suppliers to take a pro-active approach and act before arrears accumulate where they are anticipated. This includes:

- by using Fuel Direct, where available (see Chapter 11);
- accepting payments by regular instalments calculated in accordance with an agreed plan and paid other than by a prepayment meter;
- installing a prepayment meter;
- providing information energy efficiency.

It may be useful to quote these provisions when negotiating with a supplier.

Gas

The way that gas suppliers deal with customers in arrears is regulated by conditions within the suppliers' licences. A supplier must have a licence to operate, and Ofgem can enforce licence conditions. Condition 27 of the SLCs requires that suppliers publish, free of charge, details of their policies.

Condition 27 deals with how suppliers attend to customers in difficulties, and enables them to:

- distinguish (so far as is reasonably practical) customers who 'can't pay' from those who 'won't pay';
- provide customers who 'can't pay' with general information on energy efficiency;
- accept payments via Fuel Direct (see Chapter 11);
- accept the repayment of arrears in instalments, taking into account information available about a customer's ability to pay;
- offer a prepayment meter where safe and practical.

The SLCs do not oblige suppliers to recognise debtors who fall into other vulnerable categories, but do provide for opportunities for consumers to come to payment arrangements. Vulnerability may vary between customers and suppliers should consider the categories included on page 9 of the National Standards for Enforcement Agents (see Appendix 5).

Energy UK

Energy UK is the new trade association for the gas and electricity sector, established in April 2012 following a merger of the Association of Electricity Producers, the Energy Retail Association and the UK Business Council for Sustainable Energy. Its membership includes the main domestic energy suppliers in Great Britain – British Gas, EDF Energy, npower, E.ON, Scottish Power and Scottish and Southern Energy. Under the Energy UK **'safety net policy'**, no vulnerable customer should be disconnected from her/his electricity or gas supply at any time of the year. You are considered to be vulnerable if you are unable to safeguard your personal welfare or the personal welfare of other members of your household because of 'age, health, disability or severe financial insecurity'.[5]

The safety net policy compliments and supports the regulations contained within suppliers licences. Although not legally binding, the policy could be used as a negotiating tool to avoid disconnection if you believe that you should be treated as vulnerable. Examples of what constitutes 'vunerable' for the purpose of the code include:

- you care for an elderly person in your household;
- you have a disbaility or a chronic health condition;
- the household includes young children;
- a carer, social worker, health visitor or other professional has indicated that someone in the household is vulnerable.

The safety net encourages member agencies to work with charities and support agencies such as Citizens Advice Bureaux and other advice agencies to identify vulnerability.

If you are not identified as a vulnerable customer until after the disconnection has taken place, you should be reconnected as a priority. The safety net identifies 24 hours as being a reasonable timescale, or sooner if you have a smart meter.

See www.energy-retail.org.uk for more information.

3. Arrears in another person's name

You may not be liable for an electricity or gas bill which is in another person's name – eg, if your partner was previously responsible for the bill and has left home, if you are a joint tenant or sharer, or if the person responsible for the bill has died. In most cases, it will be possible to reach a settlement by way of a new contract between the supplier and the correct person.

You cannot be held liable for the bill of the previous occupier of your premises (see p65).[6] See Chapter 5 for who is liable for a bill. Under rules on joint and several liability, the supplier can try to reclaim the whole amount from one individual to an agreement. Any discount is at the supplier's discretion.

4. Arrears as a result of estimated bills

Previously, the former Energywatch indicated that where gas arrears built up over an extended period because of a succession of estimated bills, repayment of the arrears could be made over an equivalent, extended period if you would otherwise be caused hardship. This remains a sound principle and, for example, if a meter has not been read for two years, you should be allowed two years to repay the resulting bill.

The same position could be used as a reasonable basis for making repayment arrangements with electricity suppliers. If you cannot afford the rate of repayment of arrears on this basis, you should be allowed to repay the arrears at a rate you can genuinely afford (see p110). Check also your supplier's code of practice on the payment of bills and on prepayment meters. In other circumstances, you may be asked to accept a prepayment meter. This may simply be offering the choice of self-disconnection in some cases, unless the meter is a 'smart meter' (see p51). However, such cases may be referred to Consumer Focus or Ofgem for an opinion, as suppliers should try and offer you a range of options for repayment if you are experiencing genuine financial difficulty. See p97 when you are in arrears. Estimated bills are a common way to accrue arrears. The introduction of smart meters should, in theory, see the end of estimated billing as the meter will send information to your supplier about how much energy you have used.

Where arrears have accrued because of estimated billing, you should ensure that your supplier has adhered to the minimum standards for meter reading (see p84). The voluntary *Code of Practice on Accurate Bills* published by Energy UK may also be useful. It is advisable to take your own readings regularly – at least once every three months – to ensure that a supplier's estimate of your consumption is correct. Suppliers will amend estimated bills if you give them your own reading.

If arrears have arisen because of a supplier's failure to read your meter accurately, you may wish to dispute your liability for the full amount of the arrears. See Chapter 6 for information on high bills.

5. **Ways of paying your arrears**

As the supply of energy is governed by contracts, it is open to you and your supplier to negotiate and find a solution to your arrears. However, because of the large number of customers of each supplier, energy companies may find it difficult to reach individual solutions. In legal theory – and in practice – it is possible for suppliers to settle arrears by an individual payment scheme or even by writing them off, wholly or in part. This is even more likely in cases where suppliers have been at fault.

Unfortunately, it may be difficult to get a supplier to exercise any such option at first approach, since customer service staff may not be fully aware of the range of options legally available. Persistence, spread over a period of months if not years, may be necessary.

Before negotiating with your supplier, consider which way of repaying your arrears would best suit your needs. You will need to consider paying:

- through a short-term arrangement; *or*
- in instalments through a payment plan; *or*
- through a prepayment meter; *or*
- through the Fuel Direct scheme (see p104).

Consider applying for charitable assistance to repay or reduce arrears if you are experiencing serious hardship (see p114).

The ways these various options work are discussed below. Energy companies usually expect you to reach arrangements by way of telephone calls, but in all cases it is advisable to back up any conversations in writing and enter into correspondence wherever possible, keeping copies. It may be difficult to get an energy company to respond by letter, but any failure to respond will not create a good impression should the matter result in court action.

Wherever possible, deal with the supplier's legal department (if it has one), as call centre advisers will often know little about the relevant law or about ways a dispute may be lawfully settled. The legal department is very much the last resort, and tends to be used with people who threaten legal action or where a case has reached the end of resolution.

If a deadlock situation is reached, contact Citizens Advice consumer service for advice. If you are in a vulnerable situation the Extra Help Unit may help (see p223). The Energy Ombudsman may also be able to intervene where the complaint system has been exhausted (see Chapter 14).

Short-term arrangements

Where problems with hardship are likely to be temporary, suppliers often come to a short-term arrangement with you to enable you to pay your bill in instalments, based on your ability to pay, so long as the outstanding balance is paid before your next bill arrives. If you ask for this arrangement regularly, a payment plan or a prepayment meter may be a better option.

Payment plans

Payment plans usually operate with credit meters or, for electricity only, with variable tariff meters. Some suppliers allow you to have a payment plan in conjunction with a prepayment meter set to pay for current consumption only. Suppliers calculate an amount which you are required to pay on a weekly, fortnightly or monthly basis. This figure includes an estimated amount for current consumption and an amount for arrears.

Many suppliers add your arrears to your estimated annual consumption, and then divide by 12 for a monthly figure, or by 52 for a weekly figure. You may be told that this is the figure the computer says you have to repay. British Gas frequently uses £4 a week as a starting point for negotiations, but cannot insist on this amount. Its aim is to ensure that you will repay the arrears within a year. Often, the use of this formula means that you may be required to repay the arrears at a faster rate than you can afford. The overriding principle is that the method and rate of repayment should take account of your ability to pay.[7] If, for example, you can afford to repay £1.50 a week, the supplier should simply add this figure to your estimated weekly consumption.

It is also important to ensure that the amount estimated for current consumption accurately reflects your use of fuel and that the supplier does not attempt to recover the arrears more quickly than you can afford by overestimating your consumption. Take particular care to ensure that your meter is read each quarter so that you can accurately track your consumption and, if necessary, ask for a review of the rate of your payments.

In practice, most suppliers attempt to recover debts over an average of 46 weeks. This is an arbitrary figure chosen by the supplier and has no legal basis.

In light of this, it is vital that prior to contacting the supplier to implement a payment plan, you complete a full financial statement outlining your income and expenditure (see p115). This will show you exactly how much disposable income you have. Use this information to work out how much of your disposable income you can afford to use to repay your energy debt. Once you have this figure, do not agree to a payment plan for more than this. This is for two reasons: firstly, you may try and meet these payments to the detriment of feeding, heating or clothing you or your family. Secondly, if you fail to meet the payments it may make your debt situation more complex, and could prejudice any future arrangements with your supplier. Therefore resist any attempts, however persuasive, by your supplier to agree to a payment plan for more than you can realistically afford.

Prepayment meters

Prepayment meters can be reset to pay arrears over a period of time. For many prepayment meters, resetting means adjusting the meter to reclaim a fixed amount of arrears each week, irrespective of the amount of fuel used. A timing device in the meter registers the amount due towards the arrears each week. This amount is then deducted from the value of fuel paid for by inserting tokens, cards or keys, either when the meter is recharged or over the week. If you do not feed the meter every week, a build-up of these charges may result. Your supply will effectively be disconnected until you can afford to pay these charges through your meter. This is known as 'self-disconnection' (see p56).

The gas Quantum meter and similar 'smart card' electricity prepayment meters are more sophisticated in the way they are able to recover arrears. They recover an agreed fixed sum once each week and leave you with a certain minimum percentage of your credit – typically 30 per cent – for your current fuel supply. This means you always get some fuel for each credit you make.

The E.ON power card meter is set so that, where there is a build up of weekly fixed charges, you are guaranteed the use of only 10 per cent of any credit you make for your ongoing supply. The remaining 90 per cent is used towards this part of your debt. If your supplier offers this, or a similar meter, you can find out the level of this setting from the meter itself. The information booklet supplied with the meter should give details of how to obtain information from the meter.

These settings can be changed by the supplier. It may be worth pressing for a change in the settings if you are facing hardship. Smart meters are currently being rolled out across the UK and can be programmed to operate in prepayment mode. You can agree with your supplier to pay the way that best suits you. In theory, they offer greater flexibility than the old style meters. For example, you will be able to top-up credit remotely, without having to physically go out and purchase credit, reducing the risk of 'self-disconnection' because the shops are shut.

A prepayment meter can be a good option for those with energy debts. The advantage of seeking a prepayment meter is that you pay-as-you-go, and cannot therefore run into more debt. It also means that once the debt is paid off the situation cannot resurface in the future. However, the disadvantages of a prepayment meter include that if you are in serious financial distress the lights may literally go out, and prepayment customers generally do not benefit from certain discounts (such as a direct debit discount). Also, costs may be incurred if you do not yet have a smart meter and have to travel to purchase top-ups. Note too that outlets for top-ups may not be open 24 hours a day.

Fuel Direct

Fuel Direct is a system of direct deductions from income support, income-based jobseeker's allowance, pension credit or income-related employment and support allowance, before payment of the benefit to the claimant. From October 2013, it will also include universal credit. Payments are made up of a fixed sum towards arrears and an amount for current consumption of fuel. Fuel Direct is discussed fully in Chapter 11.

Consumers often complain that it can be difficult to get Jobcentre Plus offices to respond to requests for Fuel Direct. Do not be discouraged from considering this option – it is sometimes the only sensible way for payments to be made and for disconnection to be prevented. It is a useful and often cheaper alternative to prepayment meters.

The wording of SLC27.6 suggests that Fuel Direct should be used as an option, 'where available', when arrears have been incurred by vulnerable people. A supplier may be at fault if it overlooks this option, as many people who fall within a vulnerable category are likely to be on a qualifying benefit.

If you are eligible for Fuel Direct and are willing to have arrears deducted from your benefit, request that your supplier and the DWP implement this. Be prepared to make a complaint if the supplier will not implement Fuel Direct or if you face procedural obstacles or delays (see Chapter 14).

6. **Choosing how to pay your arrears**

Both gas and electricity suppliers are required to have a code of practice on payment of bills and guidance for dealing with customers in difficulty, under Standard Licence Condition 27. Additionally there is the Energy UK safety net policy which many suppliers have also agreed to adhere to see p99.

Electricity

Your supplier should offer some choice about payment method if you cannot pay your bills because of hardship. The electricity suppliers' policies towards customers in arrears should comply with the relevant licence conditions.[8] In practice, the choices may be limited, and some suppliers may not offer a range of choices, preferring to install prepayment meters. The amount of choice will depend on the policy of the supplier.

However, the broad options which should be offered are:

- a payment plan in instalments over an agreed period which takes into consideration your ability to pay;
- Fuel Direct (see Chapter 11);
- a prepayment meter as an alternative, and last resort, to disconnection.

The payment method available will also depend on your payment arrangements in the past. It is unlikely that you will obtain your choice of method if you have a succession of broken arrangements. The supplier may reasonably take the view that a prepayment meter offers the best chance of secure and regular payment without increasing arrears.

If you are not satisfied with the options made available to you, consider using your supplier's complaints procedure. Note also that Consumer Focus can intervene in disputes about the choice of a meter or method of payment, particularly if you are a vulnerable customer.

Gas

Under the licensing framework, gas suppliers are subject to similar conditions to electricity suppliers. Prepayment metering is no longer offered automatically as a last resort, and there is a commitment to the counselling of customers to find a payment method which is suitable.

In practice, you should be able to negotiate a payment plan of your choice initially, unless you have broken a previous agreement. If you do not keep to the first payment agreement made, your supplier is likely to insist you have a prepayment meter rather than renegotiate a further arrangement. However, if there are legitimate reasons why a previous arrangement was broken, such as a change of circumstances, this should not disqualify you, especially if it is the only or most suitable method for you.

7. **Arranging to pay your arrears**

Once you have established how much you owe, you need to arrange to pay the arrears. If you do not contact your supplier to make an arrangement to pay, action will be taken towards disconnecting your supply.

It is advisable to make agreements in writing, since they will take effect as variations of the consumer supply contract. Your negotiations with your supplier will be more effective if you have considered how you would like to pay your arrears. You will need to think carefully about which best suits your needs. Consider the costs of the various options to you and the practicalities of using a particular scheme. Also consider how convenient it will be for you to make your payments – it is important to make an arrangement which you can keep. Chapter 4 looks at the advantages and disadvantages of the various methods of payment, including Fuel Direct.

When you contact the supplier's debt collection department, you should be counselled so that the staff can establish the most suitable method of payment for you.[9] Be prepared to provide information about your financial situation, including a financial statement listing other liabilities such as rent, council tax, water bills, etc. Inform the supplier if anyone in your home is elderly, disabled or under five years old, or if you claim income support, or if there are any other factors which cause you financial hardship, such as multiple debts.

Arranging a payment plan

If you have not previously had any difficulty with your bill or you have previously been able to manage a payment plan, you should not be refused this as your preferred option. If paying regularly at a post office or PayPoint will be convenient for you, say so.

Make sure that the rate at which you agree to pay your arrears is realistic. If you are in a multiple debt situation, see p114. This is important, as it is unlikely that you will be offered a revised payment plan if the first arrangement breaks down. You may be forced to accept a prepayment meter instead.

Waiver, full and final settlement of arrears and estoppel

As the supply of gas and electricity is covered by contracts, general principles of the law of contract may be applied to assist you. The legal principles are complex, but there is no reason why they should not be applied to arrears. Simply giving you time to pay off arrears does not deprive the supplier of the right to take recovery action for the debt, but other principles of contract law protecting you may come into play.

In some cases, an energy company may be prepared to waive its rights to recover arrears, or remit a debt, either wholly or in part. A number of doctrines of contract law, including waiver, full and final settlement and estoppel may be of assistance to a consumer with arrears in seeking a solution. These principles have yet to be tested in relation to gas and electricity supply contracts, but for information on the general principles see textbooks on the law of contract.

A full discussion of these principles is not possible here, but the following may be of assistance to advisers as to points of law to consider and explore. Legal advice should be sought before seeking a part payment or full and final settlement based on common law principles of contract; the law relates here to England and Wales and separate advice should be sought if considering settlement in Scotland.

In many cases, a supplier may prefer to reach a final settlement on arrears on commercial grounds, rather than face the cost of recovery action through the courts for a debt. Under the small claims procedure of the county court, a supplier will not be able to recover legal costs if the sum claimed is under £5,000. This often makes procedure through the county court an uneconomic recovery option; furthermore energy companies do not want to have a reputation for being hard on consumers. The general attitude of suppliers is that they will go to court (including the magistrates' court – see Chapter 9) to impose a prepayment meter.

Some suppliers may be prepared to accept a one-off lump sum payment of arrears as settlement to a dispute. In contract law, parties may seek to be discharged of their obligations under an agreement by varying the terms and one party accepting a lesser payment. Many civil disputes are settled privately between parties without recourse to court action by entering into an agreement to conclude matters in a full and final settlement, rather than continue to court. This may be an option where you are in a position to switch supplier (although the successor company may be entitled to recover certain arrears if the debt is assigned, if a full and final settlement is not reached).

However, the legal rules can be quite complicated. Simply sending a small amount to an energy supplier is not sufficient to discharge arrears or a sum owed in interest.[10] The supplier is still lawfully entitled to recover the money, unless some benefit is derived from the part-payment.

For part-payment to represent a settlement, the company must formally agree to waive its right to recovery action in return for accepting a lump sum or by agreeing to drop some obligation on itself, such as the requirement to read a meter. Alternatively, you might agree to accept a prepayment meter, varying the terms of an existing contract, in return for the supplier accepting a lesser sum in full and final settlement of the arrears. Where a company is threatening legal action, it may be possible to pay part of the money owed in return for the company waiving its right to take legal action (thus saving itself the cost of litigation). You must make a clear offer to the supplier that you are willing to pay a smaller sum immediately to clear arrears and it is necessary for the supplier to agree and to waive the right of court action. Alternatively, the energy company may agree to waive its right to recover a sum in arrears if you have switched supplier. In some cases, you might agree to waive the right to pursue a claim against the supplier or a complaint against the supplier to Ofgem for a breach of the licence conditions. In such a case, the supplier will have derived a benefit (not being subject to a complaint or legal claim) and may agree to accept a lesser sum.

For the avoidance of doubt, your offer to settle a sum in arrears should be in writing and clearly refer to acceptance, being a full and final settlement of arrears and a waiver of further recovery action.

Any communications should be marked 'full and final settlement', including endorsing this on any final payment cheque. Ideally, the supplier should notify you, but this does not always happen. In some cases, an offer of full and final settlement will be accepted, or initially appear to be accepted. However, inadequate record keeping or changes in staff may mean that the decision on full and final settlement is not recorded, and the supplier may seek to renege on the agreement.

Example

Mrs Green is a widowed pensioner who had been a customer of one supplier for many years. Before her husband died, he switched to a new supplier. The new company failed to read the meter and sent a large estimated bill of over £750, which was carried over each quarter.

Efforts to negotiate proved fruitless, and letters went ignored. Mrs Green contacted her previous supplier who had kept records of her good payment history. Mrs Green paid sums she could afford, and repeatedly wrote to her new supplier offering to pay by instalments. No written response was forthcoming. The new supplier then threatened legal action to recover the arrears. On taking advice, she was recommended to make a payment of 10 per cent of the bill in full and final settlement. She sent a cheque for 10 per cent of the outstanding amount and the letter was clearly marked 'cash this cheque only if you accept this sum in full and final settlement of the dispute'. She also endorsed the cheque 'full and final settlement cheque'.

The new supplier cashed the cheque after Mrs Green switched supplier, returning to her old energy company with whom she had a good payment record.

Four months after she returned to her old supplier, the new energy company presented her with a fresh demand. The letter in full and final settlement was cited in negotiations. It was argued that by cashing the cheque in response to the settlement letter the supplier had accepted the offer of settlement by Mrs Green. Eventually the supplier agreed to waive recovery and wrote off the arrears when it emerged that it had not read Mrs Green's meter for over a year.

Disputes over whether a supplier has agreed to full and final settlement may come down to a dispute of fact where the energy company has accepted payment. Legal advice should be taken wherever possible.

In some cases, a supplier may agree to forego the right to recover arrears for a period and not enforce a debt in return for a lesser sum in payment. During that period, the supplier cannot go back on the agreement and take action. What is known as the doctrine of 'estoppel' operates. This provides that where a person acts in reliance of a promise made on another, that other person cannot then break the promise and take enforcement action. For example, where a supplier agrees to grant a three-month suspension on paying arrears and you act accordingly, the supplier cannot demand the money in the three months. The supplier is said to be 'estopped' from taking action in the period.[11]

Fuel Direct

Fuel Direct must also be available under the terms of the new suppliers' licence. See Chapter 11 for more about Fuel Direct.

Prepayment meters

Prepayment meters are generally available to customers in debt as an alternative to disconnection. You are not normally charged the cost of repositioning a meter to enable a prepayment meter to be fitted in these circumstances. Note that a supplier is not entitled to charge for the repositioning of a meter to meet the needs of a disabled person.

If you have previously not been able to manage a payment plan, you may be offered a prepayment meter as your only option. If this is not convenient for you, try to renegotiate another payment plan – Standard Licence Condition 27 sets out a number of alternatives including Fuel Direct.

If you feel you are not being treated appropriately, consider making use of the complaints procedures and contact Citizens Advice consumer service.

When will a prepayment meter be refused?

If you are not in arrears, you may request a prepayment meter for **electricity** at any time. You may have to go onto a waiting list until one becomes available.

There are additional safety considerations which may prevent the installation of a **gas** prepayment meter. A prepayment meter will not be installed if:

- there are any secondary (subsidiary) meters supplied with gas through that meter; *or*
- the position of the meter physically prevents installation – eg, a prepayment meter cannot physically be fitted into a semi-concealed meter box. However, the possibility of relocating the meter will be considered in this situation; *or*
- the location of the meter prevents safe operation of the mechanism, taking account of your circumstances – eg, if you are disabled and cannot cope with a meter located above a door, relocation of the meter or the control panel would be considered; *or*
- there has been no contact with you; *or*
- you have refused a prepayment meter.

It is rare, however, for a request for a prepayment meter to be refused. If it is, contact Citizens Advice consumer service. If you cannot have a prepayment meter installed, negotiate a payment plan or Fuel Direct instead.

8. **Rate of repayment**

Both gas and electricity suppliers are required to make arrangements for the recovery of debts which take into account your ability to pay. This applies whether you are offered a payment plan or a prepayment meter.

The rate of Fuel Direct deductions is often used as a yardstick to determine the period over which a debt should be repaid within a payment plan or through a prepayment meter.

If you get income support (IS), income-based jobseeker's allowance, pension credit or income-related employment and support allowance, you may wish to consider the Fuel Direct scheme, but note that this would result in fixed deductions for your arrears. This may not be appropriate if your arrears should be recovered at a lower rate.

Repayments below Fuel Direct rates

If your income is low, or roughly equivalent to basic IS levels (eg, you receive housing benefit or council tax benefit), argue that you should not repay your debt at a higher rate than the Fuel Direct rates.

There are many situations where a supplier should accept less than this level of repayment, particularly if your income is less than basic IS levels (eg, you may not be entitled to benefit because you work, but you have to pay childcare or mortgage expenses which are not taken into consideration, or your benefit is reduced because of a trade dispute, or you are an asylum seeker, or you receive less IS than other claimants or no benefit at all) or if you have multiple debts.

Suppliers are primarily concerned with ensuring that customers pay for their current consumption as the first priority, and should accept payments of arrears over extended periods of time at rates which customers can afford to sustain, even if this is very low. If you have multiple debts, your suppliers should be persuaded to treat fuel debts in the same way as other priority debts. If you cannot afford the rate of repayment sought, ask to pay at a lower rate, providing information about your income, necessary outgoings and other debts. If the supplier refuses to accept lower payments, contact Citizens Advice consumer service for advice.

If a supplier formally refuses a particular repayment rate but then goes on subsequently to accept regular repayments from you at that rate, it is arguable that an agreement by conduct has been reached. Similarly, if a supplier has promised not to take enforcement action or pursue a certain sum and you then act in reliance on that promise, it is arguable that the supplier cannot then renege on the promise. For example, if a supplier tells you that it is prepared to reduce part of a debt and you then repay the remainder, it should not be open to the supplier to take action regarding the unpaid balance at a later date. The rule on estoppels (see p109) applies.

Arrears more than six years old

Where arrears for fuel accrued more than six years ago, recovery is statute barred under the Limitation Act 1980, which imposes a six-year time limit on the recovery of contractual debts in law. The six years run from the date that the bill first fell due. Suppliers cannot instigate legal action after this date, although this does not stop them from serving a demand for a bill which is more than six years old. However, you are not under a legal obligation to pay if faced with a demand which relates to a debt more than six years old. Where legal action has been commenced within the six-year period – eg, the supplier has taken court action against you and obtained a judgment then they can enforce the judgment even after six years but may need to seek the permission of the court to do so. If the debt accrued under back-billing rules legal advice should be sought.

Paying for your current consumption

Whatever your rate of debt repayment within a payment plan, you will also have to pay for your estimated current consumption over the year. It is important that this estimate is as accurate as possible, otherwise you may end up paying more than you can afford. The requirement at Standard Licence Condition 31A for suppliers to provide detailed information about your last year's consumption will be useful here.

You can check the estimate provided by the supplier, either by using your own bills or by asking for details of the actual readings of your meter over a past period. Suppliers often have records for up to eight quarters. Try to make sure that the readings cover at least a year so that you make allowances for seasonal variations in your consumption, and any changes in your lifestyle or appliance usage. You will need to calculate the number of units of fuel you have used over the period covered by meter readings, and then divide this figure by the number of weeks in that period to calculate the number of units you use on average each week. Multiply that figure by the cost of the units of fuel. Then add on the amount of the standing charge for each week.

If you have not been in your property for long, the supplier's energy efficiency advisers should be able to advise you on the likely size of your bills if you provide them with details of the size of your home, family and the appliances you use.

Once you have joined a payment plan, ensure that your meter is read every quarter, either by you or the supplier, so that you can check the accuracy of your estimated current consumption.

9. **Lump-sum repayments**

You should not be asked to pay lump sums of money as part-payment towards arrears as a condition of being allowed a prepayment meter; nor should you be asked to pay lump sums before being allowed to pay arrears in instalments if you are unable to pay your bill because of hardship. The supplier's licence specifically provides that it must allow you to pay your arrears in instalments, taking into account your ability to pay.

However, a supplier might demand a part-payment towards a debt before agreeing to install a prepayment meter. In many situations, this will be contrary to the licence provisions. Refer a dispute arising from such a request to Citizens Advice consumer service.

10. **Breakdown of repayment arrangement**

Electricity

If a change of circumstances has occurred which has affected your ability to pay, ask the supplier to consider a revised payment arrangement. Electricity suppliers are obliged to consider this under the licence conditions. Electricity suppliers may include a statement about changes of circumstances in their codes of practice, if they have one (suppliers are not under an obligation to issue one). Note that the provisions within conditions can be enforced by Ofgem in individual cases, in contrast to the provisions within the code of practice. Any special circumstances ought to be brought to the attention of the supplier.

If your circumstances have not changed, it may have been that the level of repayment was too high in the first place. If this is so, ask for a revised payment arrangement based on a more detailed picture of your financial circumstances. Otherwise, you may be obliged to accept a prepayment meter as an alternative to disconnection.

In the event of a dispute and a threat of disconnection, contact Citizens Advice consumer service for advice.

Gas

If you cannot manage the payment level you have agreed, always try to pay something (at whatever level you can afford) when your payments are due while renegotiating a new payment arrangement. You will then be able to show willingness and to argue that it is not a payment plan that you cannot manage, but rather the level of the repayments. The supplier's policy is to avoid the build-up of debt. You are more likely to have a prepayment meter installed if the level of your debt increases.

The gas suppliers' codes of practice on paying bills state that your case can be considered again if your circumstances change. It is important to provide as much information as possible.

11. **Resisting a prepayment meter**

Some suppliers will often attempt to impose a prepayment meter on new or existing customers if:

- a security deposit is required from you, because you are a new customer with no previous payment record, or because as an existing customer you have consistently paid your bills late and you are unwilling or unable to pay the deposit;
- you claim income support or otherwise have a low income;
- you have arrears, by refusing to consider you for a payment plan or refusing access to the Fuel Direct scheme or otherwise presenting the prepayment meter as your only option;
- you have previously had an arrangement to pay arrears in instalments, but this has broken down.

In individual cases, Ofgem has a duty to make decisions about the reasonableness of the request for security, including the request for a cash security deposit or the imposition of a prepayment meter as an alternative. Standard Licence Condition 28 in both gas and electricity suppliers' licences obliges suppliers to prepare a code of practice on the arrangements they have in place for prepayment meter customers. The code should include information about where keys/cards can be topped-up and what customers should do if meters malfunction.

In individual cases, it is important to begin by reminding the supplier of its obligations and to negotiate an affordable payment plan in the first instance. Ensuring that a payment plan is affordable will reduce the chance of it failing and avoid more difficult negotiations to reinstate a revised payment plan.

Where a supplier cites the need for a security deposit, you may need to show that you will be able to manage a payment plan, perhaps by referring to other bills you have successfully managed to pay in instalments – eg, catalogue debts or consumer purchases. If negotiations fail, contact Citizens Advice consumer service.

If a supplier attempts to impose a prepayment meter on someone who will not be able to operate it, it will be in breach of its duty to supply. Action could be taken against the supplier either by complaining to Consumer Focus or by considering court action (see Chapter 14). Disconnection should not take place simply because a supplier wishes to impose a prepayment meter and in the event that a supplier seeks a warrant to enter premises, the matter should be taken to the magistrates' court for consideration as to reasonableness (see Chapter 10).

Charitable assistance to reduce your debt

British Gas, Scottish Gas, EDF Energy and npower currently offer charitable assistance to customers experiencing financial difficulty in the form of their energy trusts (see p192). Check whether your fuel supplier runs a similar scheme. Currently, you must be receiving a supply from the relevant company to be considered as eligible for their scheme. The aim of these schemes is to free individuals from fuel debts and enable them to make a fresh start. You can only ask the relevant trust to help you to clear arrears – you are usually expected to set up a regular payment arrangement to manage your future supply and prevent arrears accruing on your account again. The qualifying criteria for these trusts is relatively broad. You must be able to show that you are experiencing financial hardship, and that a payment from the trust will assist you to pay your future fuel bills. You need to complete an application form, available from the supplier's website. Not all applications are successful and it can take a number of weeks for the trustees to decide your case. Make sure that you give as much information as possible about your circumstances including why you have had difficulty paying your energy bills. You will also be required to complete a detailed financial statement listing your other commitments and any other debts you may have. Some trusts offer further help in the form of 'further assistance payments' to meet the cost of either applying for bankruptcy or a debt relief order. These can be useful if you have multiple debts and want to pursue either of these options but cannot meet the cost of doing so yourself. Check whether your supplier offers this type of help.

12. **Multiple debts**

For many people, gas and electricity arrears are just part of a bigger problem of unpaid bills. It is beyond the scope of this book to give detailed advice about debts other than those for fuel. See CPAG's *Debt Advice Handbook*. This section tells you where you may be able to get advice and outlines what you need to do if you cannot get the advice you need.

If you are seeking advice about your fuel debts, tell the adviser about all your other debts as well, or you may not get the best advice.

Visits from bailiffs

In England and Wales, this may include visits by bailiffs (in Scotland, sheriff's officers) to take away your possessions. Bailiffs cannot force entry to private dwellings in England and Wales for civil debts, and in Scotland forced entry is only possible as a last resort. Often the best advice is to keep your door closed and to negotiate with the bailiffs in writing rather than allow them in. Even if bailiffs gain entry and seize goods, the sums of money raised at auction rarely cover the bailiff and auctioneer fees and the debt remains.

Any arrangement to pay is best made with a creditor rather than a bailiff as the bailiff is likely to add fees. Under page 9 of the National Standards for Enforcement Agents (see Appendix 5), bailiffs are required to notify the creditor and report the circumstances in situations where there is evidence of vulnerability. This includes cases with local authority bailiffs collecting sums of council tax. You should contact the local authority directly to make an arrangement. If the local authority refuses to accept the money, make a formal complaint.

In Scotland, Sheriffs cannot demand entry to your home unless a Court order known as an 'exceptional attachment order' has been obtained. Forced entry cannot take place unless there is a person present who is at least 16 and is not, because of her/his age, knowledge of English, mental illness, mental or physical disability or otherwise, unable to understand the consequence of the procedure being carried out.

Energy suppliers do not have powers to force entry simply to recover money – any power of entry can only be exercised under a warrant through a magistrates' court to disconnect a supply, not to seize possessions (see Chapter 10).

Where to go for advice

Your local Citizens Advice Bureau will tell you what is available locally and can advise on multiple debt. There is also a national telephone helpline, National Debtline (0808 808 4000). Advisers will counsel you on the phone, but cannot attend court with you. However, some voluntary organisations and groups provide help with what are known as 'McKenzie friends', whereby you can be given assistance in court (see Chapter 14). Citizens Advice produces two self-help guides for dealing with multiple debts. One is for people who pay rent, the other for people with mortgages. Both include a very useful sheet to help you work out your own financial statement.

You can also consult solicitors or advice agencies who provide debt advice under the Community Legal Service Legal Help scheme. However, the scope for this assistance is being cut back. Certain charities also operate assistance schemes. Make sure that any advice you get is free and genuinely independent of your creditors.

See also CPAG's *Debt Advice Handbook*.

Helping yourself

Whether you choose to seek advice or to help yourself, you should gather together the following information and take the following steps.

Stage 1: Work out your income and essential expenditure

Firstly, add up all the money you have coming in from wages, benefits, maintenance and any other income every week or month, depending on how you get paid. Check that you are receiving all the benefits to which you are entitled, and that you are not paying too much tax. A local advice agency, Citizens Advice Bureau or welfare rights service can help you do this.

Secondly, work out what you spend each month on essentials. Ignore any payments for arrears at this stage. Include your normal payments for the following items:

– rent or mortgage and any other loans secured on your home;
– gas (your average weekly or monthly bill over the last year);
– electricity (your average weekly or monthly bill over the last year);
– transport to work;
– council tax;
– water charges (in England);
– childcare;
– food;
– clothing;
– other household expenses – eg, cigarettes, cleaning materials, etc.

Be realistic, and remember that payments for housing are a priority (eg, rent or mortgage). Work out what you need to live on over a long period and not over a week. Do not include current payments on loans, credit agreements or catalogues.

When you have done this, deduct the total of your expenses from your total income. The difference is what you have available to deal with your debts. If this is nothing, or your expenses are more than your income, seek advice (see p115).

Stage 2: Work out your debts

Make a list of everything you owe to everyone. Include:

– arrears of rent/mortgage;
– arrears of gas/electricity/water/telephone bills;
– the total amount owing (not just the arrears) on loans, credit cards, catalogues, credit agreements, etc.

Some debts must take priority because there are serious consequences if you cannot pay them. For most people these are:

– rent, mortgage or secured loans;
– council tax.

If you are in arrears with any of these, contact the people and/or organisations you owe and try to arrange repayments. If you explain your position fully, they will usually allow you a period to pay off your arrears. This may be a long period of time – particularly if you are on income support or your income is very low. You may be able to pay off mortgage arrears over the remaining term of the mortgage.[12] If you cannot reach agreements, or if you think you have agreed to something you cannot afford, seek advice (see p115).

Deduct the total of what you have to pay on these priority debts from the amount you had available to pay all the debts. If there is nothing left, seek advice (see p115).

Now divide what is left fairly between all the other people you owe money to.

Stage 3: Work out how much to pay your creditors

To work out how to share this money between your creditors, there is a basic rule: the more money you owe to one creditor, the bigger share that creditor gets.

Add up all your debts (except the priority ones you dealt with at Stage 2).

Next, work out what percentage of your total debt is made up by each individual debt. For example, if your total debt is £2,400 and you owe British Gas £120, the percentage of the total debt owed to British Gas is:

$$\frac{£120}{£2,400} \times 100 = 5\%$$

Take that percentage of the weekly or monthly amount you have available to pay your debts.

In the example above, if you have £15 a month available for debts, you should pay British Gas 5 per cent of that or: £15 x 5% = £0.75 a month.

Once you have worked out all these details, contact all of your creditors. They will all need to see your financial statement to understand why you will only be making a small payment to each of them. Electricity or gas suppliers ought to agree to accept whatever you can afford to pay using this calculation. They may try to argue that they should be priority creditors, but they must accept what you can reasonably afford to pay. Your electricity supplier may have adopted a policy of accepting low rates of repayment on a *pro rata* basis with other creditors when revising its code of practice. Check your supplier's code of practice.

See also Chapter 12, which examines issues of fuel economy and efficiency.

Administration orders

If you have multiple debts, you can apply to a county court in England and Wales for an administration order as a way of getting the county court to take over the administration of your debts.[13] This is a little used, but extremely useful, provision whereby the court will decide how much you can afford to pay to each of your creditors. You make one monthly payment to the court, which will then pay your creditors on your behalf.

To be able to obtain an administration order under the current rules:

- you must have a county court or High Court judgment against you;
- the total of your debts must be less than £5,000.

Administration orders are suitable for people with multiple debts who live in rented accommodation or pensioners on low incomes who own their own properties with no outstanding mortgage. Administration orders are not available in Scotland.

Importantly, the court can reduce the amount of overall debt paid by order so that only a percentage of the total debts are to be paid – eg, ordering that the debtor pays into the administration order 25p for each £1 owed. Thus, a person with total debts of £4,000 would only be required to ultimately pay back £1,000 under the administration order.

In terms of fuel debt, the making of an administration order by a court must be the definitive statement your ability to pay. Suppliers who seek to recover arrears outside the terms of the administration order could find themselves in contempt of court.

Suppliers, however, are not used to people putting their debts into administration orders. Always contact your supplier in advance to explain your proposed course of action. You will also need to make arrangements to pay for your current supply. The supplier will almost certainly insist that you pay using a method which offers the supplier greater security, such as a prepayment meter, Fuel Direct or through a payment plan using direct debit. The supplier will not be permitted to recover arrears through any of these methods of payment without the leave of the court, since the court will take over the payment of arrears.

To apply for an administration order, obtain form N92 from your local county court. When you have completed the form, take it back to the court, where you have to swear that the contents of the form are correct. The court will then contact all the creditors on the list and either make the order by agreement or arrange a private hearing with a district judge to consider your application. In practice, few creditors will bother to attend a hearing for an administration order, and in many cases they may write off the debt completely at this stage.

The court has powers to cancel or vary the administration order once it is granted, if you fail to pay. However, if you do encounter payment problems, contact the court immediately to seek a variation of the order.

Advantages of an administration order

- The order usually runs for a period of three years, though this is not automatic but subject to application (check with the court). Provided you have paid your monthly payments, the rest of the debt is written off at the end of this period.
- Interest is frozen on accounts.
- Your creditors cannot chase you or take other court action against you while the order runs.
- You have to make only one payment each month.
- The court can reduce the amount of each debt owed by requiring only a percentage of the debt to be paid.
- It is possible for a charity or a third party to pay off the amount owing under the administration order in a lump sum

Disadvantages of an administration order

Your name will appear on a register of court orders and you will find it hard to obtain credit. Although it is not illegal to take on more credit while you have an administration order, the court will expect you to sort out your existing situation before you start taking on new debts.

Debt relief orders

Debt relief orders (DROs), granted by the Insolvency Service, were introduced by the Tribunals Courts and Enforcement Act 2007. To qualify, you must satisfy the following qualifying criteria.

- You must be unable to pay your debts.
- Your total debts must be no more than £15,000.
- Your total assets must not be more than £300, although you are permitted to own a car or motorbike worth up to £1,000.
- Your disposable income after deducting allowable expenses, must not be more than £50 a month.
- You must be living in England or Wales, or at any time during the last three years have been resident or carrying on business in England or Wales.
- You must not have been subject to a DRO within the last six years.
- You must not be involved in any other formal insolvency procedure at the time of application for a DRO.

Under a DRO recovery action by creditors to obtain money from you is stopped and at the end of a one-year moratorium period the debts are cleared. So, for example, a supplier could not take any further action against you such as disconnection in respect of fuel arrears included in a DRO.

Certain debts are excluded from a DRO. See CPAG's *Debt Advice Handbook* for further details. Although you can include fuel arrears in the order, you will be expected to meet the costs of future fuel consumption and should include these in your expenditure figures.

To apply for a DEO costs £90 but this can be spread over six monthly instalments.

DEOs are administered by the Official Receiver through the Insolvency Service. You can only apply online through an approved third party or intermediary. These are usually debt advisers who have authority to complete the application forms.

For more information see www.bis.gov.uk/insolvency.

Notes

2. Legal protection when you are in arrears
1 Condition 26.1 SLC
2 Condition 26.2 SLC
3 Condition 26.4 SLC
4 Condition 27.5 SLC
5 Energy Retail Association, *ERA Safety Net: Protecting Vulnerable Customers from Disconnection* at www.energy-uk.org.uk/publication/finish/30/308.html

3. Arrears in another person's name
6 Sch 6 para 2 EA 1989

5. Ways of paying your arrears
7 Condition 27 SLC and codes of practice from suppliers
8 Conditions 26 and 27SLC

7. Arranging to pay your arrears
9 Condition 27 SLC
10 *Foakes v Beer* [1881-85] All ER 106; *Pinnel's Case* (1602) 5 Co Rep 117
11 *Central London Property Trust v High Trees House Ltd* [1947] 1 KB 130

12. Multiple debts
12 *Cheltenham and Gloucester Building Society v Norgan* [1996] 1 All ER 449
13 s112 County Courts Act 1984

Chapter 8

Disconnection for arrears

This chapter covers:
1. When you can be disconnected for arrears (below)
2. Protection from disconnection (p126)
3. Preventing disconnection (p128)
4. At the point of disconnection (p129)
5. Getting your supply reconnected (p131)
6. Disputes: unlawful disconnection (p133)

1. When you can be disconnected for arrears

The most important power which suppliers have for non-payment of energy bills is to cut off your supply of gas or electricity if you do not pay your bill. The power to disconnect is considered more effective than the right to recover money through the court system.

Unfortunately, large companies such as energy suppliers have difficulty distinguishing between deliberate non-payment and those who would pay but are suffering financial hardship or other problems. However, disconnection should only be a last resort in extreme circumstances and should not be used as a standard method of debt recovery.

After the highly publicised deaths of two low-income pensioners from hypothermia in the winter of 2003, the energy industry came under scrutiny from Parliament, Ofgem and the media with respect to disconnection policies applied to consumers who have arrears. In practice, few customers are disconnected as a result of a failure to pay bills.

Ofgem collects and monitors information from suppliers about the number of customers they have disconnected. Between July and September 2011 419 electricity disconnections and 128 gas disconnections had taken place in the UK.[1] This represents a very small percentage of the number of customers in fuel debt during the same period – 875,401 electricity customers and 810, 049 gas customers, and an even smaller percentage of all customers nationally. The current trend appears to be for a reduction in the number of disconnections –

Ofgem reported that disconnections decreased by 39 per cent for electricity and 58 per cent for gas from July to September 2010 for the same period in 2011.

Informing the supplier of vulnerability

To protect vulnerable customers, in April 2010 the Standard Electricity Distribution Licence Conditions were consolidated with regard to maintaining a register of vulnerable customers and, from 1 October 2010, a new Standard Licence Condition 27 applies to the disconnection of customers, with provision for the most vulnerable during winter (see p126).

It is important as a preliminary step in all cases to discover the cause of the arrears, and identify whether you fall into a vulnerable group.

If someone in your household is vulnerable as a result of age, illness, disability or poverty, inform your supplier as soon as possible, preferably before arrears arise.

Your supplier is required, at least once a year, to take 'all reasonable steps' to inform all domestic customers about the Priority Services Register (see p97) and how you can be listed on it if you are of pensionable age, disabled, have a hearing or visual impairment or have long term ill-health.[2] If you have different suppliers for gas and electricity, you need to register with both.

Although there is no fixed definition of a 'vulnerable' consumer in energy legislation, the Energy Retail Association (now Energy UK – see Appendix 1) set out a common definition of vulnerability for all energy suppliers:

> 'A customer is vulnerable if, for reason of age, health, disability or severe financial insecurity, they are unable to safeguard their personal welfare or the personal welfare of the household.'[3]

If you fit within this definition you are likely to be in receipt of one of the following benefits:
- retirement pension;
- pension credit;
- disability living allowance (personal independence payment from June 2013);
- attendance allowance;
- long-term incapacity benefit;
- employment and support allowance;
- income support (IS);
- IS with disability premium;
- income-based jobseeker's allowance;
- universal credit from October 2013.

If you are entitled to such benefits but there has been a problem with your claim, quote these provisions in initial correspondence with a supplier.

Potentially vulnerable categories include those listed in page 9 of the National Standards for Enforcement Agents (see Appendix 5) as well as those included under SLC 27 (see p126). Suppliers may also have their own definitions.

Remember that individual circumstances can vary, and that people may move in and out of vulnerable categories.

Supplier does not acknowledge a vulnerable situation

If the supplier does not respond properly to the information about vulnerability, ignores information it holds, or if there is delay, you should consider making a formal complaint (see Chapter 14). Also inform Citizens Advice consumer service.

Where a complaint involving a vulnerable person is referred to Citizens Advice consumer service, it may investigate the complaint for the purpose of determining whether it is appropriate to take any action, including:

- providing advice; *or*
- representing you with anything relating to the complaint with the supplier.

For Citizens Advice consumer service to be involved with a disconnection, you need to be the occupier or person entitled to a supply at the premises where disconnection has or may occur, or be acting on behalf of such a consumer. Citizens Advice consumer service may provide the route to the Extra Help Unit which supports vulnerable customers in cases which may then be taken up by Consumer Focus.[4]

When the supplier can disconnect – electricity

Contract suppliers can only disconnect for arrears if the contract says so. If you are threatened with disconnection, check your contract carefully.

With any remaining tariff customers, a tariff supplier may disconnect your supply if you have not paid all charges due in respect of your electricity supply[5] within 28 working days after the date of the bill or other written request to pay.[6] You must be given at least seven working days' written notice of the intention to disconnect[7] and cannot be disconnected for any amount which is 'genuinely in dispute'.[8] **'Charges due'** include any amounts for the electricity supply, standing charges, meter provision or the provision of an electrical line or plant.[9] They do not include other charges such as those for credit sale agreements or for repositioning/adapting a meter for a disabled person.[10]

They might wrongly include charges for periods when supply was disrupted and a power supplier failed to re-connect supply in a reasonable time. Check carefully that you are only being asked for the arrears for which you are liable.

Charges due can only be properly established on the basis of a meter reading. Estimates cannot be used, and you should not be disconnected on the basis of an estimated bill. However, you must ensure you pay the amount actually due, otherwise disconnection may take place. The supply can be cut off at the premises to which the bill relates.[11] Failure to give the required notice of disconnection is an enforcement matter. Contact Citizens Advice consumer service for advice.

When the supplier can disconnect – gas

Gas suppliers supplying under the terms of contracts and deemed contracts may disconnect your supply if you have not paid any charges due for gas within the 28 days following the date of the bill.[12] **'Charges due'** are any charges in respect of the supply of gas.[13] You are entitled to seven days' notice in writing of the intention to disconnect.[14] This will usually be given in the final demand, which may arrive earlier than the 28 days above. A gas supplier is not entitled to disconnect your supply for any amount which is 'genuinely in dispute'.

It is important to pay any undisputed part of the bill, as well as to maintain or establish a payment arrangement for ongoing fuel costs while reaching a resolution of the dispute.

If you have changed supplier and you owe money to your previous supplier, the previous supplier can assign some of its debt to your new supplier in certain circumstances (see p33). The new supplier may cut off your supply as though it were the previous supplier if you fail to pay. You are entitled to a minimum of seven days' notice of the new supplier's intention to disconnect.[15] There is no right to disconnect when all of the bill is genuinely in dispute.[16] You may be protected from disconnection by conditions contained in your supplier's licence if you fall into one of the protected categories (see p126).

Note that public gas transporters may also disconnect your supply in certain circumstances (see p33).

Disconnection when you pay in instalments

If you have an arrangement to pay in instalments, either for your current supply only or for your current supply plus an amount for arrears, the supplier is not entitled to disconnect for arrears while you keep to the terms of your agreement, since you are paying the amounts requested in writing.[17]

If you miss a payment, the supplier will be entitled to disconnect for arrears from 28 working days after the date of your missed payment, but only if there are still charges due (see above), and providing you have been given seven working days' notice of the intention to disconnect. If your account is in credit, based on a reading of your meter and allowing for any standing and other charges, the supplier is not entitled to disconnect.

In practice, suppliers are more likely to try to impose a prepayment meter as an alternative to disconnection. The supplier has to inform you of its intention to disconnect, subject to the notice period above, before being entitled to install a prepayment meter no less than 28 days from the date of your missed payment (see p113). A prepayment meter may be installed with your agreement at any time.

A supplier may also decide that a security deposit is required if you do not keep to your agreement to pay by instalments. The supplier has to write to you to inform you of this. The supplier must give you notice that it intends to disconnect if you do not pay a security deposit. A prepayment meter may be imposed if you do not wish to pay a security deposit. See p38 for more about security deposits.

If the breakdown of your instalment arrangement has occurred because you cannot afford to pay, you may be able to arrange another payment plan and, in any event, the supplier must offer you a prepayment meter as an alternative to disconnection, providing this is safe and practical.

Payment arrangements fail for a variety of reasons. Often it may be wholly or partly the fault of the supplier. It might have been the wrong arrangement from the outset: the commencement date may not coincide with the receipt of income; the frequency of payments may not coincide with the receipt of income; or the amount for consumption or arrears may be set too high (or too low). There may have been a change in lifestyle or appliance use. You may have been ill or in hospital. Under their licence conditions, suppliers are required to make instalment arrangements based on what customers are able to pay. Failing to keep to an agreement should not automatically preclude the possibility of another one being arranged – it is essential to establish why a previous arrangement failed.

Fuel Direct (see p168) should also be considered as a payment option. Under SLC 27.6(i) suppliers are expected to use '*where available*, a means by which payments may be deducted at source from a social security benefit received by that customer.' The use of the words 'where available' suggests that a supplier may be at fault if it overlooks or ignores this option, as Fuel Direct will be available in many more instances than current figures for its usage suggest.[18]

Complaints about disconnection

To complain about a disconnection by an energy supplier, first contact the company concerned. Energy suppliers are subject to regulations setting out how to respond to a complaint (see Chapter 14).

In some cases, Consumer Focus may refuse to investigate a complaint until you have given the supplier a reasonable opportunity to deal with it.

If you have exhausted the supplier's complaints procedure then Consumer Focus can investigate your complaint about disconnection of gas or electricity against:

- a gas transporter for:
  - disconnection of, or a threat to disconnect, your gas;
  - refusal to reconnect your supply following disconnection;
- a gas supplier for:
  - cutting off of, or a threat to cut off, your gas;
  - refusal to reconnect your supply following disconnection;
  - the failure of a prepayment system;

- a electricity supplier, distributor or licence holder for:
  - disconnection of, or a threat to disconnect, your electricity;
  - refusal to reconnect your supply following disconnection;
  - the failure of a prepayment system.

Contact Citizens Advice consumer service in the first instance (see Appendix 1). For more information on complaints, see Chapter 14.

2. **Protection from disconnection**

The following provisions may prevent disconnection in certain circumstances.
- If you are having difficulty paying your bill, Condition 27 of the Standard Licence Conditions (SLCs – see below), the supplier's code of practice and the ERA Safety net may offer some protection (see p128).
- If you claim income support, income-based jobseeker's allowance, pension credit or income-related employment and support allowance, Fuel Direct may be an option (see p168). From October 2013, this includes universal credit.
- The supplier may not be entitled to disconnect (see p133).
- If you are a tenant, your local authority may be able to help (see p207).

Condition 27 of the Standard Licence Conditions

If you are threatened with disconnection because you cannot pay your bill, condition 27 gives you the following rights.
- You are entitled to a payment arrangement to repay your arrears at a rate you can afford.
- By using, where available, a means by which payments may be deducted at source from a social security benefit such as Fuel Direct (see Chapter 11).
- To pay by regular instalments and through a means other than a prepayment meter.
- If you have not been able to manage a payment arrangement, you must be offered a prepayment meter (if safe and practical) as an alternative to disconnection. The meter must be set to recover arrears at a rate which you can afford.
- If you are a pensioner or have children under 18, you should receive protection from disconnection in winter under (see p127).
- You should be offered information about how you can reduce your charges by using the electricity supplied to your home more efficiently.

Suppliers are obliged to develop methods for dealing with customers in arrears under the terms of this condition. These set out the procedures which should be followed by each supplier and provide the practical mechanism for protecting your rights. Any departure from the methods may constitute a breach of your rights and could be referred to Ofgem for investigation (see p1).

Calculation of an instalment rate

Under SLC 27 a supplier must not disconnect you unless it has first taken all reasonable steps to arrange the payment of charges.

The calculation of instalments whether by agreement or through a prepayment meter must be based on terms of the licence conditions. The supplier 'must take all reasonable steps' to discover your ability to pay and must take this into account when calculating instalments.

This may require the completion of a financial statement setting out details of income, expenditure and debts (see p115).

The supplier must also consider:

- relevant information provided by third parties, where it is available; *and*
- where instalments will be paid using a prepayment meter, the value of all of the charges that are to be recovered through that meter.

Protection in winter for pensioners and children

Under SLC 27.10 which came into force on 1 October 2010:

'The licensee must not disconnect, in winter, domestic premises at which the domestic Customer has not paid Charges for the Supply of Electricity if it knows or has reason to believe that the customer is of Pensionable Age and lives alone or lives only with persons who are of Pensionable Age or under the age of 18.'

This condition protects households which contain pensioners or children. If you are in this situation, contact your supplier.

Other situations where disconnection should not occur

Examples of when supply will not be disconnected include:

- if you agree, and keep, to a payment plan;
- if the debt is in the name of a past customer and you have made arrangements to take over the supply;
- if you have a query about your bill and you have paid the part of it which you think is right.

In a case of part-payment you may have to negotiate and contemplate legal action to stop disconnection (see Chapter 14). An injunction could be obtained, requiring the supplier to fulfil the terms of the contract. In return you will probably be expected to give undertakings to pay for the fuel with which you are supplied until the matter is resolved.

The codes of practice may also advise you of when disconnection can be delayed by you taking action. For example, some codes of practice say that if you contact the Department for Work and Pensions or social services for help, the supplier will delay disconnection, typically for 14 or 21 days. You must tell the supplier what you are doing.

Suppliers are expected to make an effort to enable you to discuss your circumstances with them directly so that an appropriate payment arrangement can be reached to recover the debt. Suppliers are also under an obligation to offer the installation of a prepayment meter, thus avoiding the need to disconnect a supply.

The Energy Retail Association (ERA – now Energy UK, see p99) committed to an additional safety net being put in place, offering further protection for vulnerable households.[19] This includes:

- suppliers fitting a prepayment meter where safe and practical to do so, providing continued access to a fuel supply, or putting you onto the Fuel Direct payment scheme;
- if a prepayment meter is not appropriate or offers of help are refused and you continue to be at risk, then details are to be sent to social services for further support and assistance.

It may be useful to suggest these alternatives to disconnection as basis for negotiation with suppliers.

3. **Preventing disconnection**

There are reasons why you should always try to prevent disconnection.
- You cannot solve a debt problem by being disconnected. The supplier will still want the money you owe and may take court action to get it. You will also be charged the costs of disconnecting the supply.
- If you later want your supply reconnected, you will have to pay any arrears still owing, plus the costs of disconnection and reconnection.
- If the supplier has had to get a magistrate's warrant (or Justice of the Peace or Sheriff's warrant in Scotland) to disconnect your supply, you will also have to pay the costs of obtaining the warrant (although an application may be made to the court to use its discretionary power to refuse the claimed costs).
- You may have to pay a security deposit as a condition of being supplied following the disconnection.

It is always preferable to deal with your problems sooner rather than later. You are more likely to be able to obtain a solution which genuinely meets your needs if you have time to think about your proposals to the supplier, or what the supplier is prepared to offer you. If you delay resolving the problem to the point of disconnection, you will be negotiating under far more stressful conditions. At that stage, it is possible that the only way of avoiding complete disconnection will be to have a prepayment meter installed.

You may be able to prevent disconnection if:

- you contact the supplier; *and*
- you arrange to pay your arrears at a rate you can afford; *or*
- you ask the Department for Work and Pensions (DWP) to put you on the Fuel Direct scheme (see p168); a request may also be made by the supplier; *or*
- you agree to accept a prepayment meter set to collect the arrears at a rate you can afford.

In practice, disconnection most often occurs where there has been no contact between the customer and the supplier. Once you contact the supplier, the supplier must consider your situation and look for a suitable way for your supply to continue and for you to repay your arrears at a rate you can afford (see Chapter 7).

The codes of practice may make some provision for disconnection to be delayed, typically for 14 or 21 days, if you tell the supplier that you are going to ask the DWP or social services (social work in Scotland) for help with the bill.

Wherever possible, information should be supplied in writing, in addition to any conversations over the phone. In practice, suppliers expect and prefer you to contact them by phone. It is safer in terms of establishing an agreement and ensuring that the correct information is received, to confirm everything in writing, keeping copies.

If this fails you can make representations at the warrant stage if the matter goes to the magistrates' court (see Chapter 10). It is often possible to negotiate a settlement at this point so always attend court, taking an adviser or friend with you if possible.

4. **At the point of disconnection**

The supplier's right to enter your premises

The supplier may, with your consent, enter your premises to disconnect your supply, providing it has served you with a correct notice of disconnection and has published details of Standard Licence Condition 27 on its website (see p123 and Chapter 10).[20] If you do not consent, the supplier must obtain a warrant from the magistrates' court (or Sheriff Court in Scotland). The costs of the warrant will be added to your bill – these are generally around £75. Although in some cases, the supplier will disconnect your supply from the mains supply outside your property – which makes reconnection extremely expensive. It has yet to be tested in law to what extent, if any, a realistic offer to clear arrears may be grounds for a magistrates' court to refuse to issue a warrant of entry to disconnect.

Your premises must be left no less secure than they were before entry. Any damage caused by legally gaining entry must be made good or compensation paid. If the supplier fails to secure your premises and your possessions are stolen as a result, you can sue the supplier. Suppliers sometimes change locks and leave a note telling you where to pick up a key. There has been at least one case of a customer receiving compensation for overnight expenses resulting from this.

Disconnecting external meters

A warrant is not required for the disconnection of an external meter. Disconnection is lawful, providing the correct notices have been given (see p123).

Disconnecting smart meters

The new technology contained within smart meters means that suppliers can disconnect your supply remotely without visiting your home. Following its 2011 statutory consultation on this matter, Ofgem has sought to address this development by modifying and strengthening the existing protection contained in SLC 27 for all vulnerable customers.[21] Suppliers must be able to show that they have:

- taken pro-active steps to establish whether anyone in the household is vulnerable;
- made sure that written contact with you is in plain English and that it includes details of sources of help, such as Citizens Advice consumer service;
- made a number of attempts to contact you using different methods such as telephone, email, etc and at different times of the day;
- visited the property and looked for any visual signs indicating vulnerability;
- checked whether the property is unoccupied, either on a temporary or permanent basis;
- considered whether the occupancy of the property has changed.

Last-minute negotiations

If the supplier agrees not to disconnect at the last minute, but an official turns up to carry out the disconnection, the disconnection should not be agreed to, and the official should be asked to contact the supplier's office. Many suppliers will accept payment on the doorstep, but some will make an extra charge to cover their expenses.

Some electricity suppliers' disconnection officials routinely carry prepayment meters with them and will offer you one as an alternative, even at this late stage. If you accept the meter, check that it has been set to collect arrears at a rate you can afford. If it has not, ask the supplier to change the setting. Do not be put off by such statements as 'it cannot be changed' or 'it is set at the factory'. This is not the case. It is unlikely that a gas supplier would try to fit a prepayment meter straight away – the system has to be purged and re-lit first.

If you refuse to allow entry, the supplier will have to obtain a warrant or may disconnect from the road. This will cost more, unless you are able to negotiate keeping your supply and paying off the arrears at a rate you can afford in the meantime (see Chapter 7).

5. **Getting your supply reconnected**

Electricity suppliers must reconnect the electricity supply within two working days if:

- you pay your outstanding bill together with the expenses of disconnection and reconnection and any security deposit; *or*
- you reach an agreement with the supplier to pay off the arrears in instalments as a condition of being reconnected.

In the event of unnecessary delays, Consumer Focus can demand an electricity supplier to reconnect your supply within the time limit. However, there appears to be no record of legal proceedings being launched by either body – eg, by obtaining an injunction or interdict in civil proceedings. Anyone affected by the failure to restore a supply would also be entitled to bring civil proceedings for damages against the electricity supplier. The supplier will have a defence if it can prove that it took all reasonable steps and exercised all due diligence to avoid failing to reconnect within the time limit.

Gas suppliers must reconnect your supply once you have paid your outstanding bill, together with the expenses of disconnection and reconnection.

Your supply should be reconnected within a 'reasonable time'. This also applies if you can reach an agreement with the supplier to pay the arrears in instalments.

In practice, if you agree to accept a prepayment meter set to collect the arrears, the supplier will reconnect your supply. You may have to pay the expenses of disconnection and reconnection separately, but usually they will be added to your arrears.

If you do not want your supply reconnected

The supplier will continue to submit bills regardless of whether or not you want your supply reconnected. If you do not pay, it may seek recovery of the debt through the small claims court or sell the right to recover the debt on to a third party (such as a debt collecting agency). In practice, few suppliers or debt collectors try and recover through the courts, preferring to send computerised letters out in the hope of payment. The reason is that in a small claims court action legal costs cannot normally be recovered. As a result it would cost more to take a case to court than would be recovered.

In some cases the debt collector may actually be outside the jurisdiction of the county court in England and Wales, being based in Scotland. In such a case it will be uneconomic for the debt collection company to try and recover the arrears, since this will require issuing a case in the English courts which may in turn be sent to the area in which the debtor lives. This makes it too expensive to begin court action.

Assuming you are liable for the bill, try to negotiate payment in instalments prior to any court action. Otherwise, if the supplier has issued a claim in the county court, respond to the claim by providing a statement of your financial circumstances – and ask to pay in instalments. In these circumstances, the court will usually order payment in instalments. If the court has made an order for payment of the whole debt at once, you could apply to the court to have the order varied to payment in instalments.

There is a fee of £40 for this application, unless you are exempt on grounds of lack of means. The court should not order you to pay an amount you cannot afford – even if you can only afford £1 or £2 a month. You would not be liable for the supplier's legal costs if you lost in the small claims court which is why suppliers seldom ever commence recovery proceedings for sums under £5,000 (see Chapter 14). The supplier is only able to claim for its fee in starting proceedings. As of 1 April 2011, the fees are:

Sums up to £300	£35
Sums from £300-500	£50
Sums from £500-1,000	£70
Sums from £1,000-1,500	£80
Sums from £1,500-3,000	£95
Sums from £3,000-5,000	£120

In Scotland, you can apply for a 'time to pay' direction before a decree (court order). If you break this arrangement by allowing three instalments to pass unpaid, you lose the right to pay by instalments. If you allow a decree to pass without defending or seeking time to pay, then you have to wait until the supplier seeks to enforce the decree before you can ask for a 'time to pay' order. You are liable for up to a maximum of £75 of the supplier's legal costs if you lose your case, but only if the debt is over £200.

The costs of disconnection and reconnection

Charges for disconnection and reconnection must be 'reasonable' and must reflect the actual costs involved. Charges vary between suppliers. For example, British Gas charges a disconnection and reconnection fee in excess of £202 including VAT. For installing a prepayment meter as an alternative to disconnection for arrears, it charges £179. British Gas may also seek to charge £50 for a visit to premises – make a complaint if this occurs and seek to have these charges waived, particularly if British Gas is already aware of any vulnerable situation or receipt of means-tested benefits.

Ultimately, the question of what is a reasonable cost may be determined by a court; Ofgem or Consumer Focus, and the Energy Ombudsman may also examine charges. Operators may drop costs at their discretion, and in some cases (where costs appear to be excessive) it may be argued that a supplier is under a duty to mitigate its loss. Legal advice should be sought.

6. **Disputes: unlawful disconnection**

If you dispute that the gas or electricity supplier is entitled to disconnect, you can ask Consumer Focus (via Citizens Advice consumer service – see Appendix 1) to intervene. It can order the supplier to connect or continue your supply pending a decision on your dispute.

Unlawful disconnection of either a gas or electricity supply is an enforcement matter. Suppliers may be forced to comply with the law by a regulator. If the supplier ignores the order, you can apply for a court order to enforce the order (see Appendix 4).

If disconnection was unlawful, you do not have to pay the costs of disconnection or reconnection. You may also have a claim for compensation.

On occasion, a supplier may wrongly disconnect a supply, arising from a mistake by a contractor who visits a household. This can be a problem in multi-occupation buildings or where a contractor suspects the occupants are squatters. In such a case, immediately contact the supplier and be prepared to back up a demand for reconnection with an action through the courts (see Chapter 14). In such a case, an injunction may be sought to order reconnection and a claim for damages included as a result of nuisance and losses caused by being without a supply.

Prepayment meters and arrears

In theory, it should not be possible to get into arrears by using a prepayment meter. But arrears may be transferred from a previous supplier where you switch supplier or they may be set on a prepayment meter if you accept a prepayment meter as an alternative to disconnection.

A problem associated with prepayment meters is that households may disconnect themselves simply by failing to top up the meter through lack of money. Consumer Focus research found that around one in six pre-pay households, or up to 1.4 million people, live in homes that have cut off their own energy supply in the last year.[22] Almost half of these households have someone with an illness or disability, and two in five house children under 16.

Consumer Focus has urged suppliers to conduct better checks of vulnerable consumers before meters are installed – and to guarantee that they will not be cut off at night or at weekends.

Notes

1. **When you can be disconnected for arrears**
    1 Domestic suppliers' quarterly debt and disconnections – Quarter 3 2011, Ofgem
    2 Condition 26.6 SLC
    3 Energy Retail Association, *ERA Safety Net: Protecting Vulnerable Customers from Disconnection* at www.energy-uk.org.uk/publication/finish/30/308.html
    4 The government announced in April 2012 that Citizens Advice and Citizens Advice Scotland will be taking on responsibilities from the Office for Fair Trading and Consumer Focus.
    5 Sch 6 para 1(6) EA 1989; Sch 4 UA 2000
    6 Sch 6 para 1(7) EA 1989; Sch 4 UA 2000
    7 Sch 6 para 1(6) EA 1989; Sch 4 UA 2000
    8 Sch 6 para 1(9) EA 1989; Sch 4 UA 2000
    9 Sch 6 para 1(1) EA 1989; Sch 4 UA 2000
    10 Sch 6 para 27 EA 1989; Sch 4 UA 2000
    11 Sch 6 para 1(6)(a) EA 1989
    12 Sch 2B paras 7(1) and (3) GA 1986
    13 Sch 2B paras 7(1) and (3) GA 1986
    14 Sch 2B paras 7(1) and (3) GA 1986
    15 Sch 2B para 7(4) GA 1986
    16 Sch 2B para 7(3) GA 1986
    17 Sch 2B para 7(5) GA 1986
    18 See Conditions 27.5 and 27.6 SLC

2. **Protection from disconnection**
    19 Energy Retail Association, *ERA Safety Net: Protecting Vulnerable Customers from Disconnection* at www.energy-uk.org.uk/publication/finish/30/308.html

4. **At the point of disconnection**
    20 Condition SLC 27
    21 Ofgem document, *Modification of The Standard Conditions of Gas Supply Licences granted under section 23 (3) of The Gas Act 1986 and The Electricity Supply Licences granted under section 11 A (3) of the Electricity Act 1989*; Modifications of standard condition 27 ('Payments, Security Deposits and Disconnections') 23 September 2011

6. **Disputes: unlawful disconnection**
    22 Hannah Mummery and Holly Reid, *Cutting Back, Cutting Down, Cutting Off*, Consumer Focus, July 2010

Chapter 9

Theft and tampering

This chapter covers:

1. Introduction

Unlike other goods, gas and electricity are delivered to you without the supplier being present. Suppliers cannot see what you are doing with their meter or with the fuel they have supplied. This makes suppliers vulnerable to theft. Perhaps because of this vulnerability, suppliers sometimes make allegations of theft on quite flimsy evidence. The consequences of such allegations against you can be severe, as a supplier has the power to punish you by disconnecting the supply without having to go to court to prove the allegations first.

Theft from, or tampering with, a meter are both criminal offences and can result in both criminal prosecution and civil proceedings to recover the alleged debt. However, it is important to realise that not in every case of alleged tampering will you necessarily have to pay for damage or alleged stolen fuel.

A full discussion of criminal law and practice is outside the scope of this book. If you might be liable for prosecution, seek specialist legal advice.

If you are legally liable to pay for any loss caused by theft or tampering, a supplier or transporter may be entitled to disconnect the supply, although this right does not follow automatically from liability (see p143).

Ofgem considers theft and tampering to be a serious problem – not least because it estimates that each customer has to pay an additional £6 a year as a result of gas theft alone.[1]

There are already a number of regulatory arrangements in place which require suppliers to detect, investigate and prevent theft of electricity and gas. These can be found at Standard Licence Condition 12. Ofgem has said that more should be done to tackle theft and tampering and it published *Tackling Gas Theft: the way forward* in March 2012 as part of its Corporate Strategy and Plan 2010–2015.

Ofgem is working with suppliers to develop better arrangements for investigating cases of alleged theft. The changes proposed are significant. In March 2012, Ofgem launched a consultation process surrounding the introduction of additional rules for the gas market which will include new licence obligations for gas suppliers. In *Tackling Gas Theft: the way forward*, Ofgem proposes that these will include:[2]

- a new licence condition requiring suppliers to implement a central theft risk assessment service, operational by the end of 2013;
- an industry-led incentive scheme to improve the rate of theft detection to be implemented by the end of 2013;
- the development of a code of practice to regulate how suppliers conduct theft investigations to be implemented by the end of 2012.

Ofgem proposes to consider reform to electricity arrangements early in 2013.

Meter ownership

The theft of gas or electricity or interference with a meter will often cause damage to the meter itself. The supplier of the gas or electricity and the owner of the meter may not be the same company. Nearly all gas meters are owned by National Grid in its role as the main public gas transporter and electricity meters are owned by the privatised electricity suppliers in their role as distributors of electricity. If you are disconnected for theft or tampering, it will normally be one of these companies that actually carries out the disconnection even if you have a contract with a different supplier for the actual supply of gas or electricity.

2. Tampering with a meter

Evidence of tampering

Since a supply of gas or electricity is charged for on the basis of metered consumption, the most obvious unlawful method of reducing a potential fuel bill is to interfere with a meter to prevent it registering or to reduce the amount it has registered. There is a variety of possible techniques for this, including fixing wires or pipes to bypass a meter, using a wire to inhibit the rotation of the disc or making the meter run backwards so that recorded consumption apparently diminishes. There are tell-tale signs on a meter that has been tampered with – eg, the seals are cut or missing, the casing is cracked or badly scratched or a small hole has been drilled in the side. These descriptions are included not as a guide to people who might want to try it, but for advisers who may have no idea what tampering involves and may need to establish if a meter has been interfered with.

Existing electricity meters have two sorts of seals – prescribed copper seals (PCSs) and company seals. PCSs are put on a meter at the time when the meter is originally certified – conceivably some meters may still have Electricity Supply (Meters) Act seals, but PCSs have been used for all new meters in the last 30 years. Company seals are put on the meter by the meter provider. Although, in theory, electricity meters should have no seals missing, suppliers carrying out wiring work or installing meters commonly leave off company seals. So, if company seals are the only ones missing, that in itself is weak evidence of tampering.

Never assume that an allegation of tampering is correct, whatever technical evidence is quoted by the supplier. The evidence is not always clear-cut and the supplier's experts do not always get it right. You can get your own expert (look for an 'electrical engineer', 'gas engineer' or 'gas installer') to examine the meter for an objective assessment. It may be possible, if you are eligible, to obtain legal help under the Community Legal Service scheme.

Meter tampering will not always be seen when the meter is read in the normal way. All meter readers should be trained in detection, but they are only there for a short time. Holes or cracks may be on the far side of the meter in a dark cupboard and therefore difficult to spot. In some cases, the dividing up of properties into separate self-contained dwellings and the resultant variations as to the addresses of occupiers can give rise to problems.

Theft due to tampering can be detected by unusual patterns of consumption – eg, if the bills suddenly go down or if they go up after the installation of a new meter. A meter examiner employed by the meter provider will then come to look at the meter, normally accompanied by a colleague (see Chapter 10) and sometimes by the police. If they detect signs of tampering, the meter will be removed and the supply disconnected. If they cannot detect any evidence there and then, the meter may be taken away for further examination, but a replacement should be left so that the supply is not disconnected straight away. Some electricity suppliers are prepared to install another meter immediately, usually a prepayment meter. However, when a gas supply is disconnected, the system must be purged and re-lit before the supply of gas can be re-started. The people who actually carry out the disconnection are unlikely to have both the expertise and the authority to do this.

In the future, the scope for unlawful or illegal tampering with meters will be reduced with the introduction of smart meter technology, whereby the meter can be controlled remotely and the level of fuel consumption can be regulated. Although physical tampering will certainly be more problematic, the question remains whether it will be possible to hack smart meter digital technology in the same way that, for example, home computers are hacked. The householder might hack the device so that usage is under-reported, in order to pay less.

The consensus among consumer groups is that safeguards are needed to manage the 'massive collection' of consumers' data uploaded by meters and the right to privacy. A third party might seek to hack the device to obtain information about activities within the premises – eg, criminals might be able to use data about fuel consumption to establish when the property is unoccupied. The government is expected to introduce smart meter protections following a consultation process launched in May 2012. It is anticipated that these will include allowing consumers to choose who can access this information by opting out of particular kinds of data management. Additionally, Energy UK members have already launched their *Privacy Commitments for Smart Metering* document prior to the development and publication of a more formal *Smart Metering Privacy Charter*. This document can be found at www.energy-uk.org.uk and explains what information meters can collect, who the information may be passed on to and in what circumstances. For example, other industry parties in connection with supply and distribution issues, or police and law enforcement agencies in order to prevent and investigate fraud. The statement undertakes to act within the boundaries set by data protection law.

Examining the evidence and the law

If a supplier alleges that a meter has been tampered with, there are two key areas to consider.

* You must establish what exactly is alleged to show that the meter has been tampered with. In some cases it will be obvious that the only explanation for damage to a meter is tampering – eg, a hole drilled in the meter casing with a wire inserted. In other cases there may be alternative explanations – eg, if meter seals are missing, it may be that these are company seals which were never put on, or were removed by the supplier but not replaced, or have been removed by someone else. Any evidence the supplier has should be presented to you so that you can comment. However, take care in any comment you make, as it is unlikely that you will be cautioned about anything you say possibly being used against you in court.

* You must investigate whether the supplier has evidence that it was you, and not someone else, who tampered with the meter. Usually, the supplier will not know who did the tampering. If that is the case, the action it can take is more limited than if it has direct evidence against you. It will help if you can explain why it has been tampered with – eg, if you know that the meter was taken over from a previous occupier who had tampered with it or that it was damaged by builders. However, evidence that the meter was interfered with while in your custody can, depending on the circumstances, be sufficient to convict for theft of electricity.[3]

If a supplier alleges that you are liable for theft or tampering, find out which legal provision it is relying on. Different considerations apply when dealing with different parts of the law. Normally the supplier will point to particular provisions in the Gas Act, Electricity Act or Utilities Act, as appropriate, but liability can also arise under general common law principles or under your contract with your supplier.

General common law principles

In England and Wales, when you receive or take on a meter, you become 'bailee' of it. A **'bailee'** is under a duty to take 'reasonable care' of bailed property (in this case, a meter). For example, if you leave your home unlocked and a thief enters to break open a coin meter, you may well be liable to pay compensation for failing to take reasonable care.[4]

In Scotland, 'bailment' does not apply, but the concept of **'restitution'** may be used – ie, if you are in possession of goods which do not belong to you, you are under an obligation to look after them until the owner returns for them.

If you intentionally damage a meter, you could be liable to pay compensation to the supplier. The supplier can sue you, or you may be prosecuted for criminal damage, which is an imprisonable offence. On conviction, the court can order you to pay compensation to the supplier to remedy the cost of the damage.

Contractual liability for meter damage

If you are supplied under a contract, your contractual duty will be no higher than your duty as a bailee (see above), but in the past some suppliers have claimed that customers should pay for damage to a meter, even though they had done nothing wrong or were not negligent. For example, if a burglar damaged your meter, you would not normally have to pay for the damage under your duty as a bailee, unless your negligence allowed the burglar to get into your home. Read your contract carefully because the relevant term contained there may go wider. However, if the term is so wide that it could be regarded as unfair under the Unfair Terms in Consumer Contracts Regulations 1999, then it should not bind you, and you should refer it to the Director General of Fair Trading so that its fairness can be looked at (see Chapter 14). Contact Citizens Advice consumer service for advice.

Responsibility for meters under the Gas and Electricity Acts

In the case of gas, you can make your own arrangements for a meter which can be provided by a gas supplier or transporter. In the case of electricity, you can require your supplier to provide you with a meter, which can be sold, lent or hired to you. If you use a gas meter provided by someone other than a gas supplier or transporter, or if you own an electricity meter, you must keep it in proper order for correctly registering the quantity of gas or electricity supplied. This must be done at your own expense, and failure can lead to disconnection. However, in nearly all cases the meter will have been provided by a gas supplier or transporter, or hired/loaned by an electricity supplier and, under these circumstances, the meter is its responsibility.[5]

If you hire the meter, you may have to enter into a hire agreement with the supplier. Suppliers have no powers to impose conditions concerning the care of the meter in such an agreement which go further than what is allowed under the Acts or their licence conditions.

There are three specific meter offences under the Acts, each punishable by a fine of up to £1,000 on present court scales:[6]

- damaging or allowing damage to any meter, gas fitting or electrical plant or line;
- altering the meter index or register by which consumption is measured;
- preventing the meter from registering properly.

In each case, the offence can only have been committed if the act was done 'intentionally or by culpable negligence' – ie, if it was the alleged offender's fault.

If you are prosecuted for either of the latter two offences, possession of artificial means for altering the way the meter is registering will be taken as *prima facie* evidence that the alteration was caused by you.[7] If such artificial means are not found, a conviction would be difficult to obtain, especially if the case concerns a property in multiple occupation or where there has been a burglary.

3. **Theft of fuel**

Theft of gas and dishonest use or 'abstraction' of electricity are criminal offences.[8] Penalties include fines or imprisonment, offences being triable either way – ie, in either the magistrates' court or the Crown Court before a jury. You can be convicted of theft even if there is no damage or evidence of interference with a meter.[9] The offence of **'abstraction'** is committed where there is use of electricity without the authority of the electricity supplier by a person who has no intention of paying for it.[10]

The key to an offence under these offences is the question of dishonesty. If you genuinely believed you were entitled to use the fuel or had paid or would be paying for the fuel concerned, then the elements of the offence cannot be proved. The issue of what is honest or dishonest use is the standard applied by a jury as being the standards of honest, ordinary people.[11] Dishonesty in the context of an offence of abstraction requires knowledge that electricity was being consumed, coupled with an assumption that it would not be paid for, and a genuine belief and intention that electricity will be paid for – even in a case where a person reconnects a supply without the permission of the electricity company – will provide a defence.[12] Thus, if only one person in a multi-occupation household knows about the unlawful consumption but other occupants are ignorant of it, only the person with knowledge may be convicted of the offence. It is improper to infer guilt simply on the basis of a close relationship between members of a household where an offence has occurred.[13]

In the case of use of gas or electricity by squatters, it is important that the supplier is notified as to the use as soon as practicable and that an undertaking of willingness to pay is given. If a squatter moves into premises, uses electricity or gas and then moves out without an intention of paying for it, an offence will be committed. In one case, the police arrested squatters who were in the process of moving out of a property in which lights were on. The Lord Chief Justice Lord Taylor stated:

'The defence was that if a bill had come they would have paid. However, they were moving out when the police arrived. They had not apprised the Electricity Board of their arrival, their departure or their identity. In those circumstances it was open to the jury to find that they were acting dishonestly and to convict.'[14]

On conviction, a court may make a compensation order for payment of the fuel used, or the supplier may seek recovery through the civil courts. However, as with tampering, suppliers are more likely to recover the value of the stolen fuel by other means – ie, by threatening disconnection. Where the company transporting gas to your home (normally National Grid) is different from the actual supplier, the transporter also has the right to recover the value of the stolen gas.[15]

Squatting in residential premises became a criminal offence from 1 September 2012.[16] This change in the law does not change the legal position with existing supply of gas or electricity provided to a person living as a squatter where, for example, a supply has already been arranged. Provided the squatter genuinely intends to pay for the gas and electricity supplied, no offence of theft is committed.

It is also important to note that because you have your name on a gas or electricity bill it does not establish you as living at a property. You are simply a consumer of fuel under contract at the address but this does not mean you are living in the property, either as a trespasser or otherwise.[17]

Accuracy of meters and estimates of stolen fuel

In cases of alleged tampering or theft of fuel, suppliers will try to recover the cost of fuel stolen by estimating the consumption during the period of tampering or theft. This often leads to a dispute about whether or not a meter has recorded consumption accurately. Either party can refer the matter for consideration to a meter examiner (see p90).

If the consumption of fuel has been under-recorded, whether because of tampering or otherwise, extra charges will be due. Suppliers will claim that, since the meter has been tampered with, consumption must be estimated – and they often come up with extremely high estimates. If you dispute an estimate and want to challenge it, ask the supplier how the estimate was made and on what assumptions. Just because a meter has been tampered with does not necessarily mean that fuel was successfully stolen – it is still up to the supplier to prove that it was.

There are various ways in which suppliers estimate consumption. One measure is to compare your consumption during the period of tampering with your normal rate of consumption, either before the meter was tampered with or after its replacement. The comparison should be over a period of at least a year, as consumption tends to increase in winter.

This method may not be appropriate for you because, for example, your pattern of consumption has changed, or you have recently moved home, or because the supplier claims tampering began after the meter was last read or inspected. There is another method, based on the number and type of appliances you use. Suppliers make assumptions about the running costs of appliances and how often you use them, and then calculate the level of consumption in accordance with those assumptions. Look at the assumptions critically to see if they bear any relationship to actual usage. Suppliers sometimes assume the existence of appliances which you do not actually have, or assume that you use the appliances you do have for maximum periods of time and at maximum settings.

Also note when the supplier is alleging that any tampering began. Evidence of tampering may be clear, but not the start date or the period during which it took place. For example, the more times the meter has been read, the less likely it is that tampering would not have been noticed by a meter reader, which shortens the period during which the tampering is likely to have started. Under Standard Licence Condition 12, the supplier must take all reasonable steps to prevent and detect:

- the theft or abstraction of electricity at premises it supplies;
- damage to any electrical plant, electric line or metering equipment through which such premises are supplied with electricity; *and*
- interference with any metering equipment through which such premises are supplied with electricity.

As a result, all electricity suppliers must tell the owner of a meter if they spot any signs of tampering.[18]

If a meter examiner has been called in, s/he will decide the amount of extra fuel charge. You can get your own electrical expert (look for an 'electrical engineer', or consult Ofgem for licensed meter companies) to make an independent assessment for you. See Chapter 14 for other methods of solving disputes on charges.

Inspection of meters

There are two points to make about the inspection of meters which have been allegedly tampered with.

- A gas supplier is supposed to ensure that your meter is inspected at least once every two years, including a check to see if it has been tampered with.[19] If the supplier claims that the meter has been tampered with for more than two years (hence it can try to claim more than two years' worth of stolen gas), you can point out that this suggests it has breached its obligation to inspect the meter. Under standards of performance imposed by Ofgem, electricity meters should be read at least once every two years.

- In cases of alleged tampering or theft of fuel, suppliers often remove meters quickly. Electricity suppliers must keep meters they have removed because of tampering until Ofgem says otherwise.[20] Meter providers state in their relevant code of practice the minimum length of time they will keep a damaged meter. In the event of legal action, you will need to have your own expert inspect the meter, so check that the meter is being retained correctly and, if necessary, quote the code of practice.

Cloned keys and fuel credit cards

Energy UK indicated that illegal top-up keys were used 88,300 times during 2011. These are sold illegally for sums of around £50 and purport to reduce electricity consumption or alter meter readings. These keys may be sold door-to-door or in pubs or in the street. If you use one, not only will you lose the money but your supplier can detect that the energy used has not been bought legally and you will end up paying twice for your fuel. Anyone knowingly using or selling such a key meter could be prosecuted for theft or for other offences. The fuel industry has committed a significant amount of money to developing technology that can identify and disable cloned cards and keys.

You should only buy top-ups from official outlets. Energy supply companies never sell top-ups door-to-door. If you have bought a discounted top-up without realising it is illegal, contact your fuel supplier or Citizens Advice consumer service.

4. Disconnection of the supply

If a supplier alleges theft or tampering, as well as holding you liable for damage to the meter or any financial loss, it may also want to disconnect the supply until you make arrangements to pay for the loss.

However, disconnection powers arise under a number of different provisions and it is useful to find out which power the supplier is relying on. Each power has its own limitations and it is important to make sure they are not exceeded. In particular, the powers to disconnect for damage to, or tampering with, a meter, are different from the power to disconnect for arrears. The supplier should clarify which power it is exercising when seeking to disconnect a supply. For instance, longer notice must be given before disconnection for arrears takes place (see

Chapter 7), but in tampering cases only 24 hours may be given for gas and no notice at all for electricity, on the basis that the tamperer could be forewarned to get rid of the evidence. See Chapter 10 for the supplier's rights to enter your home in order to carry out the disconnection.

Injunctions

If suppliers exceed their powers (eg, by refusing to reconnect your supply unless you pay excessive charges) you may be able to get a court order (an 'interlocutory injunction') requiring the supplier to reconnect until such time as any dispute is resolved. Sometimes the threat to seek an injunction may be sufficient to persuade a supplier to reconnect.[21]

In England and Wales, injunctions are orders issued by judges through the county court and High Court. In emergency cases, these can be obtained out of court hours. For an application for an injunction, you are normally required to fill in a notice of application (on a court form) and to submit a written statement of truth with details of the disconnection. The statement is signed by you (the person seeking reconnection) and an undertaking may be required (eg, to pay for any fuel used as normal until the dispute is resolved). This undertaking must be kept. If the supplier is not represented in court, it is likely that a date for a hearing to enable the supplier to make representations will also be given.

On obtaining an injunction, the supplier should be informed as soon as practicable of the injunction by phone and by service of a written copy of the judge's order by fax or personal service (ie, handing in a copy to the supplier's office if practicable). Failure to comply with an injunction is punishable as a contempt of court by way of fine or, in an exceptional case, by imprisonment. As a consequence, suppliers will normally adhere to an injunction (this remedy may not be available in Scotland in respect of electricity – see p233).

You could also look into alternatives to disconnection. Normally it would be in your and the supplier's interests to keep the supply going and find an alternative to disconnection – eg, housing the meter in a protective box, or using security bridges to protect seals.

Note that a supplier may claim to be able to disconnect on the basis that money is owed for the damage to the meter, and that this constitutes arrears for which the general power to disconnect can be used, in the same way as if an ordinary quarterly bill was unpaid. This argument is wrong. First, this power can only be used in respect of the actual supply of gas or electricity. Second, you only have to pay for damage to a meter if it is specifically your responsibility under the legal provisions discussed on p138.

Specific powers of disconnection

There are three specific meter offences under the Electricity and Gas Acts which are discussed on p139. If any of the offences are committed in respect of a gas meter or fitting, the supplier can only disconnect the supply of the particular person who has committed the offence. This is also the case with the offence of damaging an electricity meter or electrical line or plant.[22]

However, if anyone tampers with an electricity meter so as to commit one of the other two offences, the supplier can disconnect the supply from the premises regardless of whether the person who committed the offence is the actual customer, and whether or not other users of electricity live there.

Suppliers' rights to enter your home to disconnect the supply are dealt with in Chapter 10. However, it is worth pointing out that gas suppliers and transporters do not have the right to enter to disconnect for theft or tampering unless they have given 24 hours' notice or have a warrant from a magistrate or, in Scotland, a sheriff or Justice of the Peace.

To get a criminal conviction, it must be proved beyond all reasonable doubt that an offence has been committed. However, to exercise its power to discontinue the supply, the supplier needs only to be able to prove it on the balance of probabilities – ie, more likely than not. There does not have to be an actual conviction before the power to disconnect can be used.

The supplier can only discontinue the supply until the matter has been remedied.[23] In the case of tampering with a meter, this includes paying for the cost of any damage to the meter and for any stolen fuel, but the two should be treated separately. Obviously tampering is normally done in order to reduce the fuel bill, which amounts to theft. However, if a meter has been damaged or tampered with, this does not necessarily mean any fuel has successfully been stolen and proof of damage or tampering is no proof that any money is owing to the supplier in respect of fuel. (It has been known for tampering to go wrong so that the meter actually registered a higher consumption.) Therefore, unless the supplier can show that, on the balance of probabilities, the damage in question caused financial loss other than the cost of replacing the meter, the matter will be remedied once that cost has been met.

Often the supplier will assess an amount of fuel which it thinks has been stolen, and will also demand payment for that before it reconnects. It can only do this if it can prove that there was a theft, and that it was caused by the particular damage in question.[24]

If the supplier can prove that fuel has been stolen, and can justify its assessment of its value, then it can disconnect for non-payment. However, suppliers cannot use this power if the amount charged is 'genuinely in dispute' (see Chapter 7).

Also check carefully any charges in respect of disconnection and reconnection. Gas suppliers are limited by the Gas Act to recovering their 'reasonable expenses'. Otherwise, there is nothing which says exactly what charges can be included, but they must refer directly to the disconnection and the reasons for it. Typical charges include:

- meter replacement – it is possible for tampering to take place without the meter actually being damaged, so do not pay for a meter to be replaced that is capable of being re-used without repairs;
- visits to your home – check that travel costs and the number of visits are reasonable;
- administration costs of calculating fuel used but not paid for – check that charges are reasonable;
- administration – check that this is not wholly or partly double-counted within some other charge.

Disconnection for safety reasons

Gas transporters and electricity suppliers have powers to disconnect your supply for safety reasons. A tampered meter can be in an unsafe condition (although not always, as with a meter which is simply missing its seals).

Electricity suppliers can disconnect your supply if they are not satisfied that your meter and wiring are set up and used so as to prevent danger and not to interfere with the supplier's system or anybody else's electricity supply.

Gas transporters have similar powers for 'averting danger to life or property', including dealing with escaping gas. The powers to disconnect are accompanied by rights to enter your property to inspect the relevant fittings and carry out such disconnections (see Chapter 10).

Neither gas transporters nor electricity suppliers have to give notice for disconnection in emergencies. Electricity suppliers must send you a written notice as soon as they can, telling you the reason for the disconnection. If you think the disconnection should not have been carried out, contact Citizens Advice consumer service who will refer the matter to Ofgem if a decision on the dispute needs to be enforced (see Chapter 14).

Gas transporters must send you a written notice within five days of the disconnection, telling you the nature of the defect, the danger involved and what action has been taken. If you want to object, you have 21 days to appeal to the Secretary of State for the Environment, Food and Rural Affairs against the disconnection. The meter stays disconnected until the fault is remedied or the appeal is successful. Reconnection without the consent of the appropriate authorities (ie, the gas transporter or the Secretary of State) is a criminal offence.[25]

When the supply is disconnected for safety reasons, a supplier may provide alternative appliances (eg, electric heaters and cookers) although this is unlikely if tampering is thought to be involved.

Gas suppliers are obliged by their licence conditions to provide a free gas safety check for installations and appliances for some customers up to once a year.[26] The check includes a basic examination and minor work. If any additional work is necessary, there may be a charge. To qualify, you must request the free safety check yourself, and you must:

- be over 60, registered disabled, or receiving a benefit in respect of disability; *and*
- live alone or with a person who also qualifies.

5. **Theft from meters**

Any form of interference with a meter, whether by electronic interference or some method specifically devised to obtain fuel belonging to another without payment, will constitute an offence under the Theft Acts.

Very few prepayment coin meters now remain. However, if your coin meter is broken into, you have two problems:

- convincing the supplier that you were not responsible for the theft; *and*
- the supplier may want you to pay for damage to the meter, and for the contents of the meter.

If you discover a coin meter theft, report it to the police as soon as practicable; this will help rebut allegations that you are responsible.

Suppliers' policies

Regardless of the legal position, suppliers may have policies, including those set out in their codes of practice, or staff guidelines which are more generous than the minimum provisions of the law. Some of these are not published, in order that they cannot be taken advantage of dishonestly, but it is always worth checking the policies of your gas or electricity supplier.

Insurance

Some household insurance policies cover against theft from prepayment meters, though many insurance companies are reluctant to offer such policies.

6. **Removal of meters**

Suppliers (and gas transporters and shippers) have powers to remove, inspect and re-install meters.[27] These powers may be exercised when tampering is suspected, as may the other powers discussed in this chapter. Suppliers must install a replacement meter of the same type, and so leave the supply connected on the same terms as before, unless they are exercising powers to disconnect the supply itself. Replacement rather than repair will also occur whenever the internal parts of a meter come to the end of their working life.

However, if gas or electricity is unpaid for, the supplier can disconnect the supply by whatever means it thinks fit. This includes removing the meter without replacing it. But seven days' notice must be given by a gas supplier, and two days' notice by an electricity supplier. This notice is usually given in the 'final demand'.

An electricity company is also entitled to disconnect a supply and remove a meter when legal proceedings under the Theft Act are not being pursued. A number of court decisions have held that disconnection would be justified where the supplier could produce, on the balance of probabilities, the civil standard of proof that unlawful abstraction had occurred, even though there may have been no criminal conviction.[28]

Notes

1. Introduction

1 Ofgem, *Tackling gas theft – the way forward,* Consultation, 2012

2 Ofgem, *Tackling gas theft – the way forward,* Consultation, 2012

2. Tampering with a meter

3 *Semple v Hingston* [1992] Greens Weekly Reports 21:1201

4 Sch 7 paras 10(4) and 12(1) EA 1989

5 Sch 7 para 10(2) EA 1989; Sch 2B para 3(3) GA 1986

6 Sch 6 para 4(1) EA 1989; Sch 2B para 10(1)(a) GA 1986

7 Sch 7 para 11(2) EA 1989; Sch 2B para 10(3) GA 1986

3. Theft of fuel

8 s13 (electricity) and s1 (gas) Theft Act 1968; in Scotland, the common law offence of theft

9 *R v McCreadie and Tume* [1992] 96 Cr AppR 143, CA

10 *R v McCreadie and Tume* [1992] 96 Cr AppR 143, CA

11 *Ghosh* (1982) 75 Cr AppR 154

12 *Collins and Fox v Chief Constable of Merseyside* [1988] Crim LR 247 and *Boggeln v Williams* [1978] 1 WLR 873

13 *Collins and Fox v Chief Constable of Merseyside* [1988] Crim LR 247

14 *R v McCreadie and Tume* [1992] 96 Cr AppR 143, CA at 146

15 Sch 2B para 9 GA 1986

16 s144 Legal Aid, Sentencing and Punishment of Offenders Act 2012

17 *Doncaster Borough Council v Stark and Another* [1997] CO/2763/96 5 November 1997, Potts, J; *Frost (Inspector of Taxes) v Feltham* [1981] 1 WLR 452

18 Condition 12 SLC

19 Condition 12 SLC

20 Condition 12 SLC

4. Disconnection of the supply

21 *Gwenter v Eastern Electricity plc* [1995] Legal Action, August 1995, p19

22 Sch 2B para 10(2) GA 1986

23 Condition 12 SLC; Sch 4 UA 2000

24 *R v Director of General of Gas Supply ex parte Smith* [1989] (unreported); *R v Minister of Energy ex p Guildford* [1998] (unreported)

25 ss17(2) and 29 EA 1989; s18(2) GA 1986; regs 4, 6, 7, 9 and 10 GS(RE) Regs; reg 29(4) ES Regs

26 Condition 37 SLC

5. Theft from meters

27 Sch 5 UA 2000

28 *R v Director General of Gas Supply ex parte Smith* [1989] QB 31 July (unreported); *Director of Gas Supply ex p Sherlock & Morris N Ireland* [1996] QB 29 November unreported; *R v Seeboard PLC & another ex p Robert Guildford* [1998] 18 February 1998, per Ognall, J

Chapter 10

Rights of entry

This chapter covers:
1. Entering your home (below)
2. Right of entry with a warrant (p151)

1. Entering your home

The Gas Act 1986 and the Electricity Act 1989 give suppliers and gas transporters certain rights to enter your home. Suppliers do not have any entry rights other than those under the Acts. These rights can only be exercised if:

- you consent; *or*
- the supplier obtains a warrant from a magistrates' court (in Scotland the Sheriff court, a Justice of the Peace or a magistrate); *or*
- there is an emergency.

Suppliers emphasise formally that disconnection should be a last resort. However, in practice this is not always the case, and some suppliers may seek a warrant to disconnect ahead of adopting deductions via Fuel Direct. Suppliers' licences also contain conditions requiring them to train their representatives and to ensure that they behave appropriately when visiting your home.

Suppliers and their agents should also be conversant with page 9 of the National Standards for Enforcement Agents (see Appendix 5), taking special care if a person in debt falls into a vulnerable category included in the guidance. These standards are published by The Ministry of Justice and were updated in January 2012.

These standards are intended for use by all enforcement agents, public and private, and the creditors (in this instance the fuel suppliers) who use their services. This national guidance does not replace local agreements or the legislation, and you should check any codes of practice published by individual suppliers, which may prove helpful. The standards are not legally binding. They can, however, offer a useful benchmark to determine what you can reasonably expect if suppliers instruct agencies to collect debts on their behalf.

Legal powers

Electricity and gas suppliers and gas transporters have the right to enter your home to:[1]

- inspect fittings or to read the meter – no advance notice has to be given;
- disconnect supply on non-payment of bills (this does not apply to gas transporters). Electricity suppliers must give one working day's notice, and gas suppliers 24 hours' notice (this may be waived on grounds of public safety or tampering);
- discontinue supply or remove a meter under their powers in connection with theft and tampering (see Chapter 9). Gas suppliers must give 24 hours' notice;
- discontinue supply or remove a meter where they are no longer wanted. Electricity suppliers must give two working days' notice and gas suppliers 24 hours' notice;
- replace, repair or alter pipes, lines or plant. Electricity suppliers must give five working days' notice (unless it is an emergency, in which case notice must be given as soon as possible afterwards), and gas suppliers seven days' notice.

Notice should given be in writing and can be served by post or by hand, or by attaching it to any obvious part of the premises. Once any required notice has been given, suppliers may use these rights at any reasonable time. 'Reasonable' is not defined but it probably means at reasonable times of the day – ie, not late at night, or on religious festivals and public holidays such as Christmas Day, or when the supplier knows that it would cause severe difficulty.

If they have disconnected your supply for any reason other than to do with safety, gas suppliers and transporters also have the right to enter your home to check that the gas supply has not been reconnected without consent.

Electricity suppliers do not have the power to inspect or read the meter if you have written to them asking for the supply to be disconnected and this has not been done within a reasonable time.

A gas transporter also has the right to enter your home if it has reasonable cause to suspect that gas is, or might be, escaping, or that escaped gas has entered your premises, in order to do any necessary work to prevent the escape or to avert danger to life or property.

Officials representing the supplier or transporter must produce official identification when using any of the above powers.

If you intentionally obstruct an official exercising any of the above powers of entry, you can be fined up to £1,000, although you cannot be punished if the official does not have a warrant.[2]

Suppliers must leave the premises no less secure than they found them, and must pay compensation for any damage caused.

Licence conditions

Gas and electricity suppliers operate under licences issued by Ofgem (see Chapter 1), which has powers to force the suppliers to keep to the conditions in their licences (see Chapter 14). Licence conditions state that gas and electricity suppliers must send details of their policies on entering customers' homes to Ofgem for approval.

Suppliers' codes of practice require the following.[3]

- Suppliers' representatives visiting or entering your home must be fit and proper persons – eg, they must have no relevant criminal convictions.
- Each representative must be identifiable, including by driving marked vehicles, wearing appropriate clothing and carrying a suitable photocard.
- Each representative must be fully trained about the legal powers discussed above.
- Suppliers must operate password schemes for pensioners or disabled or chronically sick customers. If you want one, you can have a password known only to you and the supplier so that you can identify genuine representatives.
- Representatives must be able to tell you where you can get further help or advice in relation to the supply of gas or electricity.[4]

Check your supplier's website for its code of practice or phone and ask for a copy.

2. Right of entry with a warrant

If you do not consent to the supplier entering your premises in accordance with any of the above rights, or there is no adult to give such consent, the supplier or transporter can get a magistrates' warrant (or the Scottish equivalent). In an emergency, a supplier does not need to get a warrant, but can obtain one nevertheless if entry is obstructed despite the emergency. The issue of a warrant is governed by the Rights of Entry (Gas and Electricity Boards) Act 1954.[5] Although the application is dealt with through the magistrates' court, the application is a civil matter, not a criminal matter.

To get the warrant, the supplier must apply to the magistrates' court or, in Scotland, to a Justice of the Peace, a magistrate or a sheriff. The warrant will be granted if the court is satisfied that:

- entry to the premises is reasonably required by the supplier;
- the supplier has a right of entry under the powers discussed above, but that right is subject to getting consent to enter;
- any conditions the supplier is supposed to meet in order to exercise the right of entry (eg, to give notice) have been met.

Also, the court must be satisfied that:

- if the right of entry does not itself have a requirement for notice, 24 hours' notice has been given after which entry was refused; *or*

- there is an emergency and entry has been refused; *or*
- the purpose of entering would be defeated by asking for consent – eg, if tampering is suspected.

In recent years, the practice has been to use the warrant system to enter the home of a customer to fit a prepayment meter rather than actually disconnect a supply. Prior to 2010, this could result in a customer in fuel poverty paying more for energy than other customers. However, discrimination in charging between those on prepayment meters and those who pay by other methods should now have been reduced.

Under the Electricity Act 1989, a warrant of entry remains in force for 28 days. If entry is not sought within this period, the warrant lapses.[6]

Notice of application for a warrant

There is no general requirement under the 1954 Act for the supplier or court to inform you that an entry warrant is being applied for, or has been issued. You have no right to be notified or to be present at the hearing. However, your supplier may state in its code of practice that it will inform you. Under the Humans Rights Act 1998 there is an arguable point that a person affected by the warrant should be notified of the hearing and given an opportunity to make representations to the magistrates' court. This point has yet to be tested, but Article 6 of the European Convention on Human Rights ensures the right to a fair trial and representation in legal proceedings which affect the rights of a person, including civil obligations. The State is under a duty to ensure the effective protection of rights.[7]

Typically a supplier will serve a notice informing you (often in rather small print) that you may attend. In practice, it prefers to obtain the warrant in the absence of the customer.

Some letters may state that the police may be in attendance. This is wrong and misleading. The police should not be involved because the warrant is a civil matter, not a criminal one. The police have no powers to enforce the warrant, as it is a private dispute between you and the supplier. Only if there is a threat of violence at the property should there be any involvement by the police, and then only to restrain a breach of the peace – eg, a fight breaking out. A complaint should be made where a letter contains such a suggestion, and it may constitute an offence under section 40 of the Administration of Justice Act 1970 (harassment of a debtor).

Contacting the supplier in advance

Wherever possible, you or your representative should contact the supplier in advance of the hearing as there is still the possibility of negotiation.

In some cases, it is known for suppliers to withdraw the application prior to the hearing, particularly if the application may be contested or if the person is vulnerable. Reference should be made to the National Standards and Enforcement Agents (see Appendix 5) in a case of vulnerability. If a supplier disregards the guidance, a complaint can be made, as well as the matter being brought to the attention of the magistrates' court.

Representations should be made in writing, and may be faxed or emailed direct to the most senior person in the energy company available, or directed to the legal department if its details can be obtained. An explanation of the vulnerability and an outline of the issues should be included.

If a defence can be shown, or there are factors which the court should consider, mention should be made of these and be prepared to provide further details, together with the intention of attending court.

Restrictions on disconnection

Standard Licence Conditions 27 for gas and electricity provide that a supplier should not disconnect in winter (see p127) and that disconnection should be a last resort. When contacting the supplier or its agent, mention these restrictions, and at court where appropriate.

The approach of the court

The court should not grant the warrant unless it is satisfied that the legal requirements have been met; but in practice, courts tend to rubber-stamp suppliers' applications for warrants in the absence of the customer. However, the Court of Appeal has emphasised the importance of carefully scrutinising warrant applications to gain entry to private homes.[8] Magistrates have a discretion under the 1954 Act and are expected to exercise that discretion reasonably in each case, considering all relevant factors, disregarding irrelevant ones and not acting perversely.[9] If you suspect that your supplier will be applying for a warrant, write to the supplier. Set out the reasons why a warrant should not be granted and send a copy to the court, asking that it be shown to the magistrate (or other Scottish court officer) who will deal with the application. Letters and representations should be addressed to the Justices' Chief Executive stating that you wish to attend the hearing and make representations at any application. Letters may be faxed to the court in urgent cases.

However, as a result of magistrates' court reorganisation and the recent closure of some courts, administration is not always efficient and it may be necessary to attend the court in advance to seek an adjournment, or alternatively on the day set for the hearing. If attending in advance, ask to speak to the duty clerk concerning the application.

Adjournments

If you cannot attend court for a good reason, you may seek an adjournment. The application should only be made if you genuinely intend to contest the warrant application at a later date. With any letter to the court you may include a request to allow an adjournment of the warrant application, to allow you to attend or be represented. In an emergency, if you cannot get to court, you may be able to obtain the adjournment over the phone. If you are in a vulnerable situation or if the disconnection is being investigated by an official body, there may be grounds for an adjournment until the matter is determined.

It is important not to leave the matter to the last minute – this is not likely to make a good impression. In cases where the energy company has been shown to have failed to respond to representations, this should be put forward as reasons for the delay.

On attending court it may be possible to negotiate with the agent representing the supplier, and in some cases it may be possible to have the warrant application withdrawn. In some cases, simply attending court and being prepared to contest the warrant will lead the supplier to withdraw the application.

You may represent yourself in court, be represented by a lawyer, or may be assisted by a 'McKenzie friend' (see p237). Magistrates' courts are familiar with the role of McKenzie friends and although they do not have a right of audience, in some cases the court may allow the friend the opportunity to speak. The McKenzie friend may assist in helping put documents and information to the court and providing a means statement as to your financial circumstances.

A warrant only allows a supplier to act exactly in accordance with its terms and, if you are unhappy with an entry by warrant, check its wording precisely. In one case, Offer (the former electricity regulator) decided that a forcible entry to disconnect supply had been illegal because the warrant only covered forcible entry if the supply was left connected.

Proportionality and Human Rights Act principles

Under European Union law, UK courts must have regard to a 'doctrine of proportionality' – ie, any legal measures applied against citizens of member states and affecting their rights must be proportional to the ends achieved.

The law has yet to be tested, but it is at least arguable that an application for a warrant to gain entry to disconnect electricity or gas may be a disproportionate measure in the case of a vulnerable household (eg, a lone parent receiving benefits). In a case of fine enforcement, *R (on the application of Stokes) v Gwent Magistrates' Court*, the High Court held that enforcement activity may be disproportionate as a measure and contrary to Article 8 of the European Convention on Human Rights (protecting rights to the home and family life).[10] Following this principle, it would appear open to a magistrates' court to decline to issue a warrant where a debt is relatively small and the hardship caused to a vulnerable household would be severe. A magistrates' court should consider the position of any children residing in the property and anyone with disabilities who may be affected. It is therefore important that a means statement and details of all persons residing in the property are provided to the court at the hearing. In the event that you are too ill to attend, send details to the court in writing in time for the hearing.

Similarly, it has not been determined whether it is correct for an energy company to pursue a warrant where another option, such as deductions from benefit under Fuel Direct, may be available.

Defects in the 1954 legislation

From anecdotal evidence and experience, it appears that a number of major suppliers have doubts as to the applicability of the 1954 Act. The legislation dates from the period when energy companies were state-owned and supplies were not provided on the modern contractual basis. The legislation as envisaged in 1954 was not designed to accomplish the instalment of prepayment meters, which amount to a change in the terms and conditions of supply. Therefore, there is an argument that the use of a warrant to fit a prepayment meter is not with the powers granted under the Act as envisaged in 1954, and that you can legitimately object to the change in the terms and conditions. Sometimes energy companies are reluctant to tackle these arguments in court and may withdraw the warrant.

If a warrant application is challenged in court, questions should also be added regarding the cost of the application. Some suppliers (or companies acting on their behalf) will add £300 or more for the cost of seeking an individual warrant against one, even though they may be making 10 or more such applications at the same time. The additional costs added should be referred to Ofgem and to Consumer Focus for examination as to fairness.

Liability for negligence and improperly obtained warrants

A gas or electricity operator is protected against liability in civil law for acts in accordance with executing the warrant. However, a gas or electricity operator who gains entry under a warrant will remain liable for any wrongful acts or defaults committed during the course of executing the warrant against the premises or where a warrant has been obtained in bad faith or for an improper purpose.[11] Therefore, a gas or electricity operator may be liable to action in negligence, trespass or nuisance where the warrant is executed against the wrong premises or where damage is caused in the process of disconnection. If a supplier knowingly tries to force entry without a warrant this will be a criminal offence, such as criminal damage. A householder who resists such entry is entitled to use reasonable force.[12]

Appeals from the magistrates' court

Rights of appeal from the magistrates' court on a point of law lie to the High Court under section 111 of the Magistrates' Courts Act 1980 (known as 'case stated' appeals) and also to the High Court by way of judicial review. Seek legal advice before attempting such an appeal.

Notes

1. Entering your name
1 Sch 6 paras 6(1) and (2) and 7(1) and (2) EA 1989; Sch 2B paras 16, 17, 23(1), 24, 24(2), 26, 27 and 27(1) GA 1986
2 s1(3) RE(GEB)A 1954
3 Code of Practice on Procedures with respect to Site Access (Electricity); Arrangements in respect of Powers of Entry; Authorisation of Officers (Gas)
4 Condition 31(1) SLC

2. Right of entry with a warrant
5 s1(3) RE(GEB)A 1954; this applies to Scotland under s11(7)
6 s101 EA 1989, amending s2 RE(GEB)A 1954
7 ECHR Article 6; *Rommelfanger v Germany* (1989) 62 DR 151 and *Diennert v France* (1996) 21 EHRR 554
8 *O'Keegan v Chief Constable of Merseyside* [2003] 1 WLR 2197
9 *Associated Provincial Picture Houses v Wednesbury Corporation* [1948] 1 KB 223
10 [2001] JPN 766 EWHC Amin 564
11 *O'Keegan v Chief Constable of Merseyside* [2003] 1 WLR 2197
12 Criminal Damage Act 1971; *Vaughan v McKenzie* [1969] 1 QB 557

Chapter 11

Fuel and benefits

This chapter covers:
1. Introduction
2. Income support, income-based jobseeker's allowance, income-related employment and support allowance and pension credit (p158)
3. Cold weather payments and winter fuel payments (p159)
4. Housing benefit (p162)
5. Impact of charitable payments on benefits (p164)
6. The discretionary social fund (p165)
7. Fuel Direct (p168)

This chapter does not apply to people who are subject to immigration control, whose immigration status may be jeopardised if they claim certain benefits. See CPAG's *Benefits for Migrants Handbook* for further details.

1. **Introduction**

This chapter deals with the limited payments and loans available within the social security system for fuel and related costs. It also covers the Fuel Direct scheme which is available to some claimants with fuel debts. It is not intended to be a comprehensive guide to the benefits system, but should help to establish if you are eligible for help with a fuel-related cost.

If you cannot afford to pay for fuel or related expenditure, obtain specialist benefits advice to ensure that you are receiving your full entitlement. Do not delay in this, as there are time limits for claiming all benefits and restricted opportunities for backdating. Do not be put off from seeking advice and do not assume that you are not entitled to any help or to more help than you are getting at present. Whatever your circumstances, your local Citizens Advice Bureau, advice centre or welfare rights service should be able to provide you with a benefits check free of charge. If you are refused a benefit and need to appeal, consult CPAG's *Welfare Benefits and Tax Credits Handbook* for detailed information and seek advice. If you are not entitled to any benefit, see Chapter 12.

From **October 2013** a new benefit, **universal credit**, will start to replace:

- income support;
- income-based jobseeker's allowance;
- income-related employment and support allowance;
- housing benefit;
- working tax credit;
- child tax credit;
- budgeting loans;
- crisis loan alignment payments.

Eventually these benefits and tax credits will be phased out entirely. At the moment, it is expected that this process will be completed by October 2017.

Benefit entitlement checks

If you need further advice or help with benefits, contact your local Citizens Advice Bureau, advice centre or welfare rights service. Alternatively, in Scotland and Wales, you can get a free benefit check from one of the government funded energy efficiency schemes.

In Wales, Nest: freephone 0808 808 2244.

In Scotland, the Energy Assistance Package Scheme: freephone 0800 512 012.

---

2. Income support, income-based jobseeker's allowance, income-related employment and support allowance and pension credit

Income support (IS), income-based jobseeker's allowance (JSA), income-related employment and support allowance (ESA) and pension credit (PC) are national 'safety net' means-tested benefits. The benefits are administered by the Department for Work and Pensions (DWP) and are key benefits if you need direct help with fuel-related costs. Although there is no specific provision within these benefits for fuel costs, entitlement to these benefits can help you qualify for other assistance, such as social fund payments. If you are on these benefits, you may be able to avoid disconnection by paying for your fuel and any arrears through the Fuel Direct scheme (see p168).

Income support

IS is a benefit for people aged 16 or over and under the qualifying age for PC who are on a low income. Only certain groups can get IS – eg, lone parents with a child under a certain age and people caring for a disabled person. You cannot get IS if you are working for 16 hours or more a week (and if your partner is working 24 hours or more a week) or if you have savings of over £16,000. Your income must be less than the set amount the law says you need to live on (known as your 'applicable amount').

Income-based jobseeker's allowance

Income-based JSA is a benefit for people aged 18 (or in some cases 16) or over and under pension age who are available for and actively seeking work and are on a low income. You cannot get income-based JSA if you are working for 16 hours or more a week (and if your partner is working 24 hours or more a week) or if you have savings of over £16,000. Your income must be less than the set amount the law says you need to live on (known as your 'applicable amount').

Income-related employment and support allowance

Income-related ESA is a benefit for people aged 16 or over and under pension age who are unable to work due to ill-health or disability. You cannot get ESA if your partner is working 24 hours or more a week or if you have savings of over £16,000. Your income must be less than the set amount the law says you need to live on (known as your 'applicable amount').

Pension credit

PC is a benefit for people who have reached the 'qualifying age'. For claimants born before 6 April 1950 this is 60. For claimants born on or after 6 April 1950 it is gradually increasing to 66 by 2020 and will eventually go up to 68. PC has two different elements:

- **guarantee credit**, designed to bring your income up to a certain level; *and*
- **savings credit**, which is intended to 'reward' you for making provision for your retirement above the basic state retirement pension.

For full details about rules of entitlement and how to calculate benefits, see CPAG's *Welfare Benefits and Tax Credits Handbook*.

---

3. **Cold weather payments and winter fuel payments**

There are two types of payments which provide extra help for fuel during cold periods of weather – cold weather payments and winter fuel payments. They have different eligibility rules.

Cold weather payments

Cold weather payments are payments made to pension credit (PC) claimants and some income support (IS), income-based jobseeker's allowance (JSA) and income-related employment and support (ESA) claimants. Cold weather payments are intended to assist with the extra costs of heating when the weather has been exceptionally cold for at least seven consecutive days.

Who qualifies

You qualify for a cold weather payment if:

- a period of cold weather has been forecast or recorded for the area in which your normal home is situated (see below);[1] *and*
- you have been awarded PC (guarantee or savings credit) for at least one day during the period of cold weather. You also qualify if you have been awarded IS, income-based JSA or income-related ESA for at least one day during the period of cold weather *and*:
  - your IS or income-based JSA includes a disability, severe disability, enhanced disability, disabled child, or pensioner premium; *or*
  - your income-related ESA includes the pensioner premium, severe disability premium, enhanced disability premium, or the work-related activity or support component; *or*
  - you are responsible for a child under five; *or*
  - you are getting child tax credit which includes a disability or severe disability element;[2] *and*
- you are not living in a care home;[3] *and*
- you are not a person subject to immigration control.

A period of cold weather

This is a period of seven consecutive days during which the average of the mean daily temperature, as forecast or recorded for that period at your designated local weather station, is equal to or below 0 degrees celsius.[4] The **'mean daily temperature'** is the average of the maximum and minimum temperatures recorded for that day.[5] The regulations divide the country into 91 areas, each covered by a weather station at which the temperatures are forecast or recorded.[6] The area your home is in is determined by your postcode.

Amount of payment

£25 is paid for each week of cold weather.[7]

Claiming and getting paid

You do not need to make a claim for a cold weather payment. The DWP should automatically pay you if you qualify. If you do not receive payment and think that you may be entitled, contact your local Jobcentre Plus office. A payment cannot be made more than 26 weeks from the last day of the winter period (1 November to 31 March) in which the cold weather period fell.[8]

Challenging a decision

If you do not receive a cold weather payment to which you think you are entitled, submit a written claim for it and ask for a written decision. If you are refused, you can ask for a revision or appeal against the decision. Do so within one month of receiving the decision.

Winter fuel payments

A winter fuel payment is a yearly tax free payment to help people pay for their heating in the winter. Getting the winter fuel payment will not affect any other benefits you may get.

Who qualifies

You qualify for a winter fuel payment if:[9]

- you are qualifying age for PC in the week beginning on the third Monday in September (the **'qualifying week'**). For winter 2012/13, this means that your date of birth is on or before 5 July 1951 and for winter 2013/14, this means that your date of birth is on or before 5 January 1952; *and*
- you are ordinarily resident in Great Britain (note: you may be entitled if you live in another European Economic Area country or Switzerland); *and*
- if a claim is required (see p162), you claim in time; *and*
- you are not excluded under the rules below.

Exclusions

You are excluded from entitlement if, during the qualifying week (see above):[10]

- you are serving a custodial sentence; *or*
- you have been receiving free inpatient treatment for more than 52 weeks in a hospital or similar institution; *or*
- you are receiving PC, income-based JSA, or income-related ESA and you are 'living in residential care'. You count as living in residential care if you are living in a care home throughout the qualifying week and the 12 preceding weeks, disregarding any temporary absences;[11] *or*
- you are a person subject to immigration control.

Amount

These are the rates that apply in 2012/13. Subject to the rules below, you are entitled to a winter fuel payment of:

- £200 if you are aged between the qualifying age for PC and 79 (inclusive) in the qualifying week; *or*
- £300 if you are aged 80 or over in the qualifying week.

If you do not get PC, income-based JSA or income-related ESA and you share your accommodation with another qualifying person (whether as a partner or friend), you will get £100 if you are both aged between the qualifying age for PC and 79, or £150 if you are both aged 80 or over. If only one of you is aged 80 or over, that person will get £200 and the other person £100. If you do get PC, income-based JSA or income-related ESA, you (and your partner if you have one) will get £200 if one or both of you is aged between the qualifying age for PC and 79, or £300 if one or both of you is aged 80 or over, regardless of whether there is anyone else in your household who qualifies.[12]

If you are living in residential care in the qualifying week and are not getting PC, income-based JSA or income-related ESA, you are entitled to a payment of £100 if you are aged between the qualifying age for PC and 79, or £150 if you are aged 80 or over.[13]

Claiming and getting paid

You should automatically receive a payment without having to make a claim if you received a payment the previous year, or you are getting a state retirement pension or any other social security benefit (apart from child benefit, housing benefit or council tax benefit) in the qualifying week.[14]

Otherwise, you must claim a winter fuel payment before 31 March following the qualifying week.[15] To ensure you receive your payment before Christmas, submit your claim before the qualifying week. A claim can be accepted in any written format but it is best to use the designated form, which you can get from the winter fuel payment helpline on 0845 915 1515 (local rate) (textphone: 0845 601 5613) or from www.gov.uk.

If you are a member of a couple and your partner is receiving IS, the payment can be made to either of you (even if your partner is under qualifying age for PC).[16]

Payments are usually made between mid-November and Christmas.

Challenging a decision

Decisions can be challenged by revision, supersession or appeal. To get a decision, you may have to submit a written claim and request a written decision.

4. **Housing benefit**

Housing benefit (HB) is a means-tested benefit intended to help low income households with rent payments. You can claim HB whether you are in work or out of work.

When housing benefit assists with fuel costs

HB does not assist with most fuel costs paid with your rent. You are expected to find the money for these charges from any other income you may have, such as benefits or earnings. However, the following charges may be met by HB.

- Service charges for communal areas – as long as it is separately identified from any other charge for fuel used within your accommodation.[17] Communal areas include access areas – eg, halls, stairways and passageways.[18] In sheltered accommodation only, rooms in common use (eg, a TV room or dining room) can also be included.[19]

- Charges for the provision of a heating system (eg, for boiler maintenance), if they are separately identified from any other fuel charge.[20]

How fuel charges are calculated

With the exception of those charges listed above, HB does not cover fuel charges which are included in your rent – eg, heating, hot water, lighting and cooking. If the amount of your fuel charge can be identified (eg, in your rent agreement, rent book or letter from your landlord), the amount specified will be deducted from the total amount of your rent before your HB is calculated.[21] As a result HB may not cover the full accommodation charges that you are contractually expected to meet. For example, if your rent is £70 a week and your rent agreement states that this includes £15 for heating, £55 would be counted as rent in assessing your entitlement to HB.

If the local council considers that the amount you pay for fuel is unrealistically low compared with the cost of the fuel provided, or if this charge contains an unknown amount for communal areas, it may instead apply a flat-rate deduction (see below). This does not apply if you are a council tenant as the regulations assume that your fuel charges are specified.[22]

A flat-rate deduction will be made if the amount of fuel charges is not specifically identified as part of your rent.[23]

Flat-rate deductions from housing benefit

If fuel charges are included in your rent, the amount of rent which is eligible for HB is calculated by making flat-rate deductions if your fuel charge:[24]

- is not readily identifiable; *or*
- is considered to be unrealistically low; *or*
- contains an unknown amount for communal areas.

Fuel deductions – weekly deductions for ineligible fuel charges (2013/14 rates)

If you and your family occupy more than one room:

Heating	£25.60
Hot water	£2.95
Lighting	£2.05
Cooking	£2.95
Total all fuel	£33.55

If you and your family occupy one room only:

Heating alone, or heating combined with either hot water or lighting or both	£15.30
Cooking	£2.95

If fuel is supplied for more than one purpose, the appropriate charges will be added together. If you are a joint tenant, the deductions will be apportioned according to your share of the rent.[25]

The local council must notify you if it has used flat-rate deductions in calculating your entitlement to benefit. It must also explain that these can be varied if you can produce evidence of the actual or approximate amount of the fuel charge.[26] The flat rate deductions can be varied accordingly. The *Housing Benefit Guidance Manual* used by local authorities says that the lower rate applies if you occupy one room, even if you may share a kitchen or bathroom.[27] Argue for the lower rate deduction if you are forced to occupy one room due to disrepair, damp or mould growth in your home.

Discretionary housing payments

The local authority which pays your HB (and/or council tax benefit – CTB) can also make a discretionary housing payment (DHP) if you require additional financial assistance with your housing costs. The onus is on you to apply and the discretion is with the local authority as to when a payment is appropriate. DHPs cannot be used to cover charges which are excluded from HB – eg, most fuel charges.

Request an application form from the local authority benefits department.

DHPs are often made on a weekly basis, to 'top up' HB or CTB entitlement. It is also possible to receive a DHP as a lump sum – eg, to cover arrears of rent or council tax.[28]

There is no right of appeal against a DHP decision, but you can ask the local authority to review its decision. If a local authority acts unreasonably regarding making a decision, it can be subject to judicial review (see Chapter 14) or you can make a complaint to the Local Government Ombudsman.

5. **Impact of charitable payments on benefits**

Charities may sometimes step in to help with fuel or reconnection costs, particularly when 'vulnerable' people have been disconnected. Many Citizens Advice Bureaux and other advice agencies can help with applications for charitable payments.

For detailed information about the effect on benefits of regular and irregular payments for fuel, and the treatment of payments as income or capital, see CPAG's *Welfare Benefits and Tax Credits Handbook*, as the rules relating to capital and income are complex.

6. **The discretionary social fund**

This section is not intended to be a comprehensive guide to the discretionary social fund. You are advised to use this section simply as a tool to help you determine where financial help may be available for different aspects of fuel and related costs. Consult CPAG's *Welfare Benefits and Tax Credits Handbook* for detailed information about the operation of the social fund.

Future changes

From April 2013 community care grants and crisis loans for general living expenses (including rent in advance) will be abolished and replaced by new local provision. The new provision will be administered by local authorities in England and the devolved administrations in Scotland and Wales. Budgeting loans will continue to be available until universal credit (see p158) is fully rolled out. As people move onto universal credit they will have access to a new system of 'budgeting advances' that will replace budgeting loans for universal credit claimants.

What is the discretionary social fund

The discretionary '**social fund**' is a government fund that makes payments to people in need. There are three types of payments available: community care grants, budgeting loans and crisis loans. Budgeting loans and crisis loans must be repaid. Payments are discretionary and the social fund is budget limited, so even if you satisfy the qualifying rules, you may not receive a payment.

The Secretary of State issues national guidance for decision makers on how to administer the social fund, interpret the law and directions, prioritise applications and on when to make payments. The guidance, together with the directions, is published in the *Social Fund Guide*. Decision makers must take account of the guidance when making decisions, but it is not legally binding.

Community care grants

You may get a community care grant if you are on income support (IS), income-related employment and support allowance (ESA), income-based jobseeker's allowance (JSA) or pension credit and you do not have too much capital (over £500, or over £1,000 if you or your partner are aged 60 or over) *and*:

- you or a member of your family or a person you or a member of your family care for are coming out of institutional or residential care; *or*
- you or a member of your family or a person you or a member of your family care for needs help to avoid going into care; *or*
- you need help to set up home as part of a planned resettlement programme following a period during which you have been without a settled way of life; *or*
- you need help to ease 'exceptional pressure' on you and your family; *or*

- you need help to allow you or your partner to care for a prisoner or young offender on home leave; *or*
- you need help with certain travel expenses.

You cannot get a grant for:
- consumption costs and standing charges for gas and electricity;
- service charges for fuel.

You may get a grant for:
- household equipment, including cookers and heaters;
- connection and reconnection charges;
- furnishings, including bedding.

These groups of claimants are given priority in the guidance:
- elderly people, particularly those with restricted mobility;
- people who have a mental illness or learning disability;
- people with disabilities or chronic or terminal illnesses;
- people who have misused drugs or alcohol;
- ex-offenders;
- families under stress, particularly where there has been domestic violence or other special factors;
- young people leaving local council care or special residential schools.

Budgeting loans

You may get a budgeting loan if:
- you have been on IS, income-based JSA, income-related ESA or PC for the past 26 weeks (disregarding one or more breaks of 28 days or less);
- you are not involved in a trade dispute;
- you do not have too much capital (the limit is £1,000, or £2,000 if you or your partner are aged over 60).

The budgeting loan must be for one or more of the following categories:
- furniture and household equipment;
- clothing and footwear;
- rent in advance and/or removal expenses;
- improvement, maintenance and security of the home;
- travelling expenses;
- expenses associated with seeking or re-entering work;
- hire purchase and other debts for any of the above items.

Crisis loans

You do not have to be entitled to IS, JSA, ESA or PC to claim a crisis loan. You may get a loan if you are aged 16 or over and require it to meet the immediate short-term needs of yourself and your family. The loan must be to meet expenses arising in an emergency, or as the consequence of a disaster, and the loan must be the only means of preventing serious damage or serious risk to the health and safety of yourself or your family. You must not have had more than two previous crisis loans for living expenses within the previous 12 months. This does not apply if it is an 'alignment payment' (loan made while you are waiting for a benefit claim to be processed) or there is a disaster or emergency which you could not have avoided.[29]

You cannot get a loan for service charges for fuel.[30] This is the only fuel-related item which is excluded. Fuel consumption and standing charges are not excluded.

Options for different fuel-related costs

Fuel bills

You cannot, in any circumstances, get a community care grant or a budgeting loan to pay for bills for the consumption of gas or electricity or any standing charges.[31] Consider applying for a crisis loan, particularly if:

- you do not qualify for Fuel Direct; *and*
- the installation of a prepayment meter is not safe or practicable; *and*
- there is a serious risk to your health if the supply is not reconnected/continued.

Connection and meter installation charges

You may be able to get a community care grant for the reasonable costs of fuel connection alongside any costs for furniture, furnishings, bedding and household equipment as part of a general start-up grant, particularly in situations where you are being resettled back into the community, are setting up home for the first time or following the breakdown of a relationship.

You should also apply for a community care grant for connection costs alone if this is your sole need. Relevant connection costs might include security deposits for the supply of your meter, or the costs of providing wiring or cables to connect your supply.

A community care grant may be made for the installation of prepayment meters, including the cost of any piping or wiring, if you have difficulty in budgeting for quarterly bills or if your family includes a child under five or with a disability.[32]

Reconnection charges

Community care grant guidance[33] says that a grant may be made if your supply has been disconnected and you are going onto Fuel Direct. If the debt leading to disconnection was caused by a breakdown in the direct payments system, ask the DWP for an ex gratia payment. (If you are not able to get a community care grant, you may be able to claim a crisis loan.)

If you are going onto Fuel Direct and cannot get a community care grant, the costs of reconnection should be added to your debt.

Re-siting a meter

There should be no charge when an electricity meter is re-sited to meet the needs of a disabled customer (see p123). A community care grant may be available for re-siting meters if a disabled person needs easier access. You may wish to consider this if your supplier refuses to re-site your meter free of charge.

Cost of replacing a damaged meter

Meter installations are not excluded items for community care grants or crisis loans.

Draughtproofing/insulation

Consider applying for energy efficiency scheme grant for these items (see p183).

Heaters

Community care grants may be made for the provision or repair of a heater to allow you to continue living in your home. Decision makers are advised to be aware of schemes to assist with energy efficiency.

Domestic appliances

The costs of installing domestic appliances may be met through a community care grant if you are moving to more suitable accommodation.

Challenging discretionary social fund decisions

If you are refused a discretionary social fund grant or loan, ask for a review of the decision. See CPAG's *Welfare Benefits and Tax Credit Handbook* for more information.

7. **Fuel Direct**

The Fuel Direct scheme allows an amount to be deducted from your benefit entitlement and paid directly to your energy supplier. To go onto the Fuel Direct scheme you must be in debt for gas or electricity and in receipt of income support (IS), income-based jobseeker's allowance (JSA), income-related employment and support allowance (ESA) or pension credit (PC).

For a Fuel Direct arrangement to be set up, the Department for Work and Pensions and your energy supplier both have to agree. The operation of Fuel Direct involves direct deduction from benefit for both current consumption and for debt recovery. The debt recovery rate is set at £3.60 (during 2013/14) a week, or £7.20 a week if you have debts for both gas and electricity.

Fuel Direct is also known as the DWP's third party deduction system.

Who is eligible for Fuel Direct

The decision to include you in the Fuel Direct scheme is made by a DWP decision maker. If you are in receipt of IS, income-based JSA, income-related ESA or PC, you are eligible for Fuel Direct. In some situations deductions can be made from contribution-based JSA or contributory ESA. You can ask to be included in the scheme or the relevant agency can include you (sometimes at the request of your supplier).

Deductions can be made from your benefit if:[34]
- your arrears for mains gas or mains electricity are greater than the IS rate for a single person aged 25 and above (£71.70 during 2013/14); *and*
- you will continue to need a fuel supply; *and*
- it is in your, or your family's, best interests for direct payments to be made.

You will normally be refused if:
- the above do not apply; *or*
- you already have a prepayment meter which has been reset to collect arrears (though if you have a prepayment meter for current consumption only, you could still have the arrears paid by Fuel Direct); *or*
- your supplier does not agree to you paying this way (but see below).

How to arrange Fuel Direct

Contact the DWP and the supplier if you want to pay by Fuel Direct. The DWP will contact your supplier to check that it agrees to you paying in this way and to get the figure to pay for your current consumption.

Before agreeing to deductions, check that you are the person liable for the bill (see Chapter 5).

If the amount of the deduction totals more than 25 per cent of your IS/JSA/ESA applicable amount or PC minimum guarantee (before housing costs), you must sign a form giving your consent for the deduction to take place. If you receive child tax credit (CTC) this calculation is 25 per cent of the total of your CTC, child benefit and IS/JSA/ESA applicable amount or PC minimum guarantee (before housing costs).[35] Do not delay returning this if you agree with the deductions.

If disconnection is being threatened, make sure that you are in regular contact with your supplier. Let your supplier know that you want to arrange or are arranging Fuel Direct. Suppliers will normally delay disconnection for a limited period if they know you are trying to do this.[36] Continue to stay in regular contact with your supplier, informing it about the progress of your application. Take the name and extension number of the person arranging Fuel Direct for you and always keep a note of when you called. It helps if you keep copies of letters/forms in the event of difficulties. If there are any delays, the supplier can be asked to delay disconnection for a longer period. Check with the DWP that your application has been received and is being dealt with. If disconnection is imminent, ask the DWP to phone the supplier to confirm that Fuel Direct is being arranged and that written confirmation will follow.

Deductions are made at the DWP office before you receive your benefit. If you disagree with any decision about deductions, you can appeal.

Deductions

Deductions can be made to cover arrears, or just to cover weekly costs after the debt has been cleared, or both.[37]

For arrears

- The maximum statutory deduction that can be made for electricity or gas is £3.60 for each fuel debt (in 2013/14).
- There is a total maximum deduction of £7.20 (in 2013/14) altogether for gas and electricity arrears.[38]

For current consumption

- Your energy supplier will advise the DWP of an estimate of your weekly consumption. This is usually calculated by looking at your consumption over the past year. It may be appropriate to look at alternative periods of time when calculating your estimated weekly consumption. If the amounts suggested seem high, ask for an explanation of the assumptions used in the calculation – errors are not uncommon. You will need to ensure that your supplier is not relying on estimated figures.
- The final decision on the amounts deducted rests with the DWP decision maker, who is not bound to accept the supplier's estimates of your current consumption.[39]
- The maximum deduction that can be made without your consent is 25 per cent of your IS, JSA or ESA 'applicable amount' or PC 'minimum guarantee' (your entitlement before any deductions for income, etc. are made). If you get CTC this calculation is 25 per cent of the total of your CTC, child benefit and IS/JSA/ESA applicable amount or PC minimum guarantee (before housing costs). This includes the combined amount of the deductions for arrears and current consumption.[40]
- If you disagree with the amounts proposed by the supplier, ask the decision maker for a different deduction. You will need to provide information about the assumptions in your own calculation. You will need to conduct your negotiations with care to ensure that the decision maker or the supplier does not assume that you are refusing to join the Fuel Direct scheme, as this could ultimately lead either to disconnection or to the imposition of a prepayment meter. If the decision maker does not agree to accept your calculations, you could always accept the supplier's calculation to ensure entry to the scheme, and then appeal to a tribunal.

Reviews of the amount of the deduction

The deduction for arrears is a fixed amount and cannot be varied. The figures for your current consumption will normally be reviewed regularly.

It is important to make sure that deductions are based on an actual reading of your meter. If the supplier bases your estimated future consumption on estimated readings of your meter, the amount of your deductions is likely to be wrong.

Ask the decision maker to review the amount of deduction if you can show that the calculation of the deduction is based on a mistake about a material fact.[41] The decision maker can ask the supplier to provide details of the basis of the supplier's calculation of estimated current consumption.

You may wish to request a review if you can provide evidence that your actual consumption is likely to be different. You may want to do this if:

- an actual meter reading shows that the supplier's calculation is based on wrong information;
- your consumption has increased or decreased because of a change in your circumstances such as the birth of a baby, a child leaving home, the need to remain at home more because of illness, a change in a heating system, major repairs or improvements to your home to aid energy efficiency – eg, loft insulation, double glazing, dry-lining of walls, draught proofing measures or changes to the way in which you use fuel as a result of energy advice.

You can request a review at any time a relevant change occurs. It is sensible to obtain the supplier's agreement to this, as this will make the decision-making process smoother.

Other direct deductions for debts

Other debts can also be paid by direct payments from benefit, and payment of these may be in competition with payments for fuel. The number of deductions for arrears is limited to a maximum of three. Regulations provide that debts will be paid in the following order of priority:[42]

- housing costs not covered by the mortgage payment scheme;
- rent arrears (and related charges);
- gas and electricity charges;
- water charges;
- council tax and community charge arrears;
- unpaid fines, costs and compensation orders;
- payments for the maintenance of children;
- repayment of integration loans;
- repayment of eligible loans;
- repayment of tax credit overpayments and self-assessment tax debts.

If you have arrears for both gas and electricity, the decision maker decides which debt takes priority.

The following debts can also be paid from benefit, but are not mentioned in the regulation governing priority between debts. You should argue that payments for gas or electricity take a higher priority than these debts:

- deductions for overpayments of benefit (but check that the overpayment is recoverable, and seek advice if necessary);
- loans from the social fund.

Change of circumstances

You have a duty to advise the DWP of any changes in your circumstances. This is a normal requirement for benefit claims, but is particularly important with respect to changes in energy supplier. If you switch your supplier for gas or electricity, you must immediately notify the DWP.

Sanctions

Benefit sanctions may affect the operation of Fuel Direct, reducing the amount of money from which it is possible to make a deduction. Benefit sanctions are potentially open to challenge by way of an appeal so you seek advice if you are sanctioned.

Universal credit

When universal credit is introduced, IS, income-based JSA and income-related ESA will eventually be abolished. It is planned that a Fuel Direct scheme will continue to operate under universal credit, allowing deductions to be made in respect of electricity and gas charges.[43]

Notes

2. **Cold weather payments and winter fuel payments**
   1 Reg 2(1) and (2) SFCWP Regs
   2 Reg 1A(1) SFCWP Regs
   3 Reg 1A(2) SFCWP Regs
   4 Reg 1(2) and Schs 1 and 2 SFCWP Regs
   5 Reg 1(2) SFCWP Regs
   6 Sch 1 SFCWP Regs
   7 Reg 3 SFCWP Regs
   8 Reg 2(6) SFCWP Regs
   9 Reg 2 SFWFP Regs
   10 Reg 3 SFWFP Regs
   11 Reg 1(2) and (3) SFWFP Regs
   12 Reg 2 SFWFP Regs
   13 Reg 2(2)(b) SFWFP Regs
   14 Reg 4 SFWFP Regs
   15 Reg 3(1)(b) SFWFP Regs
   16 Reg 36(2) SS(P&P) Regs

3. **Housing benefit**
   17 Sch 1 paras 5 and 6(1)(b) HB Regs; Sch 1 paras 5 and 6(1)(b) HB(SPC) Regs
   18 Sch 1 para 8 HB Regs; Sch 1 para 8 HB(SPC) Regs

19 Sch 1 para 8 HB(SPC) Regs
20 Sch 1 para 8 HB Regs; Sch 1 para 8
    HB(SPC) Regs
21 Sch 1 para 6(1) HB Regs; Sch 1 para 6(1)
    HB(SPC) Regs
22 Sch 1 para 6(1)(a) HB Regs; Sch 1 para
    6(1)(a) HB(SPC) Regs
23 Sch 1 para 6(2) HB Regs; Sch 6(2)
    HB(SPC) Regs
24 Sch 1 para 6(2) HB Regs; Sch 1 para 6(2)
    HB(SPC) Regs
25 Reg 12B(4) HB Regs; reg 12B(4)
    HB(SPC) Regs
26 Sch 1 para 6(4) HB Regs; Sch 1 para 6(4)
    HB(SPC) Regs
27 para A4 4.912-4.193 HBGM
28 *Gargett, R (on the application of) v
    London Borough of Lambeth* [2008]
    EWCA Civ 1450

5. The discretionary social fund
29 SF Dir 14C
30 SF Dir 23 (2)(f)
31 SF Dir 29
32 Part 2 paras 304-305 SFG
33 Part 2 para 206 SFG
34 Sch 9 para 6(1) SS(C&P) Regs
35 Sch 9 para 8(4) SS(C&P) Regs
36 See your supplier's code of practice for
    customers who need help with paying
    their bills
37 Sch 9 para 6(4) SS(C&P) Regs
38 Sch 9 para 6(2) SS(C&P) Regs
39 Sch 9 para 6(4) SS(C&P) Regs
40 Sch 9 para 8 SS(C&P) Regs
41 Sch 9 para 6(4) SS(C&P) Regs
42 Sch 9 para 9 SS(C&P) Regs
43 Reg 54 Universal Credit, Personal
    Independence Payment and Working-
    age Benefits (Claims and Payments)
    Regulations 2012 (draft)

Chapter 12

....

Energy efficiency and other sources of help

This chapter covers:
1. National energy efficiency schemes (below)
2. Energy efficiency schemes in England (p183)
3. Energy efficiency schemes in Wales (p185)
4. Energy efficiency schemes in Scotland (p186)
5. Help from the local authority (p188)
6. Other sources of help (p189)

1. National energy efficiency schemes

Energy efficiency has become an increasingly important part of the government's national energy strategy, which has the shared goals of reducing harmful emissions into the environment and tackling fuel poverty. It is widely accepted that the main cause of fuel poverty in the UK is a combination of low incomes, high fuel costs and poor energy efficiency.

Often people cannot afford to heat their homes to appropriate levels because their homes are badly insulated or in a poor state of repair, or because expensive or inefficient appliances are being used. Substantial savings in fuel bills can be achieved by introducing energy efficiency measures and adopting more energy efficient behaviours. Successive governments have seen better energy efficiency as playing a central role in improving living conditions for the fuel poor in the UK. Official statistics from the Department of Energy and Climate Change (DECC) show that in 2010, the number of fuel poor households in the UK was estimated at around 4.75 million, representing approximately 19 per cent of all UK households.[1] Since these figures were produced fuel prices have significantly increased and consumer organisations estimate that fuel poverty levels range from around 6.4–7 million households in 2012.

This chapter looks at what help and support is available, how to access it and who is eligible. See also Chapter 13 for information on how you can exercise your rights against low-standard properties.

Green Deal

The Energy Act 2011 made provisions for the introduction of Green Deal. It is designed to make energy efficiency improvements affordable by removing the upfront cost. The Green Deal is complemented by an additional initiative, the Energy Company Obligation, for low-income households and hard-to-treat properties (see p177).

The Green Deal Finance Company is a private sector consortium made up of energy companies, banks and 'trusted high street names'. It will finance the cost of the installations.

You can borrow up to £10,000, to be repaid over 25 years and will be recouped via electricity bills. One of the key principles behind the Green Deal is the **'golden rule'**, which states that savings on energy bills as a result of Green Deal installations should always equal or exceed the cost of the installation. For example, if your new energy saving measure saves you £15 a month on your fuel bill, your repayments must be £15 or less. If this golden rule is not met, Green Deal finance can only be provided up to the value of the expected savings and you will have to provide the rest of the capital costs, or will have to seek an Energy Company Obligation subsidy.

Tenants (social or private) and owner occupiers are eligible for the Green Deal. However, if you are a tenant, you should seek permission from your landlord before going ahead. Landlords are required to honour the Green Deal repayments in-between tenancies. If your landlord seeks a Green Deal assessment for the property you live in, if you are the electricity bill payer, the landlord must get your consent.

The funding package is 'attached' to the meter and the property, not the occupier. The funding will continue to be repaid if, for example, there is a tenure change. If the Green Deal measures are installed on a property that is being sold, the new owner takes over responsibility for the repayments (consent and disclosure regulations[2] provide protection for both consumers and landlords). As the Green Deal is attached to the meter not you, if you have an adverse credit history you should still be able get the finance package.

Green Deal repayments will appear on your electricity bill. If you have a prepayment meter the Green Deal charge will be collected via the meter in the same way as arrears are collected.

To take out a Green Deal, first make sure that your electricity supplier is participating in the scheme. Every supplier with more than 250,000 customers must participate – those with fewer customers can choose to do so. If you have an existing fuel debt of more than £200, the Green Deal provider has the discretion to carry out further credit checks before proceeding with a Green Deal plan.

You can still change energy supplier if you have a Green Deal plan, as long as your new supplier is participating in the Green Deal.

At the time of writing, some of the detail has still to be finalised. However, the organisations involved in delivery – utilities, finance providers and installers – will clearly need to cover their administrative costs and will expect a contribution to 'the bottom line'. It is particularly important that the basis for estimating savings for each measure installed is robust, since this will in turn form the basis (amount, timescale) for repayment of the funding package. It is expected that the interest rate on a Green Deal funding package will be approximately 7.5 per cent. Although Green Deal has a fixed interest rate, there is scope for Green Deal providers to increase the interest at agreed rates (up to 2 per cent per year) in recognition of the fact that there is likely to be an increase in savings resulting from increasing fuel prices.

The Green Deal process has four main stages.

- A trained and qualified Green Deal adviser will visit your home and conduct a survey. The adviser will take specific note of occupancy details and will identify what improvements could be made, what the financial savings should be and which measures might satisfy the golden rule.
- A tailored Green Deal plan will be produced, based on the packages available from Green Deal providers to fund the improvements. Once signed, this forms the contract between you and the provider.
- The provider will arrange for a Green Deal installer to carry out the work you have agreed to.
- You pay back the cost of the improvements over time through your electricity bill. Your electricity supplier will pass on payment to your Green Deal provider.

There are almost 50 areas of home improvement approved to receive Green Deal funding, including:

- **heating, ventilation and air conditioning** – eg, condensing boilers; heating controls; under-floor heating; heat recovery systems;
- **building fabric**: cavity wall insulation; loft insulation; flat roof insulation; internal wall insulation; external wall insulation; draught proofing; floor insulation; heating system insulation (cylinder, pipes); energy efficient glazing and doors;
- **water heating**: hot water systems; water efficient taps and showers;
- **microgeneration**: ground and air source heat pumps; solar thermal; biomass boilers; micro-CHP.

The Green Deal does not lend itself particularly well to helping the fuel poor. Many fuel poor households limit their fuel use because of low income. Accordingly, any improvements in household energy efficiency are often taken up in increased comfort levels. It may be more difficult for Green Deal assessors to estimate accurately what the potential savings, if any, are for a fuel poor household installing Green Deal measures. There will be extra help for those most in need such as the vulnerable, those on low incomes and those with homes that are expensive to treat via the Energy Company Obligation (see below).

It should be noted that there are a range of other policies and regulations that help promote energy efficiency and that will affect the impact of the Green Deal. These include the Renewable Heat Incentive (see p179), the Feed-in tariff regime (see p179, the mandated roll-out of smart meters (see p51) and building regulations. The government believes that the Green Deal will provide additional finance and complement these policies. The government expects that energy efficiency, renewable heat and electricity generation will be marketed together as a package of improvements.

Consumer protection is a key feature of the Green Deal. A Green Deal Oversight and Registration Body has been established. Its role includes:

- maintaining a register of all authorised Green Deal providers, certification bodies, advisors and installers;
- maintaining the Green Deal Code of Practice and ongoing monitoring of Green Deal participants against the Code;
- controlling the use of the Green Deal quality mark;
- producing an annual Green Deal report; *and*
- gathering evidence of non-compliance and referring participants to the Ombudsman or the Secretary of State where appropriate and imposing sanctions when directed.

See www.greendealorb.co.uk for more information or call 0300 123 1234 (England and Wales) or 0800 512 012 (Scotland).

Energy Company Obligation

To ensure that funding is available for improvements to properties where the Green Deal golden rule (see p175) is not satisfied, the Energy Act 2011 introduced powers to impose an 'Energy Company Obligation' (ECO). The ECO complements the Green Deal and seeks to alleviate fuel poverty by providing subsidies for the installation of insulation and heating measures to low-income and vulnerable households and insulation measures to local communities, where the golden rule is not met.

The ECO will particularly benefit:

- low-income and vulnerable households through the Affordable Warmth Obligation (see p178);
- those living in hard-to-treat properties where the Green Deal golden rule cannot be met through the Carbon Saving Obligation (see p178);
- those living in rural areas through the Carbon Saving Communities Obligation. This includes a target to provide a minimum of 15 per cent of its funding to rural communities.

Different measures may be used to satisfy each of the three ECO strands. Solid wall insulation and non-standard cavity wall insulation are measures which will be capable of satisfying the Carbon Saving Obligation and the Carbon Saving Communities Obligation. For the Affordable Warmth Obligation, any measure which reduces the notional cost of heating the property will count towards the target (including boiler repairs, if aftercare services are provided).

The cost of ECO will be passed on by the energy companies to all of their customers through their energy bills.

Affordable Warmth Obligation

This aims to provide free heating and hot water saving measures, insulation, glazing and microgeneration technologies to low-income and vulnerable households.

You are eligible if you are an owner-occupier or live in a private rented property and a member of your household gets:[3]

- child tax credit (CTC) and have a relevant income of £15,860 or less;
- working tax credit and has a relevant income of £15,860 or less and–
  - has parental responsibility for a child under 16 (or 16-19 in full-time education); *or*
  - is in receipt of a disabled worker element or severe disability element; *or*
  - is aged 60 years or over;
- pension credit;
- income-related employment and support allowance (work-related activity or support component), income-based jobseeker's allowance or income support and:
  - has parental responsibility for a child under 16 (or 16-19 in full-time education); *or*
  - receives one of the following qualifying components:
    - CTC which includes a disability or severe disability element;
    - a disabled child premium;
    - a disability premium, enhanced disability premium or severe disability premium; *or*
    - a pensioner premium, higher pensioner premium or enhanced pensioner premium.

Carbon Saving Obligation

This provides funding to insulate solid-walled properties (internal and external wall insulation) and homes with 'hard-to-treat' cavity walls.

It is not means-tested but will be used in conjunction with the Green Deal as the measures will not meet the golden rule due to the relatively high costs. If you are a tenant, you will have to seek the permission of your landlord.

Renewable Heat Incentive

Heat generated from renewable energy sources currently meets 1 per cent of the UK's total heat demand.[4] To reach the 2020 renewable energy target,[5] around 12 per cent of the UK's heat needs to be generated from renewable sources such as heat pumps, solar thermal panals and biomass biolers.

The Renewable Heat Incentive (RHI) is a payment for generating heat from renewable sources. RHI is set by the government, administered by Ofgem and paid for directly by the Treasury rather than passed onto consumers.

The main benefit of the RHI is a generation tariff, which is paid for every kilowatt-hour (kWh) of energy produced. The level of payment varies depending on the technology and the system size. The domestic phase of the RHI is likely to be introduced in summer 2013 and will introduce ongoing tariff support for renewable heat installations in domestic properties. By the time this phase of RHI is introduced, the Green Deal should be fully operational and payments for domestic households under this phase of RHI will be made conditional on you installing Green Deal financed thermal efficiency improvements.

Although domestic RHI will not start until 2013 the government has introduced support for households through the renewable heat premium payment scheme (see below).

Renewable Heat Premium Payment

The Renewable Heat Premium Payments (RHPP) are one-off payments intended to subsidise the installation of renewable heat technology in your home until the RHI is introduced for domestic customers (expected to be summer 2013). Basic energy saving measures such as loft and cavity wall insulation must be installed first. The amount received depends on the technology but ranges from £300 for solar thermal hot water to £1,250 for ground source heat pumps. Phase 2 of the RHPP scheme will end on 31 March 2013.

The government has set an upper spend limit of £70 million for 2012/13. Funding amounts announced in the spending review for 2013/14 and 2014/15 are unchanged.

The Energy Saving Trust (EST) is administering the RHPP on behalf of the DECC. For more information visit www.est.org.

Feed-in tariffs

Feed-in tariffs (FITs) have been introduced by the government to help increase the level of renewable energy in the UK towards the legally binding target of total energy from renewables by 2020.[6] Under this scheme energy suppliers must make regular payments to householders and communities who generate their own electricity from renewable or low carbon sources such as solar electricity panels or wind turbines.

The tariffs are paid for every kWh of electricity you generate if your own a renewable electricity system. They are applicable to households, landlords and businesses. If your system is certified by the Microgeneration Certification Scheme (MCS) it is eligible for FITs. It must also be fitted by a MCS approved installer.

FITs provide three benefits.

- A payment for electricity produced, even if you use it yourself. Tariffs are paid for up to 25 years and vary depending on the type and scale of the installation – details can be found on various websites, including DECC, Ofgem and EST. FITs payments are exempt from income tax. All generation and export tariffs are linked to the Retail Price Index.
- Additional payments for electricity exported to the grid. A payment of 4.5p/kwh is made for any surplus electricity generated and exported to the grid. This is a fixed rate (though there is the option to negotiate an alternative rate with an electricity supplier), regardless of the type of renewable technology.
- Your electricity bills will be reduced as you will be using energy produced by the renewable technology installed. Until or unless a smart meter is installed the export element will be deemed to be 50 per cent of the power generated by the renewable system.

Where ownership of a property changes, ownership of the generating technology also changes and the FITs payments will transfer to the new occupier.

To ensure complementarity with Green Deal objectives, from 1 April 2012, the full rate of FITs payments for domestic households installing solar PV became conditional on the building meeting Energy Performance Certificate (EPC) level D. An EPC survey produces information on a home's energy use and energy costs. EPCs carry ratings which measure the energy efficiency of a home using grades from A (most efficient) to G (lease efficient). The average rating at present is D.

FITs is being paid for by the energy suppliers (those with a customer base of more than 50,000 customers), however the costs for the scheme will ultimately be passed through to all electricity customers through increased prices.

Warm Home Discount

The Warm Home Discount (WHD) requires energy companies by law to give a discount on energy bills to some of their most vulnerable customers. This mandatory scheme has replaced the previous voluntary agreement with the energy companies. Over the four years of the scheme to 2015, WHD will be worth up to £1.1 billion and is expected to help around two million households a year. All suppliers with more than 250,000 customers must participate and suppliers with fewer customers can choose to participate.

Energy companies are required to provide a discount on electricity bills to a 'core group' of low-income pensioners (initially comprising those in receipt of the guarantee credit of pension credit (PC), expanding to include every pensioner in receipt of the savings credit element by 2015).

You may qualify for this energy discount if on 21 July 2012 (the qualifying date for 2012/13 discounts) if:

- your name, or your partner's name, is on your electricity bill; *and*
- you get your electricity from one of the participating energy suppliers; *and*
- you are either:
  - aged under 80 and receiving only the guarantee credit element of PC (no savings credit);
  - aged 80 or over and are receiving the guarantee credit of PC (even if you get savings credit as well).

Energy companies are also required to provide the same discount to a 'broader group' of customers, although they retain discretion over who will be eligible for the discount. The discount for customers in both the core and broader groups is £130, increasing to £140 in year four.

If you are eligible as part of the core group you do not initially need to apply for a WHD – you should receive this automatically. Alternatively, you may receive notification from the Department of Work and Pensions (DWP) that you should apply to your supplier (the DWP will provide the appropriate details when it contacts you).

Each supplier has slightly different eligibility criteria for their 'broader group' customers, though all have a focus on low-income and vulnerable people.

Contact your electricity supplier to ask if you might be eligible for a Warm Home Discount.

Warm Home Discount contact details for the biggest suppliers

British Gas (including Sainsbury's Energy)
direct debit/pay on billing customers   0800 072 8625
prepayment meter customers   0800 294 8604
email: homeenergycare.leeds@centrica.com

EDF Energy
All customers   0800 096 9000
www.edfenergy.com/products-services/for-your-home/safe-warm-and-well/
    warm-home-discount

E.on
All customers   0800 051 1480
www.eonenergy.com/At-Home/ExistingCustomers/Warm-Home-Discount

npower

All customers   0800 980 5525 or 0808 172 6999

www.npower.com/spreading_warmth/Content/WarmHomeDiscount

ScottishPower

All customers   0800 027 2700

www.scottishpower.co.uk/support-centre/service-and-standards/
   warm-home-discount

SSE (including Atlantic Energy, Scottish Hydro, Southern Electric, SWALEC, Ebico, Equipower and M&S Energy)

All customers   0800 300 111

www.southern-electric.co.uk/HelpAndAdvice/ExtraHelp/PriorityPlan

Other electricity suppliers participating in the WHD scheme are: Equigas, Manweb and Utility Warehouse.

Energy companies can also (with Ofgem approval) spend a maximum of £30 million a year on industry initiatives such as financing of organisations which refer customers in fuel poverty to suppliers, providing or funding benefit entitlement checks and also providing or funding energy efficiency measures.

The cost of the WHD scheme is passed on to customers via their fuel bills.

Advice and assistance from suppliers

The provision of guidance on energy efficiency for customers is a licence condition for domestic gas and electricity suppliers.[7] Suppliers are required to provide information on energy efficiency to customers and provide reports on those steps to Ofgem. Each supplier has to produce a code of practice on using fuel efficiently. A copy of each code should be available by telephoning the supplier. The codes say that suppliers will provide certain levels of advice on energy efficiency, including which appliances are best for using your supplies of fuel most efficiently.

Suppliers are using a range of delivery routes to meet their targets, the most successful being working directly with consumers. They also promote measures with social housing providers, retailers, manufacturers and by linking with the government programmes.

The supply companies employ trained staff offering advice on ways to save energy and cut your energy bills. In certain areas they can also arrange for a representative to visit your home and make recommendations as to ways of saving energy and money.

You may also be sent booklets on home energy efficiency, including details of grants and the supplier's own schemes. You may be asked questions about benefit entitlement and the circumstances of your household, as suppliers are now under obligations to target at least 40 per cent of their energy efficiency activity on customers in receipt of certain benefits. Research suggests that some suppliers provide more comprehensive advice than others, and the types of measures emphasised in advice may vary between suppliers. The quality of energy efficiency advice provided to consumers by suppliers is monitored by Ofgem, which has reported general improvements in recent years. Ofgem monitors progress in energy efficiency measures of the big six energy companies and publishes regular reports.

The big six suppliers

Scottish/British Gas	0845 971 7731
ScottishPower	0845 601 7836
Scottish Hydro	0800 072 7201
E.ON	0500 201 000
EDF	0800 096 9966
npower	0800 02 22 20

Details of other measures, improvements and costings are also available from the EST and from suppliers.

2. Energy efficiency scheme in England

Warm Front scheme

The Warm Front scheme will end in March 2013 and will be replaced by the Green Deal (see p175).

If you need help paying for heating and insulation improvements in your privately owned or rented home, you may be able to get money from the Warm Front grants scheme. The scheme is funded by the government and is managed by Carillion Energy Services. Warm Front provides support to vulnerable groups in, or at risk of, fuel poverty. This typically includes low-income households and families, disabled and elderly groups.

The Warm Front package covers:
- loft insulation;
- draughtproofing;
- cavity wall insulation;

- hot water tank insulation;
- heating systems:
- gas room heaters with thermostat controls;
- gas, electric or oil central heating;
- converting a solid fuel open fire to a modern glass fronted fire;
- timer controls for electric space and water heaters;
- energy advice.

To qualify for Warm Front, the property must be:
- your own home – or if you rent it from a private landlord you must have the landlord's permission;
- poorly insulated and/or not have a working central heating system;
- in England.

You or someone who lives with you must be in receipt of a one of the following qualifying benefits:
- pension credit – the guaranteed credit or savings credit element;
- income-related employment and support allowance – the support group or work-related activity component;
- child tax credit (CTC) and your income is £15,860 or less;
- working tax credit and your income is £15,860 or less; *and*
  - you are responsible for a child under 16 who ordinarily lives with you (or under 20 if s/he is in education or training); *or*
  - you get the disabled worker or severe disability element; *or*
  - you are 60 or over;
- income support or income-based jobseeker's allowance; *and*
  - you are responsible for a child under 16 who ordinarily lives with you (or under 20 if s/he is in education or training); *or*
  - you get the disability or severe disability element of CTC; *or*
  - you get a disabled child premium; *or*
  - you get the severe or enhanced element of disability premium; *or*
  - you get the higher or enhanced premium of pensioner premium.

An appointed engineer will complete a survey of the work needed at your property and will make recommendations on which energy efficiency improvements are most appropriate. You should be aware that the surveyor may find that the energy efficiency of your home is above the threshold required to benefit from the scheme. If this is the case you will not be provided with any recommendations and you will be left with details of where else you may be able to get energy advice and help.

Grants of £3,500 (or up to £6,000 if your home needs oil central heating) are available. The payment is made directly to the company that does the work. You do not have to pay anything so long as the work does not cost more than the grant. You should seek to establish the costs as soon as possible. In some cases you might have to pay towards the work but wherever possible, the scheme will try to cover these costs.

The Standard Assessment Procedure (SAP), is the government's recommended system for measuring the energy rating of residential properties. To be eligible for Warm Front your home must have a SAP rating of 63 or below.

You can find out if you qualify for a Warm Front grant over the phone; benefit checks can also be undertaken. To apply, call 0800 316 2805 (textphone 0800 072 0156) or email enquiry@carillionplc.com.

3. **Energy efficiency scheme in Wales**

Nest

Nest is the Welsh government scheme designed to make private sector households warmer and healthier. The Welsh government is committed to eradicating fuel poverty, as far as is reasonably possible, in all households by 2018. Nest ensures that everyone in Wales has access to advice and support to help them reduce their fuel bills and reduce the risk of fuel poverty.

Nest offers advice and a full home energy assessment. For the most energy inefficient homes, Nest can provide, at no cost to you, home improvements including:

- a new central heating boiler;
- insulation for a hot water cylinder;
- loft, cavity wall and solid wall insulation;
- draught proofing for doors and windows;
- renewable energy technologies such as solar panels.

To qualify for Nest, the property must be:

- your own home – or if you rent it from a private landlord you must have the landlord's permission;
- energy inefficient (F or G rated);
- in Wales.

You or someone who lives with must be in receipt of a one of the following qualifying benefits:

- child tax credit and your income is £15,860 or less;
- council tax benefit (due to be localised from April 2013);
- housing benefit;
- income-based jobseeker's allowance;
- income-related employment and support allowance;
- income support;

- pension credit;
- working tax credit and your income is £15,860 or less.

To apply call 0808 808 2244 (free from a landline or a mobile phone).

4. **Energy efficiency schemes in Scotland**

Home Energy Scotland

The Scottish government currently has two programmes to help households become more energy efficient and save money on fuel bills. These are the Energy Assistance Package and the Universal Home Insulation Scheme.

The Scottish government has created a 'one stop shop' approach to communicate its programmes – Home Energy Scotland. Home Energy Scotland is funded by the Scottish government and managed by the Energy Saving Trust (EST) via its network of advice centres.

The network will help you access grants from the Scottish government and energy supply companies and offers an energy home help service. Advice network services are provided on a regional basis by experienced and expert local organisations working under contract to the EST, giving full geographical coverage across Scotland.

To apply, call the hotline on 0800 512 012, or complete an online home energy check at www.energysavingtrust.org.uk/scotland and an adviser will call you back.

Energy Assistance Package

The Energy Assistance Package aims to help maximise incomes, reduce fuel bills and improve the energy efficiency of homes. It replaces the Central Heating and Warm Deal programmes. It is managed by the EST on behalf of the Scottish government.

The package has four stages.

- Stage 1: free energy advice by phone (0800 512 012). This is open to all households in Scotland.
- Stage 2: benefit and tax credits checks and advice on low cost energy tariffs to those at risk of fuel poverty.
- Stage 3: a package of insulation measures (cavity wall and loft insulation). You qualify if you are a homeowner or the tenant of a private landlord and you or your partner is:
  - aged 70 or over and you have no central heating; *or*
  - aged 75 or over; *or*
  - receive a qualifying benefit.

  If you are a tenant renting from a local authority or registered social landlord, similar insulation measures may be available to you funded through a partnership between your landlord, the Scottish government and energy companies. For information, contact your landlord.

- Stage 4: a package of enhanced energy efficiency measures to those who are most vulnerable to fuel poverty. These will make your home warmer and cheaper to heat and include installation of heating systems or a new boiler. You qualify if you are a homeowner or the tenant of a private sector landlord and you or your partner is:
  - aged 60 or over and you have no central heating system in your home;
  - a home owner or the tenant of a private sector landlord and you live in an energy inefficient home and you or your partner:
    - is aged 75 or over;
    - is aged 60 or over and receives a qualifying benefit;
    - has a child under 16 and receives a qualifying benefit;
    - is pregnant and receives a qualifying benefit.

Help may also be available if you live in a mobile home.

Universal Home Insulation Scheme

The Universal Home Insulation Scheme (UHIS) began in 2010, and provides varying levels of grants to local authorities across Scotland to undertake targeted energy efficiency improvements that are free to all households in defined areas.

The second phase of the scheme is currently available in areas selected and put forward by local authorities, which are also responsible for the administration of the scheme. This allows free energy efficiency measures to be offered to around 200,000 households. In addition to loft and cavity wall insulation, some of the schemes provide support for harder-to-treat properties.

In the current phase, local authorities have targeted areas that are most in need of free insulation and other energy efficiency measures. This includes rural and urban communities which have not benefited from previous insulation schemes.

In November 2011, a UHIS loan fund was also opened, offering interest free loans in UHIS areas for more expensive insulation measures, including renewables and boiler replacement to improve energy efficiency.

To find out if you live in a UHIS area and what UHIS can offer you, call the Home Energy Scotland Hotline on 0800 512 012.

Landlord boiler scrappage scheme

If your home is rented and you have a G-rated boiler, your landlord may be able to get a voucher for £400 towards replacing it. The Scottish government-funded scheme operates on a first-come first-served basis. Landlords can apply by calling the Home Energy Hotline on 0800 512 012.

5. **Help from the local authority**

Home improvement grants in England and Wales

Local housing authorities in England and Wales have discretionary powers to improve living conditions in their areas. You may be able to get a grant or discount to help you to improve the energy efficiency of your home. Your eligibility depends on what is available from your council, and in many areas you will need to be receiving a means-tested benefit. Contact your local council for more information about grants and schemes in your area.

Help from social services

In England and Wales, local councils have duties under s17 of the Children Act 1989 to provide services to safeguard and promote the welfare of children in need and promote the upbringing of such children by their families. This would include negotiating with a supplier on your behalf when necessary. The equivalent provision in Scotland is s 22 of the Children (Scotland) Act 1995.

In exceptional circumstances, this can also include providing assistance in cash; a policy not to provide such assistance in any circumstances at all would almost certainly be unlawful, and could be challenged by way of judicial review (see Chapter 14). If such payments are available, you can argue that they can be used to meet all or part of a fuel bill, to buy alternative means of cooking or heating, or to provide other aids for keeping warm, such as blankets. Social services may also be able to help you negotiate with your supplier.

In Scotland, there are also powers under section 12 of the Social Work (Scotland) Act 1968 to promote social welfare by 'making available advice, guidance and assistance' to people in need aged 18 or over. This can include giving assistance in kind or, in exceptional circumstance, in cash, where giving assistance would avoid you needing greater assistance from the local authority at a future date.

If you are seeking help from social services in an emergency – because, for example, the supplier is threatening disconnection – then you should tell the supplier. Suppliers' codes of practice allow for a delay in disconnection, normally for about two weeks, while a local council investigates whether it can help, but this delay will only happen if you ensure the supplier knows of the council's involvement.

Social workers may also have good links with and/or be prepared to make referrals to charities for you.

See also p207 on local councils' powers in England and Wales to protect occupiers and tenants when an owner or landlord fails to pay fuel or water bills.

People with disabilities

Local councils also have powers to assist adults with severe disabilities. They must decide whether or not to use these powers if asked to do so by the disabled person or her/his carer. See Disability Alliance's *Disability Rights Handbook*, for more details.

Each supplier has a code of practice on services for older and disabled people (see Chapters 1 and 14). In addition, the Disability Discrimination Act 1995 and the Disability Discrimination Act 2006 may apply in cases where a disabled person is treated less favourably than an able-bodied person.

6. Other sources of help

Energy Saving Trust

The Energy Saving Trust (EST) is an impartial organisation helping people to save energy and reduce carbon emissions. It offers free, impartial advice and information.

The EST database contains details of hundreds of energy saving grants and discounts, including those from the government and energy suppliers. The EST can help you identify available grants and discounts.

The EST has teams based in Scotland, Ireland and Wales and has a regional structure in England. Its free-phone number, 0800 512 012, will automatically put you through to your local advice centre.

Measures to save energy

The EST has produced information on the ways in which you can reduce your fuel bills. A number of these cost-saving measures are listed below.

No-cost measures	
Central heating	Turn the thermostat down by 1°C.
Hot water	Set the cylinder temperature to 60°C/140°F (though 63°C–65°C provides protection against health risks, a lower temperature may not kill all germs during hand washing); use a plug in basin/sink rather than running water.
Curtains	Close curtains at dusk to conserve heat.
Lights and appliances	Turn lights and appliances off when not in use, as standby uses electricity. Cool food before putting in the fridge or freezer, and pack empty spaces with crumpled newspaper. Fill the kettle with the amount of water you need. Wash on low temperature with full loads. Choose the right size pans for cooking, with lids on.

Low-cost measures

Fit energy saving light bulbs.

Insulate hot water tanks and pipes.

Fix dripping taps.

Draughtproof exterior doors, letter box and keyholes.

Shower rather than bath.

Home Heat Helpline

Home Heat Helpline is a free national service to help electricity and gas customers who are considered to be vulnerable. It is funded by the energy companies and is aimed particularly at those who:

- are of pensionable age;
- have young children and are on a low income; *or*
- are disabled or have a long-term health condition.

The helpline may be able to help you by:

- identifying ways to save energy;
- explaining how to access reduced and social tariffs;
- helping with applications for grants for free home insulation;
- enabling you to join the priority service register (see p97);
- helping agree a flexible payment option if you have fallen behind on bill payment;
- carrying out a benefit entitlement check;
- providing a disconnection safety.

In addition to providing support for individuals, the Helpline handles calls from care professionals, community workers and from organisations such as the Citizens Advice Bureau and housing providers.

Call the Helpline on 0800 33 66 99 (minicom 0800 027 2122). It also offers an online enquiry service at www.homeheathelpline.org.uk.

Citizens Advice

Citizens Advice has been working on the **Energy Best Deal** public awareness campaign with support from the energy regulator Ofgem and major energy companies since 2008. Energy Best Deal has now improved the confidence of over 94,000 domestic energy customers across England and Wales to shop around, reduce their bills and get help if they are falling behind with paying for their fuel. Energy Best Deal Scotland has delivered a similar service to frontline advisers throughout Scotland.

Practical presentations are delivered to low-income consumers and front-line staff who work with people at risk of fuel poverty. Sessions last about 45 minutes and include advice ranging from negotiating with utility suppliers to accessing insulation grants. Information is also provided on where to get further help on benefit entitlements.

Priority service register

Energy suppliers are required to keep a register of priority service customers who, by virtue of being of pensionable age, disabled or long-term sick, require information or advice on the special services available. See p97 for more information.

National Energy Action

National Energy Action develops and promotes energy efficiency services to tackle the insulation and heating problems of low-income households. It aims to eradicate fuel poverty and campaigns for greater investment in energy efficiency to help those who are poor or vulnerable. See www.nea.org.uk for more information.

Energy Action Scotland

Energy Action Scotland (EAS) campaigns for an end to fuel poverty in Scotland and is the only national body with this sole remit. EAS seeks to develop and promote effective solutions to the problem of cold, damp and expensive-to-heat homes. See Appendix 1 for contact details.

The Energy Ombudsman

The Energy Ombudsman is an independent body which resolves outstanding energy disputes. It is a free service which deals with complaints about energy companies that provide gas and/or electricity to your home. All companies involved in providing gas or electricity to domestic or small business consumers must be members of the scheme. See Chapter 14 for more information.

Charities

Some charities, particularly charities for ex-service personnel, offer help to meet fuel bills. It is helpful if an advice agency or social worker can write to the charity to explain your circumstances. The *Charities Digest* (available in reference libraries) lists relevant charities. Another very useful book is *A Guide to Grants for Individuals in Need*. Your local reference library also may be able to help locate useful local charities.

Turn2us (www.turn2us.org.uk) is a charitable service which can help you access grants and financial help, and has an online benefits calculator.

However, the demand for charitable payments is high. It is likely that many charities will refuse to help with fuel debts if Fuel Direct or some other budgeting scheme is available. If you are on income support or housing benefit, check that a charitable payment does not affect your benefit.

Trust funds and foundations

Some energy companies have trust funds to help customers who are in debt, or may fund projects which provide support for the fuel poor.

British Gas and Scottish Gas

All customers of British Gas and Scottish Gas with current debt are able to apply to the British Gas Energy Trust Fund. This offers grants to clear arrears of:

- domestic gas/electricity bills;
- other essential domestic bills or purchase of essential household items.

Apply online at www.britishgasenergytrust.org.uk or phone 01733 421060 for more information.

EDF Energy

All EDF Energy customers with current debt are able to apply to the EDF Energy Trust Fund. The EDF scheme also extends to customers of London Energy, Seeboard Energy and SWEB Energy.

The EDF Energy Trust offers grants:

- to clear gas or electricity debt;
- to help with other essential household bills and appliance purchases.

Download or complete a form online at www.edfenergytrust.org.uk or phone 01733 421060.

E.ON

The E.ON Caring Energy Fund aims to assist E.ON customers who are living in low-income households (a household income of less than £16,040 a year and savings below £8,000). It can offer payments in full or part to cover the cost of repairing or installing heating measures or essential household appliances.

Call on freephone 0800 051 1480 for more information.

npower

npower's Energy Trust may provide one-off payments (further assistance payments) for household bills, energy arrears or essential household appliances.

Visit www.npowerenergytrust.org.uk for more information or phone 01733 421060.

ScottishPower

No specific scheme available for individual consumers. Not-for-profit organisations can apply for funding to provide support for those in fuel poverty. Priority is given to projects aimed at helping families with young children.

Apply at www.energypeopletrust.com or call 0141 568 3492.

Notes

1. **National energy efficiency schemes**
   1 DECC, Annual Report on Fuel Poverty Statistics 2012
   2 The Green Deal (Disclosure) Regulations 2012
   3 Sch 1 Electricity and Gas (Energy Company Obligation) Order 2012 No.3018
   4 DECC, Impact of Assessment Proposals for a UK Renewable Energy Strategy-Renewable Heat URN09D/685
   5 2009 Renewable Energy Directive 2009/28/EC
   6 2009 Renewable Energy Directive 2009/28/EC
   7 Electricity Act 1989; condition 31 Standard Conditions of Electricity Supply Licence

Chapter 13

....

You, your landlord and fuel

This chapter covers:
1. Introduction (below)
2. Rent increases for fuel or fuel-related services (p195)
3. Resale of fuel by a landlord (p204)
4. Defective housing and heating systems (see p210)

---

1. Introduction

Most arrangements for payment of gas or electricity are made directly with the supplier. However, some tenants pay for fuel or fuel-related services (such as heating, cooking, lighting or hot water) indirectly through their landlord – ie, the supplier supplies the fuel to the landlord who resells it to the tenant. Frequently a landlord will:

- provide gas or electricity, pay the bill and recover charges from tenants by sharing out costs on a fixed or variable basis;
- pay the bill and recover charges from tenants by using a coin meter or other payment system; *or*
- provide heating from a central boiler and recover charges on a fixed or variable basis.

It can be more economical if your landlord provides fuel-related services – eg, a common boiler in a block of flats may be relatively cheap. However, the involvement of your landlord can lead to disputes over the amount charged for fuel or heating, or over your position if your landlord fails to pay the bills. You need to think carefully before beginning a dispute with your landlord.

Always consider the strength of your position. For a tenant, this means considering how secure the tenancy is. This depends on the type of tenancy you have (protected, statutory, assured, assured shorthold, secure or none of these). A full discussion of security of tenure is outside the scope of this book, but it is an important issue because, for example, if you have no security and start a dispute with your landlord, you could end up losing your home.

The government is encouraging tenants to occupy energy efficient homes. Since 1 October 2008, a landlord must provide an 'energy performance certificate' providing details of the energy efficiency of the home (see p218).

2. Rent increases for fuel or fuel-related services

The circumstances in which your landlord can increase your rent because of increases in charges for fuel or fuel-related services depend partly on whether you have a council or non-council tenancy. If you are a non-council tenant, your rights will also vary according to whether you took up the tenancy before or after 15 January 1989 (2 January 1989 in Scotland) – see p201. A landlord's power to increase charges for fuel or fuel-related services can be limited in one of three ways.

- Payments for fuel or fuel-related services are 'service charges', so legislation which affects service charges may be relevant.
- The courts have held that fuel charges are normally part of the rent,[1] so where legislation controls the rent, fuel charges are included.
- A tenancy agreement is a type of contract and may include limits on your landlord's power to increase charges.

For charges to be recoverable they must be agreed by both parties at the beginning of the contract or by you both agreeing during the agreement.

For the position regarding employers who provide accommodation, see p218.

Council tenancies

You have a **'council tenancy'** if your landlord is a local authority, unless you have used your 'right to buy' or if, in England and Wales, your tenancy has a fixed term of more than 21 years. Most council tenancies are called 'secure tenancies', with changes to rights of succession being made by the Localism Act 2011.[2]

In England and Wales, there is no law dealing with service charges or rent control for council tenants. The Secretary of State has the power to make regulations covering heating charges, but this has not been used.[3]

In Scotland, local authorities are limited to making service charges which they think are 'reasonable in all the circumstances'.[4] There is no definition of 'reasonable' (see p201), but if you think the charges are unreasonable, you can apply for a judicial review (see Chapter 14).

Otherwise, the only protection for council tenants is contractual. If fuel or fuel-related services are provided as part of your tenancy, a failure to provide these is a breach of contract. If there is such a breach, you can go to court to claim damages (ie, compensation) and a court order requiring the local council to obey the terms of the tenancy agreement.

The terms of your tenancy may be contained in a written statement, in which case any terms relating to fuel or fuel-related services will be clear. However, often not everything is in writing – sometimes there is no written agreement at all. You will then have to work out whether your fuel problem is covered by terms implied in your tenancy. An **'implied term'** is one which, although not written down, is considered by the courts to be included automatically in any tenancy.

Every tenancy agreement in England and Wales has an implied term that the landlord will allow a tenant to have 'quiet enjoyment' and that the landlord will not interfere with or interrupt a tenant's ordinary use of the premises. In this case, that would mean not interfering in any way with your use of fuel or fuel-related services. The Scottish equivalent is the tenant's right to full possession of her/his premises, which has the same effect.

In England and Wales, terms will also be implied by the Supply of Goods and Services Act 1982 which says that services must be provided with reasonable care and skill, within a reasonable time and at a reasonable charge.[5] Problems with fuel supply or fuel-related services can often come within these terms. In Scotland, similar terms may be implied into the contract by common law.

Local authority heating systems

All local authorities have the power to produce and sell heat, including electricity which is produced by renewable sources.[6] There is no specific protection in relation to heating charges, but the authority must:

- keep a separate account of them;[7] *and*
- when fixing the charges, act in good faith, not for ulterior or unlawful purposes, and within the reasonable limits of a reasonable local council;[8] *and*
- comply with the law on maximum charges for resale of fuel (see p204).

London boroughs have additional powers in respect of the provision of heating by hot water or steam.[9] They may prescribe scales of heating charges which apply, unless there is a specific agreement setting different charges.[10] The charges must be shown separately on rent books, demand notes or receipts, and be differentiated from rent generally.

London boroughs are not allowed to subsidise heating. When providing heat or setting charges, they must not show 'undue preference' or exercise 'undue discrimination'.[11] Some preference or discrimination is inevitable, as not all tenants paying the same charges will be provided with identical heat. To decide if the preference or discrimination is 'undue', consider:

- the cost of providing the heat to you compared with the cost of providing it to other tenants;
- the level and consistency of heat;
- restrictions or terms governing the heat provided – eg, in winter only.

If you can show undue preference or discrimination, you can recover the amount you have been overcharged by taking legal action (see Chapter 14).

If you suspect that the local authority is charging more for heat and power than the actual cost to itself, the actual costs may be obtained by use of the Freedom of Information Act 2000. Under the Act public authorities are bound to make available information within 21 days of a written request, unless the information falls into a number of restricted categories.

London boroughs have a choice to use either the general power which all local councils have, or the power which is specific to them. They have more freedom if they exercise the more general power. It is not clear how the two powers relate. If a borough has resolved to apply the general power (which came into force on 14 February 1977), then the position will be clear for tenancies starting after that date. If a tenancy started before that date and has simply continued, then a court may decide that the more detailed powers apply.

Challenging the way heating is provided

If you challenge the legality of the way a heating system is being run or charges for heat, complex legal issues arise. As well as the matters mentioned, a court can consider such matters as whether the local authority charges tenants for:

- assumed heat delivery instead of actual heat delivered, if there is a significant difference;
- heating costs which are significantly higher than those of other heating systems;
- amounts unrelated to heat delivered or assumed to be delivered.

When some heating is provided but it is inadequate, it is difficult to prove that there has been a breach of the tenancy agreement unless there is a specific agreement stating how much heating is to be provided and at what times of the year. If nothing is specifically agreed or set out in the tenancy agreement, there is probably an implied term that 'reasonable heat' should be provided, but this is extremely vague. If there is a dispute, keep a detailed diary of when the heating was sufficient, when it was inadequate or off altogether, and even when there was too much.

Tenants' group pressure

Because of the difficulties with such legal proceedings, it may be easier and more effective for tenants' associations to put pressure on a local authority to change the way it manages the heating system or the charges for it. In challenging high heating charges, these are some of the matters your tenants' association can look at:

- copies of local council committee reports on heating systems and charging policies;

- a comparison of income from, and expenditure on, individual estate systems and across a local council area;
- expenditure charged to the heating account: does it include all fuel expenditure, maintenance, insurance, caretakers' wages, interest on the cost of the system; is this consistent with other public landlords?;
- district heating systems: the number of dwellings supplied, the costs and type of fuel used;
- level of service: heating and hot water, hours per day, winter and summer, temperature standards assumed and achieved;
- method of calculation of charges: pooling of costs, property by property, flat charge, charges related to size and number of bedrooms;
- energy efficiency of dwellings: insulation quality, double-glazing; a temperature survey could be organised to find out what heat is being delivered. Temperatures in all rooms at different times of the day can be measured simultaneously in a number of dwellings.

Requests made under the Freedom of Information Act 2000 may assist in obtaining relevant information from local authorities. Where a request is made in writing, the local authority must supply the requested information within 21 days, unless it falls into an exempt category. There is a right of appeal to the Information Commissioner's Office against a refusal to supply information.

Heating standards

In England and Wales, your home has to have adequate provision of heating if it is to be regarded as 'fit for human habitation'. According to the government's guidance, **'adequate provision'** means heating which provides a temperature of 18°C in the main living room and 16°C in all other rooms when the outside air temperature is -1°C.[12] However, for England, Wales or Scotland, a local authority may provide heating to another standard which it has set for itself. These are examples of standards in use:

- Chartered Institute of Building Surveyors: from the mid-1970s, recommended 21°C in living rooms, 18°C in kitchens and 16°C in hallways and bedrooms.
- British Standards Institution (Code of Practice BS5449): 21°C in living rooms and dining rooms, 22°C in bathrooms, 18°C in bedrooms, kitchens and toilets, and 16°C in hallways.

In Scotland, a property is considered uninhabitable if is deemed 'below tolerable standard' which may include lacking in satisfactory provision for heating. Local authorities may take action regarding properties which fall below this standard under powers contained in Housing (Scotland) Act 2006.

Some landlords use their own standards. Ask your local authority what standards it uses, as these will probably be used in setting the charges.

Non-council tenancies

If your landlord is not a local authority, legislation on variable service charges and on rent control applies. The legislation on variable service charges does not apply in Scotland (see p201), but there are some court cases which give rights to tenants in this area. The provisions for rent control are different for all tenancies granted before 15 January 1989 compared with most of those granted after 15 January 1989 (2 January 1989 in Scotland).

Variable service charges in England and Wales

In England and Wales, variable service charges are covered by the Landlord and Tenant Act 1985.[13] If your landlord used to be a council but it sold the property to a private landlord, then you have similar rights under the Housing Act 1985.[14]

Variable service charge

This is an amount payable by a tenant as part of or in addition to rent – directly or indirectly for services – the whole or part of which varies according to the landlord's costs or estimated costs.[15]

This is a broad definition and includes payments for electricity or gas, whether made directly to the landlord or indirectly through a landlord's meter. As long as the rent varies according to the landlord's costs, it does not matter whether a charge is simply a share of a bill (with little or no regard to your actual consumption) or an accurate assessment of your consumption. These provisions apply to all tenants unless you are:

- a tenant of a local council or any other public authority (eg, a housing action trust), unless your lease is for over 21 years or was granted under the 'right to buy' legislation;[16] *or*
- a tenant whose rent has been registered with a service charge stated to be a fixed sum.[17]

Note that tenancies with variable service charges may have these treated as fixed-sum charges if the mechanism of variation is unreasonable.

Your landlord can recover the costs of the services s/he provides (eg, as heat, light or cooking facilities) only if the service is of a 'reasonable' standard and the costs are 'reasonably' incurred.[18] There is no one definition of 'unreasonable', but it includes something which can be proved to be excessive. What is reasonable is a question of fact and degree.[19]

If the charges are based on an estimate in advance, the estimate must be reasonable and, after the costs have actually been incurred, the charges must be adjusted by repayment, reduction of future charges or additional charges, whichever is appropriate. If they are paid in arrears, most charges cannot relate to periods of more than 18 months before.[20] Similarly, charges may not be reasonable to impose where major works are undertaken and charged to an individual tenant or leaseholder who may only have a short period left in occupation of the property.[21]

You are not liable for any costs included for any service charge which was incurred more than 18 months before a demand for payment of the service charge is served. Only if you are served with a notice in writing during the 18 months that the costs have been incurred and you are required to meet them will a right to recover the charges arise.[22]

If you think service charges should not be payable, apply to a leasehold valuation tribunal (LVT) to rule on these questions.[23] In England, the procedure before an LVT is governed by the Leasehold Valuation Tribunal (Procedure) (England) Regulations 2003. There is no prescribed form of application. A letter may suffice, providing it contains certain prescribed matters;[24] alternatively a standard form may be used which can be obtained from the tribunal. Advice should be taken before commencing an application. A landlord may agree to reduce the charges before going as far as the LVT hearing.

The county court also has the power to make declarations on the same points but you will normally be expected to use the tribunal.

Access to information

The right to challenge unreasonable charges would be almost useless without access to supporting information about how the charges are made up. You have the right to require your landlord to provide information; your request must be in writing. Your landlord must provide a written summary of costs incurred over 12-month periods, and must comply within six months of your request.[25]

If the service charges are payable by tenants of more than four dwellings together, the summary of costs must be provided by a qualified accountant.[26] This is aimed mostly at tenants such as those in mansion blocks, but it also applies if you live in a house in multiple occupation.[27]

Within six months of receiving the summary of costs, you can require your landlord to allow you to inspect accounts and receipts. You can also make copies of any documents at a reasonable charge.[28] This is particularly useful if you suspect you are being overcharged.

It may be more effective to exercise these rights through a tenants' association. If members' tenancies require them to contribute to the same costs, a tenants' association can apply to the landlord to become a 'recognised tenants' association'.[29] If the landlord does not agree to this, the association can apply to the local rent assessment committee for a certificate requiring the landlord to recognise it. It can then exercise the rights to information on behalf of its members.

County court proceedings

The county court also has the power to make declarations on the same points[30] under the Landlord and Tenant Act 1985, but you are normally expected to use the LVT. The county court has the power to transfer proceedings to the LVT where a question within the jurisdiction of the LVT arises.[31] Note that the LVT has no power to deal with costs incurred in court proceedings or subsequent to the transfer. This is a matter which the court should take into consideration when deciding whether or not to ask for or agree a transfer.

Variable service charges in Scotland

The legislation mentioned above for variable service charges does not apply in Scotland. To find out if there is any limit on your landlord's discretion to increase charges for fuel or fuel-related services, look at your written tenancy agreement if you have one. If there is a term which covers how service charges can be increased, then that will apply.

If there is no such term or it is unclear, then the courts may be prepared to introduce an 'implied term' (see p195) into the tenancy agreement. In one case,[32] the court introduced an implied term that any service charge had to be 'fair and reasonable'. The court also decided that a surveyor's certificate claiming that the charges were reasonable was not valid because it was the landlord himself who signed the certification in his role as the surveyor.

Rent control

> If it is not clear what kind of tenancy you have, refer to any standard text on the law of landlord and tenant.

Rent control is relevant to payments made to a landlord for fuel and fuel-related services because such payments are normally part of the rent; therefore, the payments can be increased only if the rent can be increased.

The Rent Act 1977 and the Rent (Scotland) Act 1984 used to provide a comprehensive system of rent control. However, they do not apply to most tenancies which started after 15 January 1989 in England and Wales, or 2 January 1989 in Scotland, as these are covered by the Housing Act 1988 or the Housing (Scotland) Act 1988. The new system of rent control under these later Acts is so loose that it is virtually useless as a tool for limiting rises in charges for fuel or fuel-related services and is not, therefore, covered in this book.

Tenancies granted before 15 January 1989 (England and Wales) or 2 January 1989 (Scotland)

There are different rent control systems for:
- tenancies which are regulated – ie, protected or statutory; *and*

- tenancies which are restricted/Part VII contracts. It is outside the scope of this book to discuss the different types of tenancy, but a restricted contract can be said to include most tenancies where the landlord is resident;
- tenancies where some form of board such as breakfast is provided are excluded altogether.[33]

Tenancies starting after 15 January 1989 (England and Wales) or 2 January 1989 (Scotland) are also regulated if they were granted:

- to an existing protected or statutory tenant (ie, regulated under the Rent Act 1977 or the Rent (Scotland) Act 1984); *or*
- as a result of a possession order made against an existing statutory tenant in 'suitable alternative accommodation' proceedings; *or*
- in accordance with an agreement made before 15 January 1989 (England and Wales) or 2 January 1989 (Scotland).

Regulated tenancies

If you are a regulated tenant under the Rent Act 1977, your position will depend on whether or not there is a registered fair rent and whether the tenancy is in a contractual or statutory phase. Once a tenancy has been granted, it is contractual until the agreed period ends (usually by a notice to quit). When this happens, a statutory tenancy arises so long as you continue to occupy the premises as your residence.

Unregistered rent

Contractual: If, at the time you were granted a tenancy, no rent had been registered, then there was no restriction on what rent might be agreed. Once agreed, the rent – including any charges for fuel or fuel-related services – can only be raised if:

- there is a rent review clause (unusual in a residential tenancy); *or*
- it is done on an application to register the rent; *or*
- you enter with your landlord into a 'rent agreement with a tenant having security of tenure'.[34] Essentially this is a new tenancy agreement, so you are effectively starting from scratch.

Statutory: When the statutory phase begins, the last contractual rent applies, but may be changed in accordance with changes in the provision or costs of services (including payments for fuel or fuel-related services) or furniture.[35] There is no set form for giving notice of any change. If you do not agree in writing to any such proposed changes, you or your landlord can apply to the county court (the Sheriff's Court in Scotland) to determine the change.[36] The court can take into account past changes when deciding on any increases.

Rather than bothering with applications to the court, if you have a serious disagreement with your landlord, it is more sensible to apply for a fair rent to be registered (see below). Alternatively, you and your landlord can enter into a 'rent agreement with a tenant having security of tenure' and the tenancy will revert to being contractual.

Registered rent

You, your landlord or both of you together can apply for a fair rent to be registered.[37] The registered rent must include any sums which are payable for services, including payments for fuel or fuel-related services.[38] It does not matter whether you make such payments to your landlord at the same time as payments for rent, at different times, or under separate agreements.

The rent officer must include service payments in the total figure for the registered rent but must state them as a separate figure.[39] Rent officers should also note, separately, costs in rent which are ineligible for housing benefit (HB) – these include gas and electricity costs, heating, hot water, lighting and cooking.[40]

The rent that is registered for fuel and fuel-related services should reflect not the cost to your landlord, but their value to you. For example, if your central heating system works poorly, the payments to your landlord can be reduced – by 50 per cent in one reported case.[41] You can argue that if your heating system runs efficiently, but is expensive because of the type of fuel used (eg, underfloor heating), your rent should be reduced to the level of a system which provides the same heat at a cheaper rate. Similarly, if the premises are poorly insulated or use energy inefficiently, this could be reflected in your rent.

The amount specified for services in the registered rent will be a fixed sum unless your tenancy has a variation clause relating to payments for services, and the mechanism for variation is reasonable (again, there is no definition of 'reasonable').[42] If there is such a clause, the amount entered in the rent register can be a sum which varies in accordance with the terms of the clause. You are then protected by the rules governing variable service charges (see p199).

Sheltered accommodation and fuel charges for communal areas

HB is not normally available towards the heating cost element in service charges but an exception is made for communal areas in sheltered accommodation. Communal areas are areas providing common access such as hallways and passageways and rooms that are in common use by occupiers of the sheltered accommodation.[43]

Restricted contracts

These are known as 'Part VII contracts' in Scotland.

The level of rent is fixed by the terms of your tenancy contract, which may be oral or written. However, you or your landlord can refer the contract to a rent assessment committee.[44] The rent assessment committee then has the power to increase or reduce the rent to a level which it considers reasonable in all the circumstances.[45] There is no definition of 'reasonable', but a 'reasonable rent' is not the same as a 'fair rent' under the same Act and will normally be higher.

The rent set by the rent assessment committee includes an assessment of any payments for services including fuel or fuel-related services. Once the rent is set, this applies for two years unless you and your landlord agree to a new application, or apply on the basis of a change in circumstances.[46] A change in the services provided would be a change in circumstances; a simple increase in gas or electricity prices would probably not be a sufficient change unless it was entirely unforeseen when the rent was set.

3. Resale of fuel by a landlord

There are specific controls on the maximum charge for gas or electricity supplied to landlords and resold to tenants (see p194 for more information on the resale of fuel). The basis on which your landlord sells you fuel will be a term of your tenancy agreement – in practice, this will not normally be set out in writing. However, it is subject to an upper limit – a landlord reselling fuel cannot recover more than the maximum charge.

Maximum permitted charges

Ofgem has the power to fix maximum charges for the resale of gas and electricity, and must publish details of any charges fixed.[47] Electricity charges have two elements: a charge for each unit consumed and a 'daily availability charge' to cover the standing charge.

Gas charges also have two elements: a charge per therm of gas used and a 'daily availability charge' to cover the standing charge. Ofgem has set the maximum price as no more than the price the landlord pays for the supply of gas, although the landlord may offer more than one rate if you have a choice to take fuel or not.[48]

If your landlord overcharges for gas or electricity, you can recover the excess through legal action. Ofgem publishes information setting out the latest maximum resale price and guidance on how to check the accuracy of what you are being charged.[49] Interest (at a rate of one per cent less than the base rate of Barclays Bank plc) is payable on any overcharge for gas supply.[50]

If your landlord undercharges, you may have to make an additional payment, but this depends on your tenancy agreement. There is no implied term (see p195) that the tenant should pay the maximum charge.

Approval of meters

Electricity meters cannot be used unless the pattern and the method of installation are as approved by regulations.[51] The meter must be tested and approved by a meter examiner appointed by Ofgem. Ofgem has the power to prosecute your landlord for failure to comply with these provisions, and s/he can be fined.

Gas meters must be of a pattern approved by the Gas and Electricity Markets Authority and stamped by, or on behalf of, a meter examiner appointed by the Authority.[52] A supply of gas through an unstamped meter is an offence subject to a fine. The Gas Act does not state who would prosecute, but presumably it would be Ofgem. There is a power to make regulations for re-examining meters already stamped and for their periodic overhaul, but none have yet been made.

Obtaining a meter directly from a supplier

If you encounter continual problems with your landlord's approach to reselling electricity or gas, you could obtain your own supply directly from a supplier. Both gas and electricity suppliers are under an obligation to provide a supply, with your own meter, if requested to do so by a consumer, although you may have to pay connection charges. If you are doing this because of persistent breaches of the tenancy agreement by your landlord, you may be able to recover the charges from the landlord as compensation for the breaches.

If you have a meter installed, this would be a tenant's **'improvement'** – ie, an 'alteration connected with the provision of services to a dwelling house'. A tenant of a secure or regulated tenancy is not allowed to make any improvement without the consent of the landlord.[53] Landlords cannot withhold their consent unreasonably. If it is unreasonably withheld, it is treated as given. If suppliers are reluctant to co-operate with you, remind them that you have these rights.

The landlord fails to pay bills

If you pay for fuel with your rent, you can be disconnected if your landlord does not pay the bill. The supplier's codes of practice should lay down a period during which disconnection action will not proceed in such circumstances. There are a number of legal remedies to deal with conflicts in this area (see Chapter 14).

The landlord is disconnected

Gas can only be disconnected at the premises for which there are arrears.[54] However, electricity can be disconnected at any premises which your landlord occupies and for which s/he is registered as the consumer (eg, at the landlord's home or workplace), for failure to pay a bill incurred at other premises.[55] Your electricity supply may, therefore, be at risk of disconnection if your landlord has arrears elsewhere. This provision is more difficult to use if the two premises in question are supplied by different companies. Remember that the supplier may not be aware that your landlord is not the occupier unless you, as tenant, provide this information. Inform the supplier of the situation. Always press for disconnection of your landlord, rather than you, if disconnection cannot be avoided.

Breach of quiet enjoyment

If you pay for fuel with rent, it will be a term of your tenancy (implied, if not written down) that your landlord maintains the supply. If your landlord fails to pay a bill and the supply is threatened or cut off, you could seek a court order to restore the supply and for damages for loss and suffering. Where action or inaction (such as failing to pay a bill) by a landlord results in a supply being cut off, the landlord will be in breach of an implied covenant to ensure a supply of gas and electricity and for breach of the implied covenant for 'quiet enjoyment'[56] (in Scotland, for having been deprived of full possession).

The covenant of quiet enjoyment protects you against both wrongful acts by a landlord and also lawful acts of other persons claiming under the landlord, by way of entry, eviction or disruption of your peaceful enjoyment of the land. Thus, interventions by fuel suppliers which have been caused by the landlord's wrongful act or omission may count as breaches of quiet enjoyment. For example, if a fuel supplier takes lawful action to cut off a supply on account of a bill which a landlord has failed to pay, a claim for breach of quiet enjoyment will be sustainable against the landlord for having allowed the situation to arise.

Breach of trust

If two or more tenants contribute to the same costs by paying a variable service charge, the sums paid to the landlord are held 'on trust' by her/him. This imposes strict obligations on the landlord as 'trustee'. Failure to pay fuel bills with this money is a 'breach of trust'.

Harassment

Your landlord is committing a criminal offence if s/he harasses you in order to make you give up your tenancy or prevent you from exercising your rights. 'Harassment' means action likely to interfere with your peace or comfort, including the withdrawal of services such as the supply of gas or electricity.[57] The offence may be committed by the landlord of a residential occupier (which is wider in meaning than a tenant) or by an agent of the landlord.

A person convicted of an offence of harassment in the magistrates' court may be jailed for up to six months or fined up to £5,000; if convicted in the Crown Court, the prison sentence may be up to two years and the fine at whatever level the court sees fit. A person who has been the victim of unlawful harassment can also sue for damages, which can be very large if you have to give up occupation.[58] Proceedings may be taken in the county court or High Court.

An injunction may be obtained from the court, ordering a landlord to restore fuel supply (see p241). In emergency cases, the injunction may be obtained outside normal court hours. Damages are also available for breach of contract and for harm caused by acts of harassment, of which the cutting off or disruption of fuel supplies may be just a part. Four different types of damages may be available in a case of harassment or unlawful eviction, depending on the facts of the case. Potential claims may include:

- special damages, representing financial loss that can be identified – eg, cost of alternative accommodation;
- general damages, to put you back in the position you would have been in if the harassment or eviction had never happened. These include damages for pain, distress and nuisance;
- aggravated damages, which are awarded for especially severe harm and demonstrate the outrage and indignation of the court at the conduct of the landlord;
- exemplary damages, awarded where a landlord has acted with a deliberate disregard for your rights and her/his behaviour is calculated to make a profit. Exemplary damages are awarded where it is necessary to 'teach a wrongdoer that tort does not pay'.[59] To sustain an action for exemplary damages other torts such as trespass, assault and nuisance would have to be shown in addition to action for breach of quiet enjoyment.[60]

Your landlord has a defence if s/he can show that s/he had reasonable grounds for interfering with your peace or comfort, or for withdrawing services – eg, the gas was turned off because of an emergency such as a nearby fire.

Local authorities are often prepared to prosecute landlords for harassment. You can ask the tenancy relations officer to intervene. In England and Wales, if a local authority refuses to prosecute, you can take out a summons yourself in the magistrates' court. However, Community Legal Service funding is available only for advice, not for representation. If a prosecution is unsuccessful, there is a risk of being ordered to pay costs.[61]

Transferring the account

If your landlord consistently fails to pay bills, the simplest solution may be for you to open an account and get the supply in your own name (see Chapter 3).

Rewiring work might be necessary if a meter is moved or a new one installed. For example, in houses in multiple occupation, considerable work would be needed to replace one main meter with separate meters for each tenant – in most cases, you would only have to pay for the costs of work to the premises you yourself occupy.

If a supply is being transferred because of a breach of the terms of the tenancy, you can claim the costs of the work as damages in a court action. Otherwise this work would be an 'improvement' (see p212).

Local authorities' powers in England and Wales

Local authorities have powers to help tenants whose landlords are endangering their gas or electricity supply through non-payment of charges. If you are seeking the help of the local authority in an emergency (eg, the supplier is threatening disconnection), tell the supplier – its code of practice may allow for a delay in disconnecting while the council investigates whether it can help, but the delay will only come into effect if the supplier knows that the council is involved.

Note: although the following section on local authorities' powers has been written for landlords and tenants, it applies where any 'occupier' has been affected by the failure of an 'owner' to pay a bill. 'Owner' has a wide definition,[62] and might cover the position where one of a number of flat-sharers is both tenant and the person responsible for paying the fuel bills.

Outside London

Local authorities outside London have the power to protect occupiers if the supply is threatened or cut off as a result of an owner's failure to pay fuel charges.[63] Once a request is made in writing, the council can make arrangements with the supplier to reconnect the supply; such arrangements can include payment of arrears and disconnection or reconnection charges.

Having arranged reconnection, the council can recover expenses plus interest from the person who should have paid in the first place. If you have an arrangement where the owner, your landlord, pays the fuel bills, the local authority can also serve notice on you to pay your rent directly to it to set off against its expenses.

Within London

London boroughs have powers to protect occupiers where an owner, usually a landlord, fails to pay a bill.[64] They can make arrangements with suppliers, including to pay the expenses of reconnecting the supply of gas or electricity. After reconnection, they have a duty, as long as they think it is necessary, to pay the supplier's charges for future consumption.

However, the boroughs have no power to pay arrears – ie, for past consumption. This can be a stumbling block, as suppliers are under no obligation to reconnect the supply while money is owed. The supplier cannot chase you for the arrears because your landlord is the customer, not you. While such arrears are outstanding, a supplier may be reluctant to reconnect a supply.

You can get round this by getting the borough to recover the arrears. The borough has the power to take proceedings to recover money owing at the time fuel was reconnected,[65] and these proceedings can be taken against either the occupier (ie, you) or the defaulting owner. If you pay your rent to the borough under these provisions, you are treated as meeting your obligation to pay rent to the owner. You cannot be required to pay more than the rent that you would otherwise be paying to your landlord.

Suppliers should be keen on this kind of arrangement and prepared to reconnect, as it means the borough does the supplier's debt-collecting and, provided you pay your rent to the borough, payment is guaranteed. Boroughs can protect themselves by 'registering a charge'[66] on the affected property to recover their expenses (including administrative costs). Local authorities usually appoint a particular officer – such as a tenancy relations officer – to deal with these matters. If they are reluctant to become involved, you can point out that they can put a charge on the property to cover their expenses and protect themselves. It is unlawful to have a blanket policy not to exercise these powers; they must consider each case individually. If you are told, 'We don't do that', you can consider judicial review (see Chapter 14).

Local authorities' powers in Scotland

There are no powers in Scotland equivalent to those in England and Wales. However, local authorities throughout Great Britain do have powers to make 'control orders' in extreme cases.[67] This means that the council can take over a house in multiple occupation from a landlord and collect the rent in order to pay for any necessary repairs and to pay bills such as fuel bills. Unfortunately, it is unlikely that a control order would be made on the basis of unpaid fuel bills alone; these powers are more typically used if there is substantial disrepair. The scope of the powers given to local authorities in Scotland under Housing (Scotland) Act 2006 has yet to be tested with respect to non-payment of fuel charges.

Social landlords

'Social landlords' are local authorities, housing associations and housing co-operatives. They provide housing mostly for people on lower incomes. Some are now taking initiatives to use the competitive market for gas and electricity to set up schemes for their tenants. It has been suggested that social landlords could get discounts by 'buying in bulk' and then passing on that discount to tenants. In fact, the Gas Act 1986 and the Electricity Act 1989 do not allow this, as someone who buys and supplies gas or electricity like this must have a licence.[68]

However, there are initiatives social landlords can take. The former regulator Ofgas produced a useful guide for social landlords on all aspects of the competitive market and Ofgem continues to apply these principles.[69] This is also relevant for tenants' associations which might want to work with their landlords to promote or introduce some of its ideas. The guide mentioned three categories of action which social landlords are taking.

- **Marketing alliances.** The landlord finds a supplier which it thinks provides a good deal for tenants and then works with the supplier to promote the deal to tenants. In return, the supplier may offer discounts or other benefits.
- **Energy service companies.** These help to fund energy efficiency improvements which should pay for themselves in lower fuel bills.

- **The landlord as an energy supplier.** Social landlords can set up a company which applies for a licence to become a gas or electricity supplier itself. Rather than make a profit, supply to tenants can be at cost price.

4. **Defective housing and heating systems**

A full discussion of legal remedies for defective housing is outside the scope of this book. However, defective heating systems and appliances, structural disrepair, use of poor materials, and inadequate insulation and draughtproofing can all contribute to high heating bills. Tackling these problems can be expensive and would rarely be a tenant's responsibility. Therefore, this section looks briefly at the legal remedies available to a tenant, dividing them into:

- repairing obligations;
- negligence;
- premises prejudicial to health;
- local authorities' other powers.

There are also regulations covering the maintenance of gas appliances by landlords which are dealt with on p217.

There are different forms of action which can be taken against a landlord, but the purpose will always be to get work carried out and/or to get compensation. Good records are important evidence and can make a big difference to the level of any compensation – keep proper records of what is in disrepair and, for instance:

- when the problems started;
- when your landlord was first told of the disrepair;
- all other occasions on which your landlord has been told about the disrepair;
- what has been done, if anything, to put things right.

If you incur extra expenses (eg, to keep warm, eating out or for replacement heaters), make notes and, if possible, keep receipts. If heating bills are higher than normal, also keep these.

Repairing obligations

Your landlord's repairing obligations may be set out in a written tenancy agreement. Tenants of councils and housing associations in Scotland have a right to a formal written lease.[70] Whether or not you have a written agreement and whatever is stated in any such written agreement, there is legislation which puts a wide range of obligations on landlords. It is unusual for written agreements to be better than the responsibilities required by legislation.

Scotland

The landlord's obligation is to make sure that any property s/he rents out is in a 'tenantable and habitable condition',[71] or 'reasonably fit for human habitation'.[72] These two phrases almost certainly mean the same thing – the property must be safe, free from damp and generally in a suitable condition for you and your family to live in. Local authorities may act in cases of properties which are 'below tolerable standard'. Private landlords in Scotland have a duty to ensure that rented accommodation meets a basic standard of repair called the 'Repairing Standard' under the Housing (Scotland) Act 2006.[73]

At the start of your tenancy, your landlords has a legal obligation to provide you with written information about the effect of the Repairing Standard provisions on the tenancy. A home will meet the Standard if:

- it is wind and water tight and in all other respects reasonably fit for human habitation;
- its structure and exterior (including external pipes) are in a reasonable state of repair and in proper working order;
- its installations for the supply of water, gas and electricity and for sanitation, space heating and heating water are in a reasonable state of repair and in proper working order;
- any fixtures, fittings and appliances provided by the landlord under the tenancy are in a reasonable state of repair and in proper working order.

The repairing obligation applies to all tenancies except Scottish secure tenancies and short Scottish secure tenancies with various social landlords and certain agricultural tenancies.[74] The landlord should inspect the property and bring it up to standard before any tenancy starts. If this is not done, you can sue for damages and/or an order of 'specific implement' to force the landlord to carry out any necessary works. Unlike in England and Wales, your landlord's duty may include carrying out works to improve the property, rather than merely repairing it, if that is necessary to comply with her/his duty. However, it is much more difficult in Scotland to get an order ('specific implement') which enforces that duty.

If problems arise after the tenancy starts, your landlord is only obliged to deal with them if s/he knows, or should know, about them. This means you should report any problems as soon as they arise, preferably in writing. If you believe your home falls short of the Standard, contact your landlord. To be able to take follow up action (eg, legal action) you must submit your letter in writing and get proof of posting.

If you cannot agree with your landlord about whether or not the standard is being met, you can take your case to the Private Rented Housing Panel (PRHP).

Private Rent Housing Panel

The PRHP is an independent body made up of lawyers, chartered surveyors and lay members. In cases regarding repairing obligations the panel offers a mediation service at venues across Scotland.

If mediation is not successful, an inspection of your home regarding the disrepair may take place and a hearing held as an alternative to mediation. It may decide:

- whether your landlord has failed to comply with the Repairing Standard or not;
- to issue an enforcement notice if your landlord has failed to comply, setting out the work to be completed;
- to reduce your rent during some of the enforcement order period.

A written decision, accompanied by a full statement of the reasons for the decision, is issued as soon as possible after the hearing or consideration of the case. You can claim the cost of reasonable travelling expenses to attend a hearing.

If an enforcement notice is issued, it will set out the repair work required, and when it must be completed (this will be at least 21 days). If your landlord fails to comply with the notice, the local authority may undertake the work (and charge the landlord).

England, Wales and Scotland

For England and Wales generally, and in Scotland in connection with the following rights, it is important to distinguish between 'repairs' and 'improvements'. If the works which are needed constitute improvements, rather than just repairs (and the case cannot be brought under the headings of 'negligence' or 'premises prejudicial to health' – see pp213 and 214), a landlord has no obligation to improve a home, and a tenant has no rights.[75]

You can take legal action against your landlord for disrepair only if s/he knows about it or should have known about it.[76] It is best to tell your landlord in writing about the disrepair (keeping copies of any letters) so that there can be no dispute about whether notice has been given.

Your rights are set out in the Landlord and Tenant Act 1985 or the Housing (Scotland) Act 1987 and the Housing (Scotland) Act 2006. (These provisions do not apply to tenancies for a fixed period of seven years or more.)

Structure and exterior

Your landlord must keep in repair 'the structure and exterior of the dwelling-house (including drains, gutters and external pipes)'.[77] This includes walls, roofs, windows and doors. If these are not kept in good repair, a house can become damp and hard to heat. In Scotland, the property must not be 'below tolerable standard' (see p211).

Installations for heating and for the supply of gas and electricity

Your landlord must keep in repair and proper working order installations for space heating (ie, central heating, gas and electric fires), for heating water and for the supply of gas and electricity.[78] This does not include fittings or appliances making use of the supply – ie, wiring and pipes would be included but not cookers or refrigerators. For tenancies which started after 15 January 1989 (2 January 1989 in Scotland), a central heating boiler in the basement of a block of flats would normally come within the repairing obligation.[79]

What you can do

If your landlord does not keep the structure, etc in good repair, you have two options.

- You can bring an action for damages and for a court order requiring your landlord to carry out the repair. Damages are calculated by assessing how much the value of the premises to you has been reduced so as to put you, as far as possible, in the same position as if there had been no breach.[80] This may involve calculating the costs of alternative accommodation, redecoration, eating out, using public baths or launderettes, together with an amount for discomfort and inconvenience arising from the disrepair. Keep a record, as far as possible, of all expenses. Most claims are made in the county court or, in Scotland, the Sheriff Court. You will need the help of a solicitor. In Scotland, you can take your case to the PRHP (see p212).

- In some cases, rather than taking your landlord to court, it is easier to do the repair work yourself and recover the costs by withholding rent to the same value. Always write to your landlord to warn her/him of what you are doing. You cannot recover the costs unless the works fall within your landlord's repairing obligations, so you must give her/him an opportunity to object or comment. Send estimates for the cost of the work to your landlord and give her/him time to comment on what is being suggested – eg, 21 days. After the work has been done, write to your landlord to warn that, unless s/he pays the costs, rent to the same value will be withheld. These costs are a 'set-off' against rent due and will not be treated by a court as rent arrears, provided the court agrees that the costs were reasonable.[81] The consequences of getting this procedure wrong can be serious, so get legal advice. Note that in Scotland, this way of retaining your rent is not available if you are a statutory tenant.

Negligence

As a tenant, you can hold builders,[82] developers,[83] architects and building engineers[84] liable for their work in building or developing your home if that work was carried out negligently[85] and it causes damage to you or your property or belongings.[86] Local authorities may also be liable for negligence if they fail to inspect properly the plans for, or the site of, your home or to enforce the appropriate building regulations.[87]

If a landlord has repairing obligations (see p210), s/he is also under a duty to make sure that anyone else who could be expected to be in the premises will not suffer harm from any disrepair.[88] Effectively, this extends the repairing obligations to your guests and members of your family, such as your children, even though they are not parties to the tenancy itself. In England and Wales, this duty is specifically extended to situations where the works are carried out before a tenancy is granted.[89] Your landlord is treated as having such repairing obligations if s/he has reserved the right to enter your home to carry out any maintenance or works of repair.[90] Unlike the repairing obligations set out in the previous section, your landlord can be liable under this duty in England and Wales not only if you have given her/him notice of any problem, but also if s/he ought to have known about it.[91]

Electricity and gas can be dangerous. Consumers are protected by safety regulations which prescribe standards and methods of installation of meters and other equipment for the supply of gas or electricity.[92] If landlords carry out work on the premises, they must comply with such standards and are also under a duty to use reasonable care to ensure the safety of those who might be affected by the work.[93]

Failure to meet the appropriate standards may be negligence. The main remedy for negligence is to claim damages in a court action. These are assessed so as to put the injured party, so far as possible, in the position s/he would have been in had there been no negligence. Legal advice is essential.

Premises prejudicial to health

The Environmental Protection Act 1990 gives a remedy to any person 'aggrieved' by a 'statutory nuisance'. The Act defines 'statutory nuisance' to cover a range of matters. For people who live in defective premises, the most relevant of these is 'any premises in such a state as to be prejudicial to health or a nuisance'.[94]

Severe damp, including condensation, is generally accepted as being prejudicial to health for the purposes of the Act. Loose or exposed wiring and draughty windows and doors are other examples of problems which can make a home prejudicial to health.[95] Health is distinguished from accidental physical injury and would cover, for instance, health problems triggered by gas leakage. There may be grey areas such as cracked electrical fittings which might result in electrical shocks.

A 'nuisance' is anything coming from neighbouring property which causes substantial interference with your use and enjoyment of your home.[96]

Local authorities have a duty to investigate complaints of statutory nuisance. The local authority may serve a notice requiring any 'nuisance' to be 'abated' – ie, put right. If the notice is not appealed against or complied with, the local authority can prosecute the person who was sent the notice and/or do the works itself. Where the offending landlord is the council itself, it may also be prosecuted under these provisions by you taking a private prosecution.

You can take your landlord to the magistrates' court or, in Scotland, the Sheriff Court.[97] Legal advice should be obtained. You must give 21 days' written warning to your landlord that you are going to take proceedings. You then 'lay an information' at your local magistrates' court giving details of the defective premises and why they are prejudicial to your health and/or that of any other occupier of the premises. In Scotland, the procedure is by 'summary application' at the local Sheriff Court.[98] At the subsequent hearing, you must prove the existence of the statutory nuisance and that your landlord is responsible. Environmental health officers can give evidence of the existence of a statutory nuisance. Expert evidence on the state of premises is sufficient to find that premises are prejudicial to health, without having to prove that you are suffering from a condition. A doctor's report explaining the danger to health may be used, and in some cases it may be useful to call the medical practitioner or other expert as a witness.

The proceedings in the magistrates' court follow the rules for criminal procedure, and a finding that a statutory nuisance exists ranks as a criminal conviction[99] – an outcome which most landlords will wish to avoid.

The court can make an order that your landlord must 'abate' the nuisance. The court has wide discretion over what work it may order a landlord to do,[100] although it must be for abating the nuisance. As explained above, repairing obligations can be limited, so this kind of action can be useful if something additional, including improvements, is needed – in some cases courts have ordered the installation of central heating, double glazing and mechanical ventilators. Where a person contravenes any requirement or prohibition imposed by an order, a fine of up to £5,000 may be imposed, together with a fine at a rate of £200 a day for each day on which the offence continues after conviction.[101]

In England and Wales, statutory nuisance proceedings are criminal and the magistrates' court can make a compensation order.[102] The order can be for up to £5,000 for things such as damaged belongings and discomfort and inconvenience, although only if the loss was suffered after you sent the 21-day notice.[103] If a court refuses to make a compensation order, it must give reasons. In Scotland, the proceedings are civil, not criminal, and the court has no power to award compensation.

There is a small risk that you might have to pay the defendant's legal costs if you lose,[104] so take legal advice before starting a prosecution. However, so long as the statutory nuisance existed at the time you started the court proceedings, you can ask for your reasonable costs to be paid by your landlord.[105] Also, lawyers can represent you in court on the basis that they will only be paid if the case is successful.[106] Therefore, although financial assistance is not available, if you can find a lawyer who will take the case on such a 'no win, no fee' basis, then it need not cost you anything.

Condensation

Condensation dampness causes severe problems for many people, particularly those living in post-war system-built flats. The dampness and consequent mould growth can be damaging to health and can destroy clothing and furnishings. Attempts to heat damp premises can lead to high fuel bills. The causes of, and remedies for, condensation are complex. Most remedies are beyond the means or control of tenants, involving substantial expenditure on, for example, structure and heating systems.

Legal remedies for condensation

In Scotland, the obligations on a landlord under the Repairing Standard (see p211) are wide enough to cover condensation. This means your landlord has to make sure that there is no condensation problem when your tenancy starts and that, if it arises during the tenancy and you report it, s/he must carry out whatever works are necessary to solve the problem.

In England and Wales, for condensation to come within a landlord's repairing obligations you must show that there has been 'damage to the structure and exterior which requires to be made good'.[107] This has to relate to the physical condition of the structure or exterior. Unless condensation has occurred over a long time and plaster has perished or window frames are rotten as a result, it may be hard to show this.

If the condensation damage is caused by inherent defects in the building (eg, because of defective materials) and if the only way to correct this is to carry out improvements, this can be ordered by the court. A landlord will not, however, be ordered to renew a building completely or to change it substantially – what will be required is a question of degree.[108] It is very unlikely that a court would order installation of a different heating system or the full range of works necessary to remedy condensation.

Therefore, in England and Wales, it will normally be more effective to prosecute under the Environmental Protection Act 1990 for a 'statutory nuisance' (see p214). It is not necessary to prove a breach of any contractual or statutory duty to use this remedy.[109] This means that a court can hold a landlord liable even if s/he is not in breach of her/his responsibilities for repairs. A court can also order works of improvement if these are necessary to abate a nuisance.[110]

Landlords sometimes argue that tenants could avoid the nuisance by changing their lifestyle or by heating premises properly. This is rarely correct. If your landlord provides ventilation or a heating system, you would be expected to use it,[111] but you would not be required to use 'wholly abnormal quantities of fuel'.[112]

Other local authority powers

Local authorities have powers to bring unfit properties within their areas up to certain minimum standards. Compared with a tenant's rights, these powers are more detailed and wide-ranging. However, the disadvantage is that you have to rely on a local authority's willingness to use its powers, which can be limited, mainly due to budget restrictions. Such financial limitations are particularly relevant where mandatory grants are available to bring homes up to the relevant standard (see Chapter 12).

In England and Wales, the relevant standard is prescribed by the Housing Health and Safety Rating System under Part I of the Housing Act 2004. Exactly what satisfies each of these standards is further defined in government guidance (see p198).

In Scotland, the relevant standard is the 'tolerable standard', which is less comprehensive.[113]

Once a property has been identified as falling below the relevant standard, local councils have duties to inspect and make arrangements for dealing with it.

If you feel that your home falls below the relevant standard, contact your local authority to urge it to take action.

Maintenance of gas appliances

Landlords often provide gas fires and other gas-fired appliances to their tenants. Your landlord must maintain any such appliance or installation pipework owned by her/him in a safe condition so as to prevent risk of injury to any person.[114] Your landlord has to also ensure that each appliance is checked at least every 12 months by a registered gas engineer.[115] Your landlord must give you a copy of the gas safety record within 28 days of it being carried out or before you move in.

Gas Safe Register is the statutory gas registration body in Great Britain. It lists all gas engineers who are qualified to work legally and safely on gas appliances. By law all qualified gas engineers must be on the Gas Safe Register and carry a photo ID card with their licence number and the type of work they are qualified to do. The register is at www.gassaferegister.co.uk or you can call 0800 408 5500.

Using the Ombudsman

For more information about the Obudsman, see Chapter 14.

Local Government Ombudsman

In addition to legal remedies you can also make a complaint to the Local Government Ombudsman (LGO) against a local authority where it fails to carry out it duties and obligations. You are first expected to follow the appropriate procedure laid down in the authority's published complaints process. The LGO is a free service.

The LGO examines and investigates complaints if you have suffered injustice caused by unfair treatment or service failure by a local authority. It may recommend that an award of compensation is paid.

The LGO may investigate maladministration in respect of housing by any local authority until 31 March 2013.

Details and complaint forms can be obtained from. www.lgo.org.uk. The LGO advice team can be contacted on 0300 061 0614.

Housing Ombudsman

To complain about a housing association or a registered social landlord, you may take your complaint to the Housing Ombudsman Service. The Housing Ombudsman provides a free and impartial service investigating complaints brought against social landlords and may recommend that an award of compensation is paid. You must exhaust all stages of the social landlord's complaints procedure before contacting the Ombudsman.[116]

Single Housing Ombudsman Service

From 1 April 2013 all complaints arising from housing services provided by both local authoritites and registered social landlords will come under the jurisdiction of a single Housing Ombudsman Service. These are changes established under the Localism Act 2011 which will also make awards of compensation enforceable in the courts.[117]

Local housing authorities will become 'registered providers', which is the legal status of housing associations and other bodies registered with the regulator of social housing.

For more information see www.housing-ombudsman.org.uk.

Scottish Housing Regulator

In Scotland, complaints may be investigated by the Scottish Housing Regulator which has jurisidiction to cover complaints made by tenants involving local authorities and registered social landlords. See www.scottishhousingregulator.gov.uk for more information.

Deductions from wages by an employer who provides accommodation

If your employer provides accommodation and deducts costs for fuel from your wages, the basic agreement covering such an arrangement is your contract of employment. A written contract of employment should be provided within eight weeks of starting a job and should set out the terms and conditions.

Deductions to cover fuel costs from your wages by your employer may be unlawful if your earnings fall below the minimum wage as a result. The Court of Appeal ruled that deductions made for gas and electricity from wages paid to workers at a holiday resort were unlawful where the wages fell below the statutory minimum wage.[118]

Energy performance certificates

Since 2008, 'energy performance certificates' (EPCs) are required when buildings are constructed, sold or rented out. Landlords are required to make available EPCs to prospective buyers and tenants at the earliest opportunity.[119] Once issued, an EPC is valid for 10 years.

An EPC must be accompanied by recommendations for the improvement of the energy performance of the building to give you an idea of the amount of energy needed to heat the property.[120] Certificates for homes in England and Wales may be disclosed to or by the Energy Savings Trust.[121]

Notes

2. Rent increases for fuel or fuel-related services

1 *Montague v Browning* [1954] 2 All ER 601
2 Part IV HA 1985; s160 LA 2011
3 s108 HA 1985
4 s211 H(S)A 1987
5 ss13–15 Supply of Goods and Services Act 1982
6 s11 LG(MP)A 1976; Sale of Electricity by Local Authorities (England and Wales) Regs 2010 No.1910; Sale of Electricity by Local Authorities (Scotland) Regs 2010 No.1908
7 s12(4) LG(MP)A 1976
8 *Bromley LBC v GLC* [1982] 1 All ER 129
9 Part III London County Council (General Powers) Act 1949
10 s22 London County Council (General Powers) Act 1949
11 s20(3) London County Council (General Powers) Act 1949
12 DoE Circular 6/90, Local Government and Housing Act 1989, Area Renewal, Unfitness, Slum Clearance and Enforcement Action, Annex A, Guidance Notes on the Standard of Fitness for Human Habitation
13 ss18–30 LTA 1985
14 ss47–51 HA 1985
15 s18 LTA 1985
16 s26 LTA 1985
17 s27 LTA 1985
18 s19 LTA 1985
19 See *Russell v Laimond Properties Ltd* (1983) 269 EG 947; *Levitt and another v London Borough of Camden* [2011] UKUT 366 (LC)
20 s20B LTA 1985
21 *Scottish Mutual Insurance Co v Jardine* (1999) ECGS 43
22 s20B(1) and (2) LTA 1985; *Brent London Borough Council v Shulem B Association Ltd* [2011] EWHC 1663; *Gilje v Charlgrove Securities* [2004] 1 All ER 91
23 s19(2A) and (2B) LTA 1985
24 Leasehold Valuation Tribunal (Procedure) (England) Regulations 2003
25 s21 LTA 1985. This provision has been amended by a new s21 inserted by Sch 12 Housing and Regeneration Act 2008, but at the time of writing it is not yet in force.
26 s21(6) LTA 1985
27 s38 LTA 1985; 'dwelling' is defined as a building or part of a building occupied as a separate dwelling. Provided the occupants of a house in multiple occupation are tenants with exclusive occupation of at least a room, their landlord would have to provide certified accounts.
28 s22 LTA 1985
29 s29 LTA 1985
30 s19(4) LTA 1985
31 Sch 12, para 3 Commonhold and Leasehold Reform Act 2002
32 *Finchbourne Ltd v Rodrigues* [1976] 3 All ER 581
33 *Otter v Norman* [1989] AC 129
34 s51 RA 1977; s34 R(S)A 1984

35 s47 RA 1977; s31 R(S)A 1984
36 s47(2) RA 1977; s31(2) R(S)A 1984
37 s67 RA 1977; s46 R(S)A 1984
38 s71(1) RA 1977; s49(1) R(S)A 1984
39 s72A RA 1977
40 Sch 1 paras 4 and 5 HB Regs
41 *Metropolitan Properties Co Ltd v Noble* [1968] 2 All ER 313
42 s71(4) RA 1977; s49(6) R(S)A 1984
43 *Oxford City Council v Basey* [2012] EWCA 115
44 s77(1) RA 1977 – this refers to rent tribunals but rent assessment committees now exercise the powers of rent tribunals under s72 HA 1980; s65(1) R(S)A 1984
45 s78(2) RA 1977; s66(1) R(S)A 1984
46 s80(1) RA 1977; s68 R(S)A 1984

3. Resale of fuel by a landlord
47 s44 EA 1989
48 *The resale of gas and electricity: guidance for resellers*, Ofgem, October 2005
49 *The resale of gas and electricity: guidance for resellers*, Ofgem, October 2005
50 para 3 *Direction made under s37 of the GA 1986 as to maximum prices for reselling gas*, Ofgas, 15 February 1996
51 The Meters (Approval of Pattern or Construction and Method of Installation) Regulations 1990 SI No.791
52 s17 GA 1986
53 s97 HA 1985; s57 H(S)A 1987; s81 HA 1980; s101 R(S)A 1984
54 Sch 2B para 7(3) GA 1986
55 Sch 6 para 1(6) EA 1989
56 See *Perera v Vandiyar* [1953] 1 All ER 1109; *McCall v Ablez* [1986] 1 QB 585
57 s1 Protection from Eviction Act 1977; R(S)A 1984 as amended by s38 H(S)A 1988
58 s27 HA 1988; s36 H(S)A 1988
59 *Rookes v Barnard* [1964] AC 1129 at 1227; and this may be applicable where a landlord has a history of wrongful behaviour
60 *Kenny v Preen* [1963] 1 QB 499 at 512, CA
61 s18 Prosecution of Offences Act 1985
62 s19(8) Greater London Council (General Powers) Act 1972; s33(5) LG(MP)A 1976
63 s33 LG(MP)A 1976
64 s19 Greater London Council (General Powers) Act 1972 as amended by s42 of the London Local Authorities Act 1990.
65 s19(3)(b) Greater London Council (General Powers) Act 1972

66 Registering a charge means to attach a charge to the title of the property at the Land Registry so that the owner cannot sell the property without paying off the charge.
67 HA 1985 and H(S)A 1987
68 s4 EA 1989; s5 GA 1986
69 *Gas Competition and your Tenants: a guide for social landlords*, Ofgas Bulletin for Social Landlords, No.1, April 1998

4. Defective housing and heating systems: tenants' rights
70 ss53 and 54 H(S)A 1987
71 Erskine's Institutes II/4/63
72 s27 H(S)A 2001
73 s13 H(S)A 2006
74 s12 H(S)A 2006
75 *Ravenseft Properties Ltd v Davstone Holdings Ltd* [1979] 1 All ER 929
76 *O'Brien v Robinson* [1973] AC 912
77 s11(1)(a) LTA 1985; Sch 10 para 3(1)(a) H(S)A 1987
78 s11(1)(b) and (c) LTA 1985; Sch 10 para 3(1)(b) H(S)A 1987
79 s11(1A) LTA 1985; Sch 10 para 3(1A) H(S)A 1987
80 *Calabar Properties v Stitcher* [1984] 1 WLR 287
81 *Lee-Parker v Izzett* [1971] 1 WLR 1688; *British Anzani (Felixstowe) Ltd v International Marine Management (UK) Ltd* [1980] QB 137
82 *Gallagher v McDowell Ltd* [1961] NI 26
83 *Batty v Metropolitan Property Realisations* [1978] QB 554
84 *Cedar Transport Group v First Wyvern Property Trustees Co* [1981] EG 1077
85 s1 DPA 1972
86 *Murphy v Brentwood DC* [1990] 3 WLR 414
87 *Murphy v Brentwood DC* [1990] 3 WLR 414
88 s4 DPA 1972; s3 Occupiers' Liability (Scotland) Act 1960
89 s3 DPA 1972
90 s4(4) DPA 1972
91 s4(2) DPA 1972
92 GS(IU) Regs; Meters (Approval of Pattern or Construction and Method of Installation) Regulations 1990 SI No.791
93 *AC Billings & Son v Riden* [1957] 3 All ER 1
94 s79(1)(a) Environmental Protection Act 1990
95 But see *R v Bristol City Council ex parte Everett* 13 May 1998 – a dangerous staircase is not a statutory nuisance

96 *National Coal Board v Neath BC* [1976] 1 WLR 543

97 s82 Environmental Protection Act 1990

98 Sheriff Court Summary Application Rules 1993 SI 1993/3240 r.4

99 *Herbert v Lambeth LBC* (1991) *The Times*, 21 November 1991

100 *Whittaker v Derby Urban Sanitary Authority* [1885] LJMC 8

101 s82(8) Environmental Protection Act 1990

102 s35 Powers of Criminal Courts Act 1973

103 *R v Liverpool Crown Court ex parte Cooke* [1996] 4 All ER 589

104 s18 Prosecution of Offences Act 1985

105 s82(12) Environmental Protection Act 1990

106 *Thai Trading v Taylor* [1998] *The Times*, 6 March 1998

107 Dillon LJ in *Quick v Taff Ely BC* [1985] 18 HLR 66

108 *Ravenseft Properties Ltd v Davstone Holdings Ltd* [1979] 1 All ER 929

109 *Birmingham DC v Kelly* [1985] 17 HLR 572

110 *Birmingham DC v Kelly* [1985] 17 HLR 572

111 *Dover DC v Farrar* [1980] 2 HLR 32

112 *GLC v LB Tower Hamlets* [1983] 15 HLR 54

113 s14 H(S)A 1987; see www.scotland.gov.uk/Publications/2003/09/18167/26257 for guidance

114 Reg 36(2) GS(IU) Regs

115 Reg 36(3)(a) GS(IU) Regs

116 Sch 2 HA 1996 as amended by s180 LA 2011

117 ss181-182 LA 2011

118 *Leisure Employment Services Ltd v Revenue and Customs Commissioners* [2007] EWCA Civ 92

119 Reg 5 EPB(CI)(EW) Regs

120 Reg 10 EPB(CI)(EW) Regs

121 Reg 2 Energy Performance of Buildings (Certificates and Inspections) (England and Wales) (Amendment) Regulations 2009 SI 1990

Chapter 14

Remedies

This chapter covers:
1. Introduction (below)
2. Negotiations (p224)
3. Ofgem (p229)
4. Office of Fair Trading and unfair terms (p231)
5. Using the civil courts (p233)
6. The Energy Ombudsman (p245)

1. Introduction

This chapter rounds-up the remedies available if you are in dispute with a supplier of electricity, or a supplier or transporter of gas. The ultimate arbiters of such disputes are Ofgem and the Energy Ombudsman or the civil courts. Consumer Focus works for a fair deal for energy consumers, though in 2013 a number of its services will be delivered in conjunction with Citizens Advice (see p228). Advice and guidance previously obtained through Consumer Direct is now provided by the Citizens Advice consumer service.

Ofgem is an independent regulator, not acting on behalf of you or the supplier, so you cannot instruct it what to do.

The statutory remedies described in this section have limitations. For all practical purposes, taking your own legal action will sometimes be a better way of asserting your rights (see p233). However, it will cost time and money, unless you are eligible for Community Legal Service funding, which may be available for some disputes although after April 2013 will be subject to further restrictions.

However, in circumstances where your remedy lies with the Office of Fair Trading (see p231), you do not currently have individual remedies. If you believe that any of the terms in your contract with your supplier are unfair, you can complain to the Office of Fair Trading, which has powers to stop a supplier relying on any such terms under the Unfair Terms in Consumer Contracts Regulations 1999. These regulations were brought in under a European Union Directive and have been written so that only the Director General of Fair Trading can enforce them.

The first step in any dispute is to approach the supplier or transporter and attempt to negotiate with it, being prepared to make a complaint if necessary. Advice may be obtained from Citizens Advice consumer service (see Appendix 1) which also provides a route to obtaining assistance from Consumer Focus (see p229).

Consumer Focus is also a particularly important source of support for vulnerable customers. Currently Consumer Focus also has powers to deal with energy cases received from vulnerable consumers.[1] Consumer Focus can also deal with cases where you have been disconnected or are threatened with disconnection, including prepayment off-supply cases.[2] Consumer Focus' 'Extra Help Unit' (EHU) can assist vulnerable customers to resolve individual complaints (eg, when facing the threat of disconnection) and has statutory powers and responsibilities to help investigate the most urgent energy complaints from vulnerable consumers. To receive assistance from the EHU, your case must be transferred from the Citizens Advice consumer service. The Consumers, Estate Agents and Redress Act 2007 defines a vulnerable consumer as being someone that it is not reasonable to expect to pursue the complaint themselves.

It is anticipated following legislative changes that the EHU will become the responsibility of Citizens Advice Scotland in 2014.

In many situations Citizens Advice consumer service is still able to help potentially vulnerable consumers by providing advice and indicating the most effective ways forward. However, transfer of your case to the EHU should be possible if you are not able to pursue your complaint with the supplier because of the urgency of the situation (eg, enforcement action is taking place) or where your circumstances mean that you are unable to deal with the matter. The EHU may also be appropriate where the complexity of the problem requires expert help.

Although most of Consumer Focus's cases are referrals from the Citizens Advice consumer service, it also accepts a small number of cases from other sources including Members of Parliament and Ofgem.

Consumer Focus has been able to act where large numbers of customers are affected, though how this will role will be carried out in the future is unclear. In March 2010, Consumer Focus threatened legal action against npower for overcharging between 2007 and 2008. Customers were overcharged when their two-tier tariff charged them at the higher rate for the first 6,357 units of energy used rather than the contractual maximum of 4,572 units. As a result, the average customer was about £47 worse off. Consumer Focus considered that under the conditions of npower's gas supply licence, the supplier was required to notify customers of any changes that would make them 'significantly worse off' and give them the chance to switch if they were unhappy with the new terms. However, in May 2007 npower failed to inform its customers of the change. The Consumer Focus intervention resulted in a settlement without recourse to the courts, and nearly two million customers receiving compensation at the end of November 2010.

The regulatory body, Ofgem, if approached directly, will refer all complaints in the first instance to Consumer Focus. If enforcement action is considered appropriate, Consumer Focus will make a recommendation to Ofgem, which may or may not take action, giving reasons and details.

There are some problems which may require a referral to the Office of Fair Trading (see p231). There are also some circumstances where it may be necessary to take court action (see p233).

However, it may be that the quickest and most satisfactory outcome will be obtained by negotiations and/or activating the complaints procedure of the supplier. Any involvement by Consumer Focus or Ofgem may depend upon this approach having been exhausted first.

2. **Negotiations**

Negotiating with the supplier or transporter can be the most appropriate way of resolving a problem or dispute. To negotiate effectively, you will need to rely on a range of documents which, in their different ways, provide 'rules' about how suppliers and transporters should behave. Chapter 1 gives background information on sources of law, and on Consumer Focus and Ofgem, and it may be useful to read it first, together with any information and guidance originally issued by the National Consumer Council from 2008.

If you contact the supplier, keep a record of the person/section you contacted. Putting your complaint in writing is preferable (making sure you keep a copy of all correspondence) and essential if you wish to pursue a complaint.

Using codes of practice and policy statements

Suppliers are subject to regulations which govern how they handle a complaint from a customer. The Gas and Electricity (Consumer Complaints Handling Standards) Regulations[3] set down standards for the handling of complaints and the supply of information to consumers. Every supplier has to conform with the regulations; it should have a code of practice based upon the regulations for handling complaints. It must provide a copy of its complaints handling procedure, free of charge, to any person who requests a copy and must have its complaints procedure in a prominent position on its website.[4]

If you have asked an adviser or another person to make the complaint for you, it will be necessary to give them a signed authority to act for you.

Suppliers have also produced other codes of practice, as required by their licences, and staff may be more familiar with these than with the precise provisions of the law. So long as the provisions of a code of practice support your case, it may be easier and more effective to quote these; alternatively extracts from the Standard Licence Conditions may be quoted where appropriate. Each code of practice has to be approved by Ofgem before being used.[5]

Each supplier should have codes of practice on:

- payment of bills;
- services for elderly or disabled people;
- using fuel efficiently;
- complaints procedures.

Each gas and electricity supplier should also have codes of practice on prepayment meters and site access. Each supplier also produces various documents on its policies and other useful information. It is obliged to publish information regularly about its performance compared with targets set by Ofgem and by itself. Use these if they support your case, but always be cautious – as a summary of the law, they will not always be accurate.

Also, as the supply of gas and electricity is carried out by contract, not by statutory duty, provisions as to unfair contract terms apply. If you believe that a term in your contract is unfair, you can use this to support any negotiations (see p231).

Failure to follow a code of practice or an inadequate code of practice is not automatically negligence or a civil wrong in itself, but it can be evidence in support of such a claim.[6]

Making a complaint

Where you have a problem with the conduct of an energy company, and you cannot get it resolved or correspondence is ignored, make a complaint. This is important as the regulators will expect you to use the complaints service, if you are capable, before contacting them (although the EHU may assist you if you cannot make a complaint yourself and you fulfil the criteria for extra help – see p223).

Making a formal written complaint is often an effective step in resolving a problem.

Regulations lay down minimum standards for dealing with complaints by suppliers.[7]

Definition of a complaint

'Complaint means any expression of dissatisfaction made to an organisation, related to any one of its products, its services or the manner in which has dealt with any such expression of dissatisfaction, where a response is either provided by or on behalf of that organisation at the point at which contact is made or a response is explicitly or implicitly required or expected to be provided thereafter.'[8]

This definition is wide enough to include an independent subcontractor used by an energy supplier to carry out certain tasks – eg, the enforcement of warrants of entry and the fitting of prepayment meters. Thus, if a subcontractor behaves wrongly, a complaint can be made under the regulations to the supplier who appointed her/him.

A complaint may be made about any of the following.

- Billing – including accuracy of bills, frequency of billing, estimated bills, inaccurate bills, sending bills to the wrong address and issuing bills to the wrong person.
- Sales – including misleading sales information and behaviour of sales staff.
- Transfers – problems that occur when switching suppliers.
- Meters – including faulty meters, inaccurate meter readings and problems with fitting and changing meters. ·
- Prices – increases of prices on agreed contracts, misleading price information, problems with direct debits and credits, payment schemes, lack of notification of increases.
- Access – problems with access to low-income schemes, special tariffs and government schemes.
- Debt – problems with debt, disconnection and payment of arrears and failure to apply for Fuel Direct deductions where available.
- Customer service – inconsistent or inaccurate information, failures by staff, delay in responding to enquiries, website failures, problems with prepayment cards.

A supplier is required to have a complaints procedure in place and must comply with it relation to each consumer complaint it receives.[9] The procedure must:[10]

- be in plain and intelligible language;
- allow for complaints to be made and progressed orally (by phone or in person) or in writing (including email);
- describe the steps it will take to investigate and resolve your complaint and the likely time this will take;
- provide for an internal review of your complaint if you are disatisfied by the response.

The supplier must also give the names and contact details of the main sources of independent help, advice and information. To be independent the advisers must not be connected with the energy company.

Your right to refer your complaint to a qualifying redress scheme from the point at which the supplier notifies you in writing that it is unable to resolve your complaint to your satisfaction should be explained.

Research shows that many complaints can be resolved at the initial contact or within a couple of days. The complaints that suppliers are unable to resolve so quickly are more likely to be recorded by the supplier as a complaint. Ofgem focuses on those complaints that remain unresolved by the end of the working day after the complaint has been recorded. Ofgem statistics show that on average 13 per cent of complaints are unresolved after one working day from the complaint being received.[11]

Recording a complaints

On receiving your complaint, a supplier must electronically record that the complaint has been made. It must record the date, whether the complaint was made orally or in writing and your name and contact details or those of the person making the complaint for you.[12]

Where the supplier is licensed by Ofgem, details of the complaint must be recorded along with details of you and your account, together with a summary of any advice given and any agreement on future communication.[13]

Where you have made a complaint but the supplier cannot find your complaint, the supplier must record the fact that it is unable to trace your complaint.[14]

Where a supplier has recorded that your complaint is resolved but subsequent contact from you contradicts this, the supplier must not treat your complaint as a resolved complaint until it is demonstrably a resolved complaint.[15]

If you reach the position where the complaint is not resolved, the supplier must issue a letter saying this. In the energy industry, this is known commonly as a 'deadlock' letter. However, in reaching this point, the supplier must also set out the different remedies available to you under the complaints handling procedure, which must include:

- an apology;
- an explanation;
- the taking of appropriate remedial action by the regulated provider; *and*
- the award of compensation in appropriate circumstances.

If you have been adversely affected by a failure of a licenced supplier to comply with its marketing obligations,[16] you may be awarded compensation under its complaints procedure.[17]

When a complaint is treated as received

Your complaint and any subsequent communication must be treated as having been received:[18]

- where contact is made orally (by phone or in person), at the time at which it is received by that regulated provider;
- where made in writing (including by email) and it is received:
  - before 5pm on a working day, on that day;
  - after 5pm on a working day or at any time on a day that is not a working day, on the first working day immediately following the day upon which it is received.

Consumer Focus and Citizens Advice consumer service

Consumer Focus is the successor body to the National Consumer Council. It also took on the responsibilities of Energywatch and the regulatory body for postal services Postwatch. It was originally envisaged that establishing a single voice for consumers would provide a stronger and more effective policy voice at national and EU level.[19] Consumer Focus operates with respect to England, with Consumer Focus Scotland and Consumer Focus Wales operating in Scotland and Wales.

In April 2012, the Department for Business, Innovation and Skills announced reforms to consumer protection.[20]

- Citizens Advice will represent consumers' interests in unregulated services, taking on responsibilities and resources from Consumer Focus and the OFT. This process has already started, and since 2 April 2012, Citizens Advice has been responsible for the '**Citizens Advice consumer service**', providing phone (08454 04 05 06) and web-based (www.adviceguide.org.uk) consumer advice.
- A new National Trading Standards Board is to be created.
- A new regulated industries unit (RIU) will be created by April 2013 to take over Consumer Focus' work in energy and postal services.
- Consumer focus will cease to exist after April 2014.

Standards of performance

Failure by suppliers to comply with overall standards of performance can result in regulatory action. Suppliers are regulated through the Standard Licence Conditions (SLCs). If there is widespread evidence of suppliers flouting or avoiding their obligations under the SLCs, Ofgem and Consumer Focus would be expected to act.

There are two kinds of standards of performance – 'overall' and 'individual'. '**Overall standards**' are targets laid down by Ofgem to measure the supplier's general performance. Failure to comply with overall standards is a matter between the supplier and Ofgem and is unlikely to affect you directly. '**Individual standards**' are rules of performance (eg, Electricity (Standards of Performance) Regulations 2010) which, if they are breached, normally entitle you to a small payment in compensation in appropriate cases (see Appendix 2).

Electricity

Standards apply to all electricity suppliers. Suppliers provide online information and leaflets describing them – some may also include additional standards which the supplier has set for itself. The standards set down by the law cover:

- failure of the distributor's fuse;
- restoring supply where disconnection was the supplier's fault;
- providing a supply;
- providing an estimate of charges for connection of a supply or moving a meter;
- giving notice when the supplier has to interrupt a supply;

- dealing with voltage complaints;
- dealing with meter disputes;
- responding to complaints about prepayment meters not working;
- responding to requests or queries about charges or payments;
- making and keeping appointments;
- giving notice to consumers of their rights under this scheme.

The standards require the functions under each of these headings to be carried out within a certain number of working days. Failure to do so entitles you to a fixed sum, from £22 (for most matters) up to £50. There is a list of the time periods and compensation payments in Appendix 2.

However, these payments are normally maximum payments. If failure to meet the standards causes you to lose more than £22 or £50, you can still claim the larger amount. If necessary, you can go to court (see p233). If there is any dispute between you and the supplier over these standards or the payments, contact Citizens Advice consumer service for advice (see Appendix 1).

Gas

Minimum standards are laid down in regulations for gas. As with electricity, there are some automatic levels of compensation. The customer relations manager in each British Gas region has the authority to settle claims for breach of these standards, up to £5,000.

3. Ofgem

Enforcement matters

Ofgem has powers to order suppliers and gas transporters to do anything it considers necessary to ensure they comply with certain provisions of the Acts or any conditions in their licences. The matters covered by these powers are called 'enforcement matters' and include:[21]

- giving and continuing to supply electricity;
- connecting premises to a supply of gas;
- paying interest on security deposits;
- keeping meters in proper working order;
- producing codes of practice or other arrangements to deal with customers in default.

The list of enforcement matters seems more limited than it really is. For instance, disputes about responsibility for bills are not specifically mentioned, but may be covered indirectly because one remedy for a supplier in a dispute is to disconnect you and disconnection may be an enforcement matter. Ofgem can intervene in a dispute if it is likely to end up being an enforcement matter, but it cannot currently intervene in individual billing disputes. However, when the Energy Bill

2012/13 is enacted, Ofgem will have great enforcement powers. The Bill introduces a scheme for Ofgem to impose consumer redress orders for breaches of licence conditions by suppliers (see p46).

The conditions in suppliers' and transporters' licences are not enforceable by individual consumers because they are obligations arising between the respective supplier and Ofgem. Many disputes will arise directly under the relevant Acts, but those that only involve breaches of licence conditions will have to be referred to Ofgem. If necessary, Ofgem's exercise of its powers can be judicially reviewed. In certain circumstances the suppliers may also be judicially reviewed (see p242).

Obtaining an order from Ofgem

When an enforcement matter arises, Ofgem can make one of two kinds of order: a 'provisional order' or a 'final order'. Making a provisional order is quicker than a final order, so you should press for the former.

If you think a supplier or transporter may be in breach of an enforcement matter, contact Citizens Advice consumer service in the first instance. Unless the matter is considered 'frivolous', there should be an investigation. If satisfied that there has been a breach, the matter will be referred to Ofgem, who will make either a provisional or final order.

Ofgem cannot make an order if:

- it thinks that its general duties laid down by the Acts do not allow it; *or*
- the breaches in question are trivial; *or*
- it is satisfied that the supplier or transporter has agreed to, and is taking all steps necessary to, comply with its obligations.

Ofgem must tell you if it decides not to make an order. In deciding whether to make an order, Ofgem must take into account, in particular, your lack of other remedies and the loss or damage which you might suffer during the consultation period, which has to take place before a final order is made. If you would otherwise be without a supply, a provisional order will normally be appropriate.

If a provisional order is made and complied with, Ofgem will only confirm it as a final order if further breaches are likely to occur.

Before making a final order or confirming a provisional order, Ofgem must serve you and the supplier/transporter with a copy of the proposed order and allow 28 days for representations. If it wants to modify the original proposal, Ofgem must either get the consent of the supplier/transporter or serve copies and allow a further 28 days. A similar procedure must be gone through to revoke a final order.

Ofgem must also comply with the ordinary legal rules about natural justice which govern public or government organisations (see p242). In one case, a decision by the previous gas regulator Ofgas was quashed by the High Court because it did not tell a consumer that it had interviewed an important witness, nor did it give the consumer a chance to reply to what the witness had said.[22]

You are entitled to a copy of any order when it is made.

A supplier/transporter can appeal to the High Court (Court of Session in Scotland) against the making of an order. Although you would not necessarily be directly involved, you can be added as a third party – this is a technical procedure for which you will have to get legal advice.

The supplier has a duty to obey any order. This means you can sue for a breach if Ofgem does not enforce its own order. Ofgem can also enforce its orders by ordinary civil action against the supplier/transporter, which would be easier and cheaper for you, if you cannot obtain Community Legal Service funding to do this yourself.

Each case is decided on its merits. As mentioned above, cases will rarely, if ever, reach this stage because suppliers will want to avoid formal (and public) action.

Breach of conditions relating to payment difficulties

All suppliers' licences require them to compile methods to deal with customers in arrears. These matters are dealt with elsewhere in this book, but it is worth pointing out that a supplier's failure to comply with these 'methods' is an enforcement matter because it is a breach of the relevant condition.

4. **Office of Fair Trading and unfair terms**

As your fuel supply is provided under a contract with the supplier, the law relating to contracts, including regulations covering unfair terms, applies. A full discussion of contract law is outside the scope of this book, but this section deals with the Unfair Terms in Consumer Contracts Regulations 1999.

These regulations apply to any standard term in a contract which has not been individually negotiated,[23] or which does not accurately implement a provision of any relevant legislation.[24] Contracts are normally deemed or offered in accordance with a pre-determined scheme, which obviously means that terms have not been individually negotiated. The 1999 Regulations extended the power to investigate and challenge unfair contract terms in order to allow other bodies to share the enforcement task with the Office of Fair Trading. These currently include local authority trading standards departments, Consumer Focus and Ofgem. The power is to challenge for the general protection of consumers, not individuals.

The test of fairness

A '**standard term**' (one that has not been individually negotiated) is unfair 'if, contrary to the requirement of good faith, it causes a significant imbalance in the parties' rights and obligations arising under the contract, to the detriment of the consumer'.

The requirement of good faith embodies the general 'principle of fair and open dealing'. It does not simply mean that a term should not be used in a deceitful way. Suppliers are expected to respect consumers' legitimate interests in drafting contracts as well as negotiating and carrying them out. An imbalance to the detriment of the consumer may arise wherever a term gives powers or safeguards to the supplier which could put the consumer at a disadvantage, whether or not actual harm is currently being caused.

Transparency is also fundamental to fairness. Any written term must be expressed in plain, intelligible language, and if there is doubt as to the term's meaning, the interpretation most favourable to you must be taken. It is possible that this would require the supplier to translate the relevant terms into languages other than English, but this has yet to be tested. Terms may be considered unfair if the language used could mislead the ordinary person, or if you are not given an adequate chance to read them before becoming bound by them.

Action may also be taken against a supplier which engages in an unfair trading practice under the Consumer Protection from Unfair Trading Regulations 2008.[25] These cover unfair commercial practices which affect the operation of consumer choice, referred to as a **'transactional decision'** in the regulations. A transactional decision has a broad meaning covering any decision taken by a consumer, whether it is to act or to refrain from acting, concerning whether, how and on what terms:

- to purchase, make payment in whole or in part for, retain or dispose of a product; *or*
- to exercise a contractual right in relation to a product.

'Commercial practice' is also given wide meaning and includes a trader's act omission, course of conduct, representation or commercial communication (eg, advertising and marketing) which is directly connected with the promotion, sale or supply of a product to or from you.[26] The unfair practice can occur before, during or after the transaction, whether or not the transaction ultimately takes place. Thus, unfair atttempts to influence you through marketing and cold-calling and steps that might be taken to stop you exercising your rights can be caught by the regulations.

The test of whether a commercial practice is misleading includes whether it contains false information and whether if decives you into a transaction you would not have otherwise taken.[27] This includes the marketing of a product (including comparative advertising) which creates confusion about any products, trade marks, trade names or other distinguishing marks of a competitor. Importantly, it may also cover the failure by a fuel supplier to comply with a code of conduct if it has indicated that it is bound by the code of conduct, and the breach causes you to enter into a transaction that you otherwise would not have done so.

If a trader engages in a commercial practice which is misleading it is guilty of an offence and may be prosecuted by the trading standards department of a local authority.

In 2012, the Court of Appeal upheld the conviction for an offence under these regulations by Scottish and Southern Energy.[28] The company was held liable for misleading statements made by a trainee salesperson working for a linked company, Southern Electric Gas Ltd, operating in an area with a considerable population of elderly consumers and which had been designated by the local council as a 'no cold calling zone'. The Court of Appeal ruled that both companies could potentially have been prosecuted and that Scottish and Southern Energy fell within the definition of a 'trader' under the regulations as South Electric Gas Ltd was held by it as a subsidiary company.

5. **Using the civil courts**

There are two types of civil court action in the field of fuel rights – ordinary court action or judicial review. In England and Wales, the relationship between the consumer and the supplier is also based on contract law, with remedies available through the civil courts.

In Scotland, ordinary court action may only be available against a supplier which supplies under a contract. It is likely that a Scottish Sheriff Court would not allow an action for breach of statutory duty, as that is a type of action which has not previously existed in Scottish law.

In Scotland, a consumer's relationship with a public electricity supplier/ regional electricity company or transporter is statutory, and so any claim is based on a breach of a statutory duty (see Chapter 1). This means that you have to pursue your remedies through Ofgem. On the other hand, Ofgem is subject to judicial review. The procedure for judicial review is more flexible and easier to use in Scotland than in England and Wales, so you should still have an effective remedy.

Legal funding

In theory, in England and Wales, Community Legal Service funding is available for taking court action if you have a strong enough case and qualify on financial grounds. The number of people eligible for legal assistance has been dramatically reduced and the Legal Services Commission will only fund as part of the Community Legal Service, subject to restrictions laid down in law and guidance.

Substantial cuts in legal aid will take effect in April 2013, amid government estimates that the number of civil cases reaching court can be reduced by half a million each year.

Until these changes occur, in principle, provision may be made for:

- legal help;
- help at court;
- legal representation – this can be either investigative help or full representation;
- such other services as are authorised by specific orders or directions from the Lord Chancellor.

A successful grant of legal aid will cover all your legal costs and protect you against an order to pay the other side's legal costs if you lose. However, in many cases only an increasingly limited amount of help may be granted, if any. If your income is above the basic level of benefit, you will have to make a contribution to these costs. A legal aid application form and a means form will be filled in. However, you are not required to give a large amount of information on your means if you are in receipt of an income-related benefit. You should bring letters and documents establishing your entitlement to benefit with you together with proof of identification if you are applying for legal aid from a legal aid provider such as a solicitor or law centre. More details are set out in the General Funding Code and the Manual published by the Legal Services Commission in England and Wales.

In Scotland, the Scottish Legal Aid Board provides civil assistance. Eligibility is based upon disposable income after essential expenses have been paid. For more details, see www.slab.org.uk.

In practice, it may be very hard to find a solicitor or advice and assistance funded by legal aid in many areas. It may also take time for an application for legal aid assistance to be processed.

Emergency legal representation

Assuming a legal aid provider can be found it may be necessary to apply for emergency legal representation (ELR) in many cases involving energy problems. The first thing to check in an emergency case is whether a legal aid provider has power to grant ELR. If it does, an emergency grant should be made.[29] If it does not have the power, an emergency application will have to be made to the local Legal Services Commission Office, though in genuine emergencies, ELR can be granted over the phone or by fax. Before applying, your adviser must ensure that the legal aid application form and the means assessment form are completed.

To justify a grant of ELR it must be necessary to do the work before a substantive application for legal representation can be made and determined (typically one month). An emergency certificate will only be granted if:

- there is a risk to your physical safety or that of any family member or your home;
- there is a significant risk of a miscarriage of justice, unreasonable hardship or irretrievable problems in handling the case;
- there are no other appropriate options available to deal with the risk.

An emergency legal aid certificate lasts for four weeks. This period cannot be extended, except by the Legal Services Commission. For more information, see www.legalservices.gov.uk.

Using the small claims procedure in the county court

England and Wales

Most civil claims are unlikely to qualify for legal assistance if the amount claimed falls below £5,000. This means that you may have to act for yourself. Every year thousands of people represent themselves in small claims hearings, though until recently they have not often been used by energy consumers. In England and Wales, small claims are heard in the county court which deals with civil cases where up to £50,000 is involved (claims of £50,000 or more are heard in the High Court).

Where a dispute involves less than £5,000 – as with many consumer matters – it will be dealt with under the arbitration procedure in the county court. This is popularly known as the small claims court. A small claims hearing normally takes the form of a hearing in private in chambers – ie, the judge's private room.

There are leaflets available explaining how to bring a claim in the county court which may be obtained from your local county court if you are in England or Wales. It is important to refer to these leaflets to begin with as they set out the basic things you need to know in bringing a claim. For example, if you are owed money or should be paid compensation, a claim can be commenced through the county court to obtain a judgment to settle the legal rights of the parties. Once a judgment is obtained action can be taken if the party does not follow the terms of the judgment – eg, in a claim for compensation by paying the money owed. Any person subject to a judgment becomes a judgment debtor until the money is paid and enforcement proceedings to recover the money can be commenced against the person, whether it is a human being or a 'legal person' such as a company. The county court provides a system of enforcement for judgments whereby bailiffs can be instructed to seize goods from the judgment debtor or whereby bank accounts or other property may be seized to satisfy a judgment.

Helpful information can also be found at Her Majesty's Courts and Tribunals Service website (www.justice.gov.uk) and in leaflets available from the county court.

The small claims court is a relatively informal procedure, suitable for people who are not represented by a solicitor. This might be appropriate if an unlawful disconnection has caused you a relatively small loss or your landlord has been charging more than the maximum resale price for gas or electricity.

Other claims might include where you have a dispute with an energy company about the amount you have paid or where there has been a failure of supply which has resulted in damage such as loss of frozen food where electricity has been cut off. Or you may have a dispute about the amount of gas or electricity consumed at your home which you cannot resolve with the supplier.

Neither side can claim legal costs beyond the court fees involved and, as a result, suppliers tend to settle these cases rather than spend money on contesting them which will not be recoverable.

The court staff should always be willing to help you with the procedure for issuing a claim (Citizens Advice or other local advice agencies may also help). When the claim form is issued, a court fee is normally payable. However, if you are on income support, income-based jobseeker's allowance, pension credit, income-related employment and support allowance or, from October 2013, universal credit, you may be exempted from paying any fee on application to the court (see p244). You will need to complete claim forms which will require you to set down the details of your legal claim.

If you are not receiving any of these benefits, you can apply for remission or reduction of a fee if you would otherwise suffer undue financial hardship because of the exceptional circumstances in your case. Copies of the form are then lodged in court on payment of the fee (unless this is waived) and a copy is sent to the other side (known as the defendant). The issue of the form requires the defendant to either admit the claim or to defend it. In either case, the defendant must reply to the issue of the proceedings. If the defendant does nothing, after 21 days you may be entitled to claim judgment in default. This means you can obtain your judgment without having to argue the case in court, simply because the defendant has failed to reply.

Experience suggests that fuel suppliers will rarely contest proceedings in the small claims court, as the cost of sending someone to attend the hearing will often exceed the amount of the money concerned. In some cases involving relatively small sums (eg, less than £500), the supplier may not even contest proceedings. This is a factor which encourages the settlement of a dispute. Small claims may be particularly suited to the recovery of deposits.

Under the rules of civil procedure, each side is entitled to see the written evidence and documents used in a claim before the hearing. Each side is expected to list its documents and to make copies available. Neither side should be taken by surprise by written evidence at the hearing.

In bringing a claim relating to overcharging or a failure to supply for which you have been charged, you should gather together all your energy bills. If you no longer have them, request them in writing from your supplier. Also bring a copy of all correspondence and the contract with the energy company. These documents should be organised in date order.

Look at the agreed price for supply and work out whether the company has charged the correct rate for units over 12 months. Check whether it has charged more. Use April 1 to March 31 as the starting and finishing dates. Look especially at any periods where there may have been overcharging. You will need to produce these documents if a case goes as far as Court; prior to any hearing you should also send the other side copies all documentary evidence on which you intend to rely.

For each year, work out how many units over the limit you have been charged and multiply them first by the higher rate and then by the lower rate. The difference is the amount that you should claim for overcharging.

Check whether the supplier has ever given you an explanation of its charging methods. If not, state that you believe that you have been wrongly charged from when you became a customer, to the present day. Calculate your entire usage over the period and work out how much it would have cost when your supply started. Then work out how much you have actually paid. The difference between the two figures is what you should claim. Such cases may also arise from under-charging leading to the supplier suddenly trying to recover money with a demand for a lump sum.

The rules of court encourage parties to try and settle their cases without recourse to court proceedings – at any stage parties can negotiate and make settlement proposals to each other to avoid litigation.

If the matter goes as far as a small claims court hearing, each side has an opportunity to present her/his case. Any written evidence which is presented should normally be served on the other side before the hearing.

Methods of service

The Civil Procedure Rules set out the various methods of service that can be used. The usual method of service is by first class post, with the documents deemed served two days after posting. Other methods of service which may be used include:

- personal service – where a document is physically handed to the party. If the party is a limited company or a corporation the document can be handed to a person who has as a senior position in the organisation;
- leaving the document at the correct address;
- fax, email or document exchange – but a party may have to consent to service by these methods.

Electronic communications can be used to send copies of documents for filing at the County Court and each County Court should have a designated email address for this.

Witness statements should also be sent to the other side in advance of the hearing. For example, you might wish to call an electrician or meter reader as a witness in a case and it will be necessary to submit a written witness statement of what s/he will say first. Each side gives its evidence to the court and has an opportunity to question the other (a process known as cross examination). The judge may also ask questions of the parties.

A party to a hearing is also entitled to quiet assistance from a friend to help present her/his case. The friend is entitled to take notes, suggest questions and give quiet advice on the conduct of the case. The friend may be legally qualified but this is not essential. Such assistance is known as having a 'McKenzie friend', derived from the case of *McKenzie v McKenzie*,[30] and courts are generally familiar with the concept. (McKenzie friends often assist debtors in debt recovery proceedings in certain courts.) The McKenzie friend has no right to address the court but, in practice, the courts may allow a McKenzie friend to address the court if a litigant has difficulties. The right to speak is a discretionary one, and anyone granted the right to speak must not abuse the privilege. In particular, it is crucial that any statements made to the court relate to the facts and points of law in the case and are not directed as a general attack on the energy company and its policies. If the right to a McKenzie friend is abused (eg, by making political or personalised attacks), it may be withdrawn. It is important to be polite at all times.

If you succeed in your claim, the court fee is added to the amount which the other side has to pay you. In England and Wales, unlike other court proceedings, only limited costs can be reclaimed. This means that, even if you lose, you will not have to pay the other side's own legal representation costs (ie, each side is responsible for its own costs). As a result, some companies may be prepared to settle a case out of court. If a settlement offer is made, it should be considered seriously (the rules of court are designed to encourage settlements between the parties).

Advice should be taken, since a favourable verdict in court cannot be guaranteed or a lesser sum might be awarded. The details of any settlement should be in writing and marked as 'full and final settlement'.

A small claims court judgment takes effect like any other judgment of the county court and can be enforced through the court.

If there is a difficulty with procedure or a point of law, it may be necessary to refer to the rules of court. The rules of procedure for the county court and copies of relevant forms and statutes are set out in the County Procedure Rules. For the county court, there is the *County Court Practice*, published annually (this is known as 'the Green Book', because it has a green cover). The book is complex, but in practice it is a standard reference work for lawyers and judges as well as for litigants. Most large libraries in England and Wales will hold a copy. This covers many different situations and types of proceedings and only a small part will be relevant. In most cases there is never a need to refer to the book, only when a difficulty arises. The Civil Practice Rules are also available at www.justice.gov.uk/courts/procedure-rules/civil.

Scotland

Scotland also has a small claims procedure for sums up to £3,000 using the Sheriff Court. Procedure is governed by the small claims rules with standard forms known as summonses to be completed. The forms can be obtained from the Sheriff Court clerk at the Court or downloaded from the Scottish Courts Service website (www.scotcourts.gov.uk). The person bringing the action is known as a pursuer and the person who is being taken to court is known as the 'defender'. The details can be amended before a hearing takes place. It is also possible to apply for time in order to try and reach a settlement to the case. Bringing the case to a temporary halt in this way is known as 'sisting' the case.

If the defender does not respond to proceedings, Form 11 should be completed setting out the order you wish to obtain. If a party fails to appear at a small claims hearing, the sheriff can grant an order, known as a decree. In Scotland, no costs are payable if the claim is under £200, but costs can be awarded up to £150 if the claim is over £200.

Disputes over £5,000

In other county court proceedings (involving sums of more than £5,000), each party will have to pay its own costs, and the unsuccessful party will also have to pay the other party's costs. These may be substantial and while individuals can represent themselves it is advisable to instruct a solicitor. Note that even if you are successful, not every cost incurred will be recoverable; only essential costs incurred in litigation will be obtainable. Where excessive cost bills are issued by solicitors, these may be challenged through the courts in a process known as taxation. The court will formally review a bill and determine whether the costs incurred are just and reasonable and may deduct items from the bill.

As with small claims, the rules of court encourage parties to settle their cases out of court.

Claims for harassment

An important case which indicates that the courts will not tolerate heavy-handed and intimidating actions by energy suppliers was the judgment in *Ferguson v British Gas*[31] where the Court of Appeal ruled that legal threats issued by British Gas could constitute harassment and could be subject to both civil proceedings and a crime under the Prevention of Harassment Act 1997.

In *Ferguson,* over a period of months British Gas sent bills and threatening letters to the claimant who was a former British Gas customer who had switched to npower. The letters demanded money she did not owe. The threats included to cut-off her gas supply, to start legal proceedings and to report her to credit reference agencies. Despite repeatedly writing and phoning British Gas the threats continued, including after she complained to Energywatch and twice to the chairman of British Gas. As a result she wasted many hours, and, more importantly, was brought to a state of considerable anxiety. By January 2007 she had instructed a solicitor but still no response was received. As a consequence she began legal proceedings claiming £5,000 for distress and anxiety and £5,000 for financial loss due to time lost and expenses in dealing with British Gas and that the course of conduct amounts to unlawful harassment contrary to the Protection from Harassment Act 1997. British Gas attempted to have the claim struck out.

The Court of Appeal ruled that the course of conduct by British Gas was capable of amounting to unlawful harassment. There was a case which could go to trial and the conduct was sufficiently serious to consider that an offence might also have been committed.

Excuses raised by British Gas that it could not be blamed for letters issued by a computer or that it was a company, and should be treated as different to an individual who issued threatening letters, were rejected by the court.

The court ruled that a company such as British Gas could be held responsible for mistakes made by its computerised debt recovery system and the personnel responsible for programming and operating it. The company could be held liable in the same way that a human being could be.

The court also indicated that harassment could be a crime as well as a tort or civil wrong[32] and that in 'any well-documented case, what is sufficient for the one purpose is likely to be sufficient for the other'. This ruling opens the way in future for energy companies that allow harassment of debtors to take place to be prosecuted under the Protection from Harassment Act 1997. It was further observed that, 'The primary responsibility should rest upon local public authorities which possess the means and the statutory powers to bring alleged harassers, however impersonal and powerful, before the local justices.' This means that trading standards departments could prosecute where wrongful debt collection turns into harassment.

A wrongful attempt at debt enforcement by an energy supplier can also result in damages for slander or libel if statements are made by a supplier are untrue and may damage your reputation.[33]

Injunctions and damages

This section describes the remedies you can get through the ordinary courts. Before taking this approach, however, you need to know how they relate to the remedies available from Ofgem.

Determinations by Ofgem are final, and once a determination has been made you cannot sue a supplier or transporter over the same matters. Whether you can sue a supplier at the same time as Ofgem is using its enforcement powers is not so clear. In practice it should rarely, if ever, be necessary to duplicate proceedings in this way. However, in theory, Ofgem could refuse to make an order to reconnect your supply, so you would need to get your own court order while Ofgem considers what else it might order the supplier or transporter to do or not to do. A court could, and almost certainly would, refuse to consider a case if it felt that Ofgem was dealing with it in a way which seemed to be adequate at the time.

In practice, you will have to consider at the very start which route you should take: determination, enforcement, or your own legal action. Whether or not to use the enforcement powers is Ofgem's decision (subject to judicial review) but you can take the lead on the other two routes.

Injunctions/interdicts

An '**injunction**' ('**interdict**' in Scotland) is an order made by a court which either prohibits someone from doing something (a 'prohibitory' injunction) or instructs someone to do something (a 'mandatory' injunction). For example, if a supplier or landlord illegally cuts off your supply, you could ask for an injunction to get it reconnected.[34] Failure to obey an injunction is contempt of court, punishable by fines, or even imprisonment in extreme cases.

In urgent cases an injunction may be obtained by a claimant in the absence of the other side (what is known as an *ex parte* injunction), where, for example, locks have been changed on a property without permission or a meter has been unlawfully removed. The injunction is obtained by going to court and making an appointment for an urgent hearing. A standard form is provided, and you are asked to provide evidence in the form of a statement of truth. Normally, the claim for an injunction will be part of an action for damages. The application is made before a judge who makes a decision as to whether the injunction should be granted and gives directions about how the other side (known as the defendant) is to be notified with her/his decision.

Although there are some situations in which an injunction is granted almost as a matter of course (eg, illegal eviction), you have no 'right' to an injunction. Injunctions are within a court's discretion and whether or not they are granted depends on the overall circumstances of the case.

The most common situation in a dispute with a supplier is where you will be asking for an 'interim' injunction (or 'interim' interdict in Scotland). This would be when you need a temporary court order quickly, usually valid until the whole case can be put properly before the court in a fully prepared trial. In the county court in England and Wales, an injunction can be sought using Form N1 (Notice of Application) and wherever possible include a signed witness statement and copies of any relevant documents. In Scotland, specialist legal advice should be sought as the law relating to interdicts is complex.

An example where it might be necessary to threaten or seek an injunction is where a supplier starts action to disconnect a supply by mistake – eg, where action is taken against the wrong address. Normally, you will have had a warning but the situation can arise where a supplier or its agent has obtained a warrant against the wrong address and begins steps to disconnect. Or you come home from a holiday to find you have been disconnected in error by warrant concerning another customer.

During normal court opening hours a hearing can usually be obtained very quickly. You should try and give as much notice as possible to the energy company. Fax and email a letter to the supplier where circumstances allow, addressing it to the legal department. The threat of applying for an injunction may be sufficient to obtain a suitable response from the supplier and make applying for the injunction unnecessary.

In this situation, neither you nor the supplier/transporter will have time to present your case fully, and the court will have to make up its mind without hearing the evidence in full. The court will consider the 'balance of convenience' – ie, whether you or the supplier/transporter has more to lose or gain from the refusal or granting of an interim injunction, including whether a later award of damages will make up for any such loss.[35] For example, where a supplier threatens disconnection, the court will balance the inconvenience to you of being disconnected against the inconvenience to the supplier of having to continue to supply someone regarded as a bad customer. A court will almost always consider the balance to be in your favour if you are prepared to agree to a prepayment meter at least until your dispute is resolved.[36] If an immediate injunction is granted you will be asked to serve the supplier with notice of the order immediately by phoning them or faxing a letter; a copy of the order will also be drawn up by the court. Failure to obey an injunction will put the supplier at risk of contempt proceedings for which it may be fined or individuals may be jailed as a punishment. In emergency situations, injunctions can be obtained outside normal court hours. The court will have a phone number to contact in such cases and injunction can be granted by a judge over the phone.

Damages

As well as, or instead of, an injunction, you can claim damages (ie, monetary compensation) for a supplier or transporter's abuse of its powers or failure to comply with its statutory or contractual duties.[37] If your supply is accidentally cut off, you may be able to claim damages for negligence and damage which has come directly from the interruption of electricity or gas supply (but not for the pure supply interruptions themselves).

In a case of failure to supply, damages would cover compensation, not only for the distress and discomfort of being without a supply but also for additional expenses (eg, take away meals) and the loss of specific items (eg, fridge/freezer contents). Interest can also be claimed on any sum awarded in damages.

A claim for negligence may also arise where a supplier has caused damage or breached safety rules and damage to a person or property has resulted. In *Smith and others v South Eastern Power Networks plc and other cases* [2012] what is safe is judged as an objective question by reference to what may be reasonably foreseen by a reasonable and prudent employer. It is also crucial that any breach of duty, including breaches of codes of practice or duties imposed by statute, can be shown to be responsible for causing the damage for which compensation is sought.[38]

Judicial review and the Human Rights Act 1998

Public bodies, such as Ofgem, have both statutory duties which must be performed and powers which allow for a large element of discretion. There is usually no right of appeal against a failure to perform a 'power', or as to how that discretion is exercised. However, this does not mean that nothing can be done.

Such administrative matters are subject to control by judicial review[39] on the grounds of illegality, irrationality or procedural impropriety (see below).

The exercise of any 'public' powers by any of the principal bodies discussed in this book can be subject to judicial review. This includes not only Ofgem, but also the suppliers themselves. That the suppliers should be subject to judicial review in appropriate circumstances is probably a radical suggestion and the limits of the law have yet to be tested. Legal advice will be essential.

An **'illegal decision'** is one where the decision-making body has not been given the legal power to do what it has done – ie, if it has gone outside its remit or what it was set up to do.

An **'irrational decision'** is one which is so unreasonable that no reasonable authority could make it. In legal jargon, this is 'Wednesbury' unreasonableness, named after the court case in which the principle was established.[40] This principle requires a decision-making body to:

- consider all relevant factors;
- disregard irrelevant factors;
- not act perversely.

Challenges may also be brought on grounds of 'procedural impropriety' where a public body fails to follows its own rules. This can include breaches of 'natural justice' making decisions which are biased or unfair or which have the appearance of unfairness and prejudice to any impartial observer. If a decision-making body fails to adhere to the requirements of natural justice or the Wednesbury principles, then its decisions may be challenged in the High Court by way of judicial review. In Scotland, an application is made to the Court of Session.

Breach of one or more of these principles gives the court the power to overturn an authority's decision. It is important to realise that a court cannot overturn a decision simply because it thinks it would have come to a different decision. The court does not put itself in the place of the decision maker, but merely ensures s/he has kept within the boundaries of the law. It is possible for two different, even contradictory, decisions to lie within those boundaries so that it would be equally lawful for the decision maker to choose either.

Applying for judicial review is a two-stage procedure, governed by Order 54 of the Civil Procedure Rules. An applicant must first apply for leave (ie, permission for judicial review) by lodging an application with supporting documents and written evidence at the Administrative Court at the High Court in the Strand, London or in local centres of the High Court such as Leeds. A judge then considers the papers and decides whether leave should be granted – ie, permission to take the case on to a full judicial review hearing. In Scotland, the application is made to the Court of Session which sits in the Parliament House in Edinburgh.

In England and Wales, the court can make an order overturning a decision ('quashing' order) or requiring the body which is being judicially reviewed to do or not to do something ('mandatory' or 'prohibitory' order) in the same way as an injunction (p241). In Scotland, a decision can be quashed by 'reduction', and a 'declarator' ('declaration' in England and Wales) can be issued establishing the legal position. If damages could be claimed on ordinary principles, the court in judicial review proceedings may also award them, although they are rarely claimed.

It is important to realise that judicial review is a discretionary remedy and that different courts may or may not grant a remedy.

Applications for judicial review in England and Wales must be made promptly to the High Court and, in any event, within three months of the relevant decision. The three-month period can be extended, but only where there are strong mitigating circumstances (delays in the granting of public funding may, on occasion, be such a reason, but this cannot be relied upon). Even if leave is granted, the court may still refuse relief at the full judicial review hearing. In Scotland, applications must be made to the Court of Session; there is no specific time limit, but applications must not be unduly delayed.

The Human Rights Act 1998 applies to public authorities whose functions are of a public nature – such as regulators and suppliers. The Public Law Project (see Appendix 1) may be able to comment and advise on the Act, fuel regulators and suppliers; this is an area which requires further research and investigation. Rights protected under the Human Rights Act are those contained in the European Convention on Human Rights. These include the right to property (Article 1), the right to a fair hearing (Article 6) and the right to privacy and family life (Article 8).

Remission of court fees

If you are on income support, income-based jobseeker's allowance, pension credit, income-related employment and support allowance or working tax credit (but not getting child tax credit), you are entitled to apply for a fee remission when beginning county court proceedings. Proof of entitlement to benefit may be established by a current letter from the Department for Work and Pensions which can be produced at the court office. If you are turned down on an application for remission of fees, there is normally a right of appeal. An application for a remission is made on Form EX160, which can be downloaded from the HM Courts and Tribunals Service website.

If there is an emergency matter that needs an urgent decision of the court, the court manager can grant a remission without supporting evidence when the form is submitted to court. You are likely to be required to provide evidence within five days of the remission being given.

Complaints about National Grid

If your complaint is about any aspect of the operation of the National Grid or its employees and agents, you can use its free complaints service. National Grid will investigate your complaint and respond to you within 10 working days. If it is not possible to investigate the complaint within the 10 days, it will inform you when a response can be expected. If no response is forthcoming, there may be grounds for compensation under National Grid's standards of service provisions.

6. **The Energy Ombudsman**

The Energy Ombudsman is an independent body which resolves disputes and complaints after negotiation has failed.

The Energy Ombudsman can deal with complaints about bills for your gas and electricity services, complaints about a supplier's sales activity or about problems when changing your energy provider.

You can only refer your complaint to the Ombudsman if you have tried to resolve it with your energy provider but have received a 'deadlock letter' or eight weeks have passed since you first made your complaint to your provider. The Energy Ombudsman expects you to have fully exhausted the supplier's complaints process first. In 2011/12 69 per cent of contacts with the Ombudsman were deemed outside the scope of the scheme, many because they were started prematurely.[41]

If you have been unable to resolve your complaint with your energy supplier within eight weeks you may submit your complaint in writing to the Ombudsman. Include all relevant documents. It is also a good idea to include a chronology of events, listing key events in order, with the date on which they occurred. This provides a summary of what happened and when which assists the Ombudsman in analysing the situation. If you have incurred financial losses, submit copies of receipts, bills and invoices you have had to pay to corroborate what you claim.

If the Ombudsman decides to make an award, and you accept it, your supplier has to abide by the decision. The Ombudsman can ask your supplier to provide any or all of the following:

- a service or some practical action that will benefit you;
- an apology or explanation;
- a financial award up to £5,000 (£5,000 will only be payable in exceptional cases; normally any award will be much lower);
- all of the UK's major energy providers are members of the Ombudsman scheme, which means that they have to abide by any decision that it makes regarding your complaint.

Energy Ombudsman in 2011/12[42]

In 2011/12 the Energy Ombudsman resolved more than 6,600 complaints – 34 per cent were resolved informally and 66 per cent were formally resolved following an investigation by an officer for the Ombudsman.

71 per cent of all resolutions required by Energy Ombudsman included both a financial payment and other action to resolve the complaint; 21 per cent involved a non-financial

settlement only; 3 per cent involved a financial award only; and 5 per cent required no action.

Of the complaints receiving a financial award: 1,662 resulted in a payment of between £1 and £50; 1,579 between £51 and £100; 703 between £100 and £200; 183 between £501 and £1,000; 48 between £2,001 and £3,000; and 44 complaints received the maximum award of £5,000.

Any remedy arising from a decision by the Ombudsman normally has to be accepted in 28 days; it is possible to ask for a decision to be reviewed if you are unhappy with any aspect of it.

Back-billing

One area which generates cases to the Ombudsman is the serving of estimated bills and late bills where a customer has not been properly billed for a long period. It should be noted that the energy Ombudsman generally expects you to pay for energy you have legitimately used and to take steps to sort out the problem with the company first including by way of a complaint. The voluntary code on back-billing allows for back-billing for up to one year. The Ombudsman advises that you should continue paying, and only withhold the part of the bill which is in dispute. If you have a low income, pay what you can afford and also prepare a means statement. However, in cases of late back-billing the Ombudsman may investigate and negotiate which can result in the bill being reduced (depending on the mistake and degree of failing or negligence by the supplier) or an award of compensation made as a settlement. Although the Ombudsman expects energy legitimately used to be paid for, a financial award may still be made which can defray the cost of such a bill.

For more information and an online complaints form, visit www.energy-ombudsman.org.uk.

Notes

1. Introduction
1   s12 CEARA 2007
2   s13 CEARA 2007

2. Negotiations
3   SI 2008 No.1898
4   Reg 10 GE(CCHS) Regs
5   Conditions 27 and 39 SLC
6   *Smith and others v South Eastern Power Networks plc and other cases* [2012] EWHC 2541 QBD(TCC) 17 September 2012; *Thompson v Smiths Shiprepairers (North Shields) Ltd* [1984] QB 405
7   GE(CCHS) Regs
8   Reg 2 GE(CCHS) Regs

3. Ofgem
9   Reg 3(1) GE(CCHS) Regs
10 Reg 3(3) GE(CCHS) Regs
11 Ofgem document, *Complaints handling: audit, research and performance*, 2009
12 Reg 4(1) GE(CCHS) Regs
13 Reg 3(3) GE(CCHS) Regs
14 Reg 4(5) GE(CCHS) Regs
15 Reg 4(6) GE(CCHS) Regs
16 Condition 25 SLC gas and condition 25 SLC electricity
17 Reg 3(4) GE(CCHS) Regs
18 Reg 4(4) GE(CCHS) Regs
19 Lord Truscott, Parliamentary Under Secretary of State for Energy, Lords Hansard, 18 December 2006
20 Department for Business, Innovation and Skills, *Empowering and protecting consumers*, April 2012
21 Condition 2 SLC
22 *R v Director-General of Gas Supply ex parte Smith* [1989] (unreported)

4. Office of Fair Trading and unfair terms
23 reg 3 UTCC Regs
24 Sch 1 para (e)(i) UTCC Regs
25 SI No 1277

5. Using the courts
26 Reg 2(1) CPUT Regs
27 Reg 5 CPUT Regs
28 *R (on the application of Surrey Trading Standards) v Scottish and Southern Energy plc* [2012] CA, Criminal Division 16 February, 16 March
29 Funding Code Part 3 section 12.2.1
30 [1971]
31 *Ferguson v British Gas* [2009] EWCA Civ 46
32 At para 52
33 *Say v British Gas Services Ltd* [2011] All ER (D) 216
34 *Gwenter v Eastern Electricity plc* [1994] *Legal Action*, August 1995, p19
35 The principles are set out in *American Cyanamid v Ethicon Ltd* [1975] AC 396
36 *Gwenter v Eastern Electricity plc* [1994] *Legal Action*, August 1995, p19
37 *Faulkner v Yorkshire Electricity plc* [1994] *Legal Action*, February 1995, p23; *Gwenter v Eastern Electricity plc* [1994] *Legal Action*, August 1995, p19
38 *Smith and others v South Eastern Power Networks plc and other cases* [2012] EWHC 2541 QBD(TCC) September 17 2012
39 RSC Order 54 Rules of the Supreme Court (England and Wales)
40 *Associated Provincial Picture Houses v Wednesbury Corporation* [1948] 1 KB 223

6. The Energy Ombudsman
41 Ombudsman Services, *Resolving consumer disputes: Annual report and account 2011/12*, 2012
42 Ombudsman Services, *Resolving consumer disputes: Annual report and account 2011/12*, 2012

Appendix 1

Useful addresses and publications

Energy suppliers' contact numbers

British Gas	0800 048 0202
Ebico	0800 458 7689
Ecotricity	0845 555 7100
EDF Energy (including customers of Seeboard and SWEB)	0800 096 9000
E.ON	0333 202 4426
First Utility	0845 215 5000
Good Energy	0845 456 1640
Green Energy	0845 456 9550
Loco2energy	0845 074 3601
npower	0800 073 3000
OVO Energy	0800 599 9440
Scottish Hydro	0845 300 2141
Scottish Power	0845 2700 700
Spark Energy	0845 034 7474
SSE (including customers of Equigas/Equipower, Atlantic, Severn Trent Energy, Southern Electric)	0845 7444 555
SWALEC	0800 052 5252
Utilita	0845 450 4357
Utility Warehouse	0844 815 7777

Fuel campaigning and information organisations

Energy Saving Trust (EST)
Helpline: 0800 512 012
www.energysavingtrust.org.uk

EST England
21 Dartmouth Street
London SW1H 9BP
Tel: 020 7222 0101

EST Scotland
2nd Floor, Ocean Point 1
94 Ocean Drive
Edinburgh EH6 6JH
Tel: 0131 555 7900

EST Wales
Wales Albion House
1 Caspian Point, Caspian Way
Cardiff Bay CF10 4DQ
Tel: 029 2046 8340

Home Heat Helpline
Helpline: 0800 33 66 99
www.heatinghelpline.org.uk

National Energy Action
Level 6, West One
Forth Banks
Newcastle upon Tyne NE1 3PA
Tel: 0191 261 5677
www.nea.org.uk

Energy Action Scotland
Suite 4A Ingram House
227 Ingram Street
Glasgow G1 1DA
Tel: 0141 226 3064
www.eas.org.uk

National Energy Foundation
Davy Avenue
Knowlhill
Milton Keynes MK5 8NG
Tel: 01908 665 555
www.nef.org.uk

Public Utilities Access Forum
c/o NEA
Level 6, West One
Forth Banks
Newcastle upon Tyne NE1 3PA
Tel: 0191 261 5677
www.puaf.org.uk

Fuel and energy industry bodies

Ofgem
9 Millbank
London SW1P 3GE
Tel: 020 7901 7000
www.ofgem.gov.uk

Ofgem – Scotland
3rd Floor, Cornerstone
107 West Regent Street
Glasgow G2 2BA
Tel: 0141 331 2678

Gas Safe Register
PO BOX 6804
Basingstoke RG24 4NB
Tel: 0800 408 5500
www.gassaferegister.co.uk

Energy UK
Charles House
5-11 Regent Street
London SW1Y 4LR
Tel: 020 7930 9390
www.energy-uk.org.uk

Solid Fuel Association
7 Swanwick Court
Alfreton DE55 7AS
Helpline: 0845 601 4406
www.solidfuel.co.uk

Consumer and debt advice and information

Citizens Advice consumer service
PO Box 833
Moulton Park
Northampton NN3 0AN
Tel: 08454 04 05 06
Welsh speaking line: 08454 04 05 05
www.adviceguide.org.uk

Consumer Focus
Victoria House
Southampton Row
London WC1B 4AD
Tel: 020 7799 7900
www.consumerfocus.org.uk

Energy Saving Trust (EST)
Helpline: 0800 512 012
www.energysavingtrust.org.uk

Office of Fair Trading
Unfair Contract Terms Unit
Fleetbank House
2–6 Salisbury Square
London EC4Y 8JX
Tel:08457 22 44 99
www.oft.gov.uk

Which?
www.which.co.uk

Legal advice

Community Legal Advice
Helpline: 0845 345 4345
www.gov.uk/community-legal-advice

Law Centres Federation
www.lawcentres.org.uk

Public Law Project
150 Caledonian Road
London N1 9RD
Tel: 0845 345 9253
www.publiclawproject.org.uk

Specialist advice organisations

Age UK
Tavis House
1-6 Tavistock Square
London WC1H 9NA
Helpline: 0800 169 6565
www.ageuk.org.uk

Child Poverty Action Group
94 White Lion Street
London N1 9PF
Tel: 020 7837 7979
www.cpag.org.uk

Shelter
88 Old Street
London EC1V 9HU
Helpline: 0808 800 4444
www.shelter.org.uk

Turn2us
Helpline: 0808 802 2000
www.turn2us.org.uk

Useful publications

Energy Best Deal, Citizens Advice and Ofgem

Debt Advice Handbook, CPAG

Disability Rights Handbook, Disability Alliance

Welfare Benefits and Tax Credits Handbook, CPAG

Universal Credit: what you need to know, CPAG

CPAG's *Welfare Rights Bulletin* is published every two months by CPAG. It covers developments in social security law and updates the *Welfare Benefits and Tax Credits Handbook* between editions. It is sent automatically to CPAG Rights and Comprehensive members. For subscription and membership details contact CPAG.

Articles on social security can also be found in *Legal Action* (Legal Action Group's monthly magazine) and the *Journal of Social Security Law* (Sweet and Maxwell, quarterly).

For CPAG publications contact: CPAG, 94 White Lion Street, London N1 9PF, tel: 020 7837 7979, email: bookorders@cpag.org.uk, order online at www.cpag.org.uk/bookshop

Appendix 2

Guaranteed standards of performance: electricity

The following table summarises the guaranteed standards of performance currently applying in the electricity sector in accordance with the Electricity (Standards of Performance) Regulations 2010

Regulation	Service	Required performance	Payment (domestic customers)
Reg 5	Electricity supply fails during normal weather conditions because of a problem on the distribution system.	Restore it within 18 hours of first becoming aware of the problem.	£54 plus £27 for each additional 12 hours you are without supply.
Reg 6	Electricity supply fails during normal weather conditions because of a single incident on the distribution system affecting 5,000 premises or more.	Restore it within 24 hours of first becoming aware of the problem.	£54 plus £27 for each additional 12 hour period that you are off supply to a maximum of £216.
Reg 7	Electricity supply fails because of a problem on the distribution system due to severe weather.	Lightning events – when a distributor experiences at least 8 times the normal amount of faults in 1 day – supplies will be restored within 24 hours. Non-lightning events – when a distributor experiences between 8 and 13 times the normal amount of faults in 1 day – supplies will be restored within 24 hours.	£27 plus a further £27 for each additional 12 hours without supply to a maximum of £216.

		Non-lightning events – when a distributor experiences at least 13 times the normal amount of faults in 1 day – supplies will be restored within 48 hours. Any severe weather events where at least 35% of exposed customers are affected – supplies will be restored within a period as calculated using a formula based on the number of customers affected as set out in the Regulations.	
Reg 8	Rota disconnection	No more than 24 hours without electricity during the period covered by a rota disconnection event.	£54
Reg 11	Electricity supply fails because of a problem on the distribution system and you are without power for three hours or more, on four or more different occasions in any a 12-month period.		£54
Reg 12	Main fuse between the incoming supply cable and your meter has or might have failed.	Attend within three hours on weekdays. Attend within four hours at weekends and bank holidays.	£22
Reg 14	Power switched off to work on the network for planned maintenance.	Two days' notice.	£22 (if notice not given or electricity switched off on a different day).

Reg 15	Problem with the voltage of the electricity to your premises.	An explanation within five working days or offer to visit you to investigate within seven working days.	£22
Reg 19	If the supplier needs to visit you, or if you request a visit from it, you will be offered an appointment during the morning or afternoon or within a two-hour time band.		£22 (if appointment is not made or kept).
Reg 21	Any guaranteed standards that the supplier has failed to meet (other than those for which you have to make a claim for payment).	Send payment either directly to you or to your electricity supplier within 10 working days – except in the case of regulation 7, when payment will be issued as soon as is reasonably practicable.	Additional £22 (if failed to notify you, or your supplier, or fail to send a payment within the timescale).

Making a claim

To make a claim under regulations 5, 6, 7, 8, 11 or 14, contact your electricity supplier for details of the claims process.

If you have a dispute with your distributor about whether you should receive a payment which you cannot resolve with it, refer the case to Ofgem to request a formal decision.

Appendix 3

Reading your meter

Electricity

There are four types of electricity meter in common use.

Standard credit meter

A standard meter measures electricity consumption in kilowatt hours (kWh) – the number of units of energy used in an hour. With this type of meter, all electricity units are charged at the same rate 24 hours a day. Most standard meters have an electronic or digital display showing a row of numbers. Older meters may have a dial display with four or more dials, each with a pointer.

Variable rate credit meter

A variable rate meter operates on the same principle as a standard meter but gives more than one reading display – ie, to show daytime, normal or peak electricity use, overnight or low off-peak use and (if appropriate) controlled circuit use. Customers with a variable rate credit meter will have either one or two meters showing up to three sets of numbers. The majority of these meters will have electronic or digital displays showing rows of numbers. A few customers may still have two dial display meters installed – one each for peak and off-peak consumption.

Prepayment meter

A prepayment meter measures electricity use in exactly the same way as a credit meter. A prepayment meter has a digital display screen which can show a range of information

Smart meter

A smart meter is an electronic meter. It operates in the same way as a credit meter in terms of registering electricity consumption. Many smart meters have visual displays to highlight energy consumption levels. Most have a digital display which can show a range of information.

Reading your meter

The numbers on electronic and digital displays should always be read from left to right. Write down the first five numbers shown. Red numbers, or numbers after a digital point, should be ignored.

If you want to work out how much electricity you use, write down the numbers and take a note of the date. The next time you take a reading subtract the second reading from the first and you will know how many units (kilowatt hours) you have used in the period since you took your first reading.

The same principle applies for reading dial meters. These should also be read from left to right, ignoring the final (usually red) dial. Write down the number closest to each pointer. If the pointer is between two numbers, write down the lower number, but if the pointer is between 9 and 0, write down 9.

If there are two rows of numbers, the top row is usually for off-peak and may be marked 'low' or 'night'. The bottom row is usually for peak and may be marked 'normal' or 'standard'.

Some variable rate meters have only one digital display. This type of meter will usually show the charging rate that's currently in use. These meters should have a button that will cycle through the readings for the different rates.

If you are working out how much electricity you have used, make sure you note clearly which reading is which.

Prepayment meters normally display the amount of credit remaining for use. To obtain a reading from a prepayment meter, you will have to press a button on the meter to change the digital display. Pressing the button repeatedly will allow you to cycle through the display screens (to return to the original screen, stop pressing the button). Every prepayment meter provides a range of information but all are configured slightly differently. However, most use letters to count the display screens and include displays for:

- current credit;
- total credit accepted – ie, amount topped up onto meter;
- reading for rate 1;
- price per unit for rate 1;
- reading for rate 2 (if appropriate);
- price per unit for rate 2;
- standing charge;
- amount available for emergency credit;
- debt repayment level (if appropriate).

Note: you may have to insert your key/card/token to view all the displays.

Gas

There are three types of gas meter in common use.

Standard credit meter

The majority of gas customers have a credit meter which records the amount of gas used. Gas consumption is measured in units. For many older meters – imperial meters – gas usage is measured in cubic feet. For newer metric meters, gas usage is measured in cubic metres.

Most standard meters have an electronic or digital display showing a row of four or five numbers. Older meters may have a dial display with four or more dials, each with a pointer.

Prepayment meter

A prepayment meter measures gas use in exactly the same way as a credit meter. A prepayment meter has a digital display screen which can show a range of information.

Smart meter

A smart meter is an electronic meter. It operates in the same way as a credit meter in terms of registering gas consumption. Many smart meters have visual displays to highlight energy consumption levels. Most have a digital display which can show a range of information.

Reading your meter

The numbers on electronic and digital displays should always be read from left to right. Red numbers, or numbers after a digital point, should be ignored.

If you want to work out how much gas you use, write down the numbers and take a note of the date. The next time you take a reading subtract the second reading from the first and you will know how many units you have used in the period since you took your first reading.

The same principle applies for reading dial meters. These should also be read from left to right, ignoring the final (usually red) dial. Write down the number closest to each pointer. If the pointer is between two numbers, write down the lower number, but if the pointer is between 9 and 0, write down 9.

Prepayment meters normally display the amount of credit remaining for use. To obtain a reading from a prepayment meter, you will have to press a button (this may be marked 'A') on the meter to change the digital display. Pressing the button repeatedly will allow you to cycle through the display screens. Every prepayment meter provides a range of information but all are configured slightly differently. However, most use letters to count the display screens and include displays for:

- current credit;

- last credit (most recent amount topped up. Displays on some meters may also show how much was paid towards gas consumption, emergency credit repayment and debt repayment);
- total credit accepted – ie, amount topped up onto meter;
- reading;
- price per unit;
- standing charge;
- amount available for emergency credit;
- debt repayment level (if appropriate);
- debt remaining.

Note: you may have to insert your key/card/token to view all the displays.

Submitting meter readings

If you want to provide meter readings to your supplier, you can do this online or over the phone. This will help ensure that any bills you receive are accurate, that weekly/monthly payment amounts are appropriate and will help prevent debt building up on your account.

Calculating your costs

Before you can calculate the cost of your electricity and gas consumption, you will need to know what your tariff (the amount you pay for every kilowatt hour) is. You will find the specific name for your tariff on your fuel bill or your annual statement. Alternatively, you can phone your supplier to ask. Depending on the type of tariff you have, you will usually have a standing charge to pay along with the cost of your ongoing fuel use. This will also be shown on your bill and annual statement as a daily charge.

For gas consumption, you need to check your meter to see whether you have an old imperial meter or a newer metric meter. If it's an imperial meter measuring gas in cubic feet, it will usually have the words 'cubic feet' or 'Ft³' shown somewhere on the front of the meter. If it's a metric meter measuring gas in cubic metres it will usually show the words 'cubic metres' or 'M³'.

Your tariff for gas will be in kilowatt hours, so the readings from your gas meter need to be converted into kilowatt hours, so that you can then work out how much the fuel you use is costing. You can do this by:

- multiplying units used by 2.83 to give the number of cubic metres of gas used (if the meter is a newer metric one measuring gas in cubic metres this part of the calculation is not needed);
- multiplying by the temperature and pressure figure (1.02264);
- multiplying by calorific value (approximately 39.5, though the exact calorific value can be found on a gas bill);
- dividing by 3.6 to get the number of kilowatt hours (kWh).

Appendix 4

Draft court claim

This appendix gives a precedent for a court claim in England and Wales against an electricity supplier for breach of their duty to supply or against a gas or electricity supplier for breach of contract. Hopefully, this will be useful for legal advisers who are not familiar with this area of the law. This draft claim is put in the county court which is where most claims will be heard.

IN THE _____ COUNTY COURT

Case No: _____

BETWEEN:

A.N. OTHER   Claimant

and

-X- ELECTRICITY PLC

-Y- GAS PLC   Defendants

PARTICULARS OF CLAIM

1. The Defendants are [*gas/electricity*] suppliers and are licensed to supply [*gas/electricity*] to an authorised area, within the meaning of the [*Gas Act 1986/Electricity Act 1989*]. The said authorised area includes the premises known as and situate at [*your address*] ('the premises') which are [*owned/occupied*] by the Claimant.

2. [*For electricity supplied under contract:–*]
The Defendants supply electricity to the Claimant in accordance with their Designated Supply Contract as defined by Condition 42 of the Second Tier Electricity Supply Licence.

[For gas:–]

The Claimant has been a customer of the Defendants since *[insert date when you started paying the bill at present address]* and is now supplied pursuant to a contract in accordance with the Gas Acts 1986 and 1995.

3. *[For gas or electricity supplied under contract:–]*

It is an express term of the said contract that the Defendants shall give a supply and continue to give a supply to the Claimant.

4. In breach of the *[provisions of the Electricity Act 1989/said term of the contract]* set out in paragraph 3 above, the Defendants have failed to *[give/continue supply to the premises]*.

PARTICULARS OF BREACH

[Set out here concisely the facts of the situation on which you would rely as supporting your case in a trial – below is an example]

On 30th October 2012, representatives of the Defendants came to the premises and found a hole in the side of the *[electricity/gas]* meter. The meter was removed by the said representatives on the same day. The Claimant has been without a supply since then.

The Defendants demanded the sum of £ *[INSERT SUM?]* for the damage to the meter and for disconnection and reconnection charges and this was paid on 10th November 2009.

The Defendants claim, by letter dated 14th November 2012, that the Claimant owes the further sum of £*[INSERT SUM]* in respect of *[electricity/gas]* supplied but not registered on the damaged meter and refuse to reconnect supply until this sum is paid. The Claimant does not know how this sum is calculated and genuinely disputes that any part of it is owed.

5. Further, the Defendants are in breach of *[Schedule 6 paragraph 1(9) of the Electricity Act 1989/Schedule 2B paragraph 7(5) of the Gas Act 1986 – can't disconnect when sum genuinely in dispute]*.

PARTICULARS OF BREACH

The Claimant relies on the particulars set out in paragraph 4 above.

6. By reason of the matters aforesaid, the Claimant has suffered loss, damage, nuisance, inconvenience, anxiety and distress.

PARTICULARS OF DAMAGE

[Again, what follows below is an example]

The Claimant lives at the premises with her husband, John, and two daughters: Helen (5 years old) and Joanna (3 years old). John and Joanna both suffer from asthma which is made worse by cold conditions.

The Claimant has been unable to use the central heating system at the premises and has had to buy coal and paraffin to heat the premises this costs an average of £00.00 a *[day/week]*.

Because there is no working cooker or fridge/freezer, the Claimant and her family have had to eat meals at restaurants. On average, £00.00 more is spent on each meal than if it had been made at home.

7. Further, the Claimant claims interest pursuant to section 69 of the County Courts Act 1984 on such sums as may be found due to the Claimant, at such rate and for such period as the court shall think fit.

AND THE CLAIMANT CLAIMS:

1. A declaration that the Claimant does not owe the Defendants the sum of £00.00 or any other amount in respect of the supply of *[electricity/gas]*;

2. An injunction requiring the Defendants to install a new meter at the premises and to restore supply forthwith;

3. Damages; and
4. Further and other relief as the Court sees fit
5. Costs

6. Interest pursuant to the County Courts Act 1984 section 69 as aforesaid.

Dated this _____ day of _____ 201_____

Signed _____

Solicitor for the Claimant

Appendix 5

National Standards for Enforcement Agents (page 9)

Vulnerable situations

- Enforcement agents/agencies and creditors must recognise that they each have a role in ensuring that the vulnerable and socially excluded are protected and that the recovery process includes procedures agreed between the agent/agency and creditor about how such situations should be dealt with. The appropriate use of discretion is essential in every case and no amount of guidance could cover every situation, therefore the agent has a duty to contact the creditor and report the circumstances in situations where there is potential cause for concern. If necessary, the enforcement agent will advise the creditor if further action is appropriate. The exercise of appropriate discretion is needed, not only to protect the debtor, but also the enforcement agent who should avoid taking action which could lead to accusations of inappropriate behaviour.
- Enforcement agents must withdraw from domestic premises if the only person present is, or appears to be, under the age of 18; they can ask when the debtor will be home – if appropriate.
- Enforcement agents must withdraw without making enquiries if the only persons present are children who appear to be under the age of 12.
- Wherever possible, enforcement agents should have arrangements in place for rapidly accessing translation services when these are needed, and provide on request information in large print or in Braille for debtors with impaired sight.
- Those who might be **potentially** vulnerable include:
  - the elderly;
  - people with a disability;
  - the seriously ill;
  - the recently bereaved;
  - single parent families;
  - pregnant women;
  - unemployed people; *and*

– those who have obvious difficulty in understanding, speaking or reading English.

Issued in January 2012 by the Ministry of Justice.

Appendix 6

Abbreviations used in the notes

AC	Appeal Cases
All ER	All England Reports
CEARA 2007	The Consumers, Estate Agents and Redress Act 2007
CP(CCCBP) Regs	The Consumer Protection (Cancellation of Contracts Concluded Away from Business Premises) Regulations 1987 No.2117
CPUT Regs	The Consumer Protection From Unfair Trading Regulations 2008 No.1277
Crim LR	Criminal Law Reports
DPA 1972	The Defective Premises Act 1972
EA 1989	The Electricity Act 1989
EA 2010	The Electricity Act 2010
EPB(CI)(EW) Regs	The Energy Performance of Buildings (Certificates and Inspections) (England and Wales) Regulations 2007 No.991
EG	Estates Gazette
ES Regs	The Electricity Supply Regulations 1988 No.1057
E(CSP) Regs	Electricity (Connection Standards of Performance) Regulations 2010 No.2088
E(SP) Regs	The Electricity (Standards of Performance) Regulations 2010 No.698
G(SP) Regs	The Gas (Standards of Performance) Regulations 2005 No.1135
GA 1986	The Gas Act 1986
GA 1995	The Gas Act 1995
GE(CCHS) Regs	The Gas and Electricity (Consumer Complaints Handling Standards) Regulations 2008 No.1989
GS(IU) Regs	The Gas Safety (Installation and Use) Regulations 1998 No.2451
GS(RE) Regs	The Gas Safety (Rights of Entry) Regulations 1983 No.1575
HA 1980	The Housing Act 1980
HA 1985	The Housing Act 1985

HA 1996	The Housing Act 1996
HB Regs	The Housing Benefit Regulations 2006 No.213
HB(SPC) Regs	The Housing Benefit (Persons who have attained the qualifying age for State Pension Credit) Regulations 2006 No.214
HBGM	The Housing Benefit Guidance Manual
HLR	Housing Law Reports
H(S)A 2006	The Housing (Scotland) Act 2006
JSI	Joint Statement of Intent on Direct Payment for Fuel
LA 2011	The Localism Act 2011
LG(MP)A 1976	The Local Government (Miscellaneous Provisions) Act 1976
LTA 1985	The Landlord and Tenant Act 1985
LVT(P)(E) Regs	The Leasehold Valuation Tribunal (Procedure) England) Regulations 2003
PESL	Public Electricity Supply Licence
QB	Queen's Bench Reports
RA 1977	The Rent Act 1977
RE(GEB)A 1954	Rights of Entry (Gas and Electricity Boards) Act 1954
R(S)A 1984	The Rent (Scotland) Act 1984
SCGSL	Standard Conditions of Gas Suppliers' Licences
SFCWP Regs	The Social Fund Cold Weather Payments (General) Regulations 1988 No.1724
SFG	The Social Fund Guide
SFWFP Regs	The Social Fund Winter Fuel Payments Regulations 2000 No.729
SLC	Standard Licence Conditions 2001
SS(C&P) Regs	The Social Security (Claims and Payments) Regulations 1987 No.1968
STESL	Second Tier Electricity Supply Licence
TLR	Times Law Reports
UA 2000	The Utilities Act 2000
UTCC Regs	Unfair Terms in Consumer Contracts Regulations 1994 No.3159
WLR	Weekly Law Reports

Index

How to use this Index

Entries against the bold headings direct you to the general information on the subject, or where the subject is covered most fully. Sub-entries are listed alphabetically and direct you to specific aspects of the subject.